WHEN LAST
on the
MOUNTAIN

The View from Writers over 50

EDITED BY VICKY LETTMANN AND CAROL ROAN

WHEN LAST
on the
MOUNTAIN

The View from Writers over 50

EDITED BY

VICKY LETTMANN AND CAROL ROAN

HOLY COW! PRESS :: DULUTH, MINNESOTA :: 2010

Cover and text design by Clarity (Duluth, Minnesota).

We wish to acknowledge these authors for their permission to include the following:
"Crossword" by Elaine Handley was published in *The Dos Passos Review*, Volume 5, Number
1, Spring 2008; "Hair Inspection" by Dahlma Llanos-Figueroa, is reprinted from *Growing
Up Girl*, Michelle Sewell, editor (Girlchild Press, Washington, DC, 2006); "Wrong Color,
Right Size" by Charles Henry Lynch, first appeared in *The Evening Street Review*, Number 1,
Summer, 2009; "Signs" by Brent Robison, appears in his collection of linked short stories,
The Principle of Ultimate Indivisibility (Bliss Plot Press, 2009); and "Uncle Sterry" by Michael
Shorb, originally appeared in *The Sun*, Issue 112, March, 1985.

First printing, 2010

10 9 8 7 6 5 4 3 2 1

ISBN 978-0-9823545-2-0

This project is supported in part by grant awards from the Paula and Cy DeCosse Fund of
The Minneapolis Foundation, The Elmer L. & Eleanor J. Andersen Foundation,
The Ben & Jeanne Overman Charitable Trust, and by gifts from generous individual donors.

Holy Cow! Press books are distributed to the trade by:
Consortium Book Sales & Distribution, c/o Perseus Distribution,
1094 Flex Drive, Jackson, Tennessee 38301.

For personal inquiries, write to:
Holy Cow! Press, Post Office Box 3170, Mount Royal Station,
Duluth, Minnesota 55803.

Please visit our website: www.holycowpress.org

Library of Congress Cataloging-in-Publication Data

When last on the mountain : the view from writers over 50 /
edited by Vicky Lettmann and Carol Roan.
p. cm.
ISBN 978-0-9823545-2-0 (pbk. : alk. paper)
1. Authors—Literary collections. 2. Aging—Literary
collections. I. Lettmann, Vicky Hodges. II. Roan, Carol,
1931-
PN6071.A9W47 2010
810.9'35244—dc22   2010016986

Contents

III. VOWS

IV. THE PASSAGE OF TIME

V. A TIME TO LIVE

VI. FLIGHT

Editor's Preface

I first met Vicky during a heat wave in Russia. In June 2006, with the dusty windows opened to the street sounds of St. Petersburg, I looked around the room and saw, with relief, that I would not be alone. At seventy-five, I was the oldest member of the fiction workshop, but at least the woman seated across the table from me was not forty years younger.

We had more in common than age: we were both teachers and writers; each of us held an advanced degree from Indiana University; each of us had three grown children. Vicky was a Southerner transplanted to the Midwest, I was a Midwesterner transplanted to the South. We shared a love for literature, a joy in writing, and the perspective that is a long life's gift.

The value of that perspective became more evident over the next year as we read each other's work. Vicky's poetry could not have been written at a younger age; my stories had been told and retold for twenty years before I began to put them on paper. Although much of the new work we read by younger writers was intriguing, we longed to hear the voices of older writers who in the last decades of their lives were asking questions and searching for the insights that were relevant to our own lives.

The idea for an anthology was born in a telephone conversation when one of us asked, "If our years of experience have inspired each other and our own writing, might other older writers want to join us?"

They did. Older writers sent us 2,100 submissions from across the country, from Qatar and Canada, from Mexico and Israel, from Switzerland, England, Japan, Australia, and a small island in the Pacific. Many of their cover letters were filled with gratitude for the project.

Writers in their fifties, sixties, seventies, and eighties, and four writers in their nineties responded to our question. Two ninety-three-year-olds, Bonnie Barrett and Frances Saunders, who are still writing and still submitting their work, are represented in the pages that follow.

Six days a week, for six months, our mailboxes were filled with gifts. One day we found poetry from Glen Sorestad, who was Saskatchewan's first poet laureate; another day brought stories from James E. Stanton, whose "Draper and the Dragon" is his first publication.

How to choose from such an outpouring? We began with only three criteria—that the writer be over fifty, that the work have literary merit and be unpublished—but we soon found that we were drawn to those pieces written with courageous self-acceptance and understanding. The early submissions of two essays, Tom Hansen's "The Wisdom of Fifty" and Kaye Bache-Snyder's "When Last on the Mountain," set the tone of the book and, in the latter case, furnished the eventual title. When Jim Perlman at Holy Cow! Press became interested in the anthology, we dropped the restriction on previously published work and added, among others, Charles Lynch's "Wrong Color, Right Size."

Our next question became how to choose between five gemlike poems from one contributor or three rousing stories from another, and how to create a coherent flow out of such disparate elements as the raucous hilarity of Ann Chandonnet's "Estrogen: A Letter" and the disturbing effects of dementia in Thomas Shane's story, "Wandering Off."

After many shufflings and reshufflings, the collection began to organize itself along a timeline from memories of the past through observations of the present to intimations of the future.

In Section I, "Family Stories," the writers focus inward on memories of their families—an unwanted sister, an adored cousin, a grandmother—and on two family rituals.

In Section II, "Current Events," the focus is on the impact of events outside the family. We have arranged these selections chronologically, beginning with memories of the Great Depression and FDR's election in the '30s; through those of World War II, the segregation of the '40s and '50s, Vietnam and the demonstrations of the '60s; concluding with memories of the '70s.

Sections I and II contain memories and stories of the past. In Sections III to V, the focus is on the present, on life after fifty. We begin with a kiss and a "Vegas Wedding" at sixty and end Section III with two poems that manage to find wry humor in widowhood.

We divided the next two sections by perspective, as we did the memories sections. In Section IV, "The Passing of Time," the writers give their responses to the effects of aging, disease, and loss. One faces the death of parents in a poignant essay, "Seven Days in May." Others plan their wardrobes in "When I'm Old" and in two poems with the same title, "Dress Code."

The perspective shifts outward in Section V, "A Time to Live." Here, writers look at the effects that aging has had on their relationships and views of the world. In Bruce Barton's story, "O World Unknowable," the narrator finally becomes reconciled to his son's "predisposition." At eighty-three, Ruth Harriet Jacobs finds compassion for both a tattooed girl and her mother in "Naked Encounter." Louise Jaffe, in "Some Somes," leads us to Section VI by wondering whether the world ought not to begin again.

We cannot know our future. We can only imagine it, as Tracy Robert does in "The Curse of Ambrosia," an excerpt from her science fiction novel, or plan for it, as Pulitzer-prize nominee Sarah Getty does in her "Chant for Folding Clothes." Although the writers in Section VI, "Flight," are facing the possibility of nursing homes and the inevitability of death, they are doing so with grace and humor.

All the writers who responded to this project have given us more than we can repay. We have marveled at and been strengthened by the richness of their work. They have inspired us with tears and laughter and a new appreciation of the writing craft. We are not, it seems, over the hill at fifty, but viewing life in all its glory from a mountaintop.

Carol Roan, Editor

The Survey

Joyce Sutphen

Asked me if I was 18 or over
and I said yes, yes, I'm over 18
(and over the rainbow
and over my head in trouble . . .)
and then the survey wondered
if I was male or female
(those were the choices) and
said please indicate, which I did,
and then it wanted me
to give my age in decades
lined up, waiting to put their
brackets around me—

How would I describe myself?
Select all that apply it said,
and my household income?
The survey wanted to know how
much money I had and then
it would subtract something for
each child under the age of 18.
That part made sense. After that
the survey was all business,
and I preferred not to answer except
to say that the time of day was
early morning, long before lunch.

ONE

FAMILY STORIES

Sharing a Room with Your Sister

Judith Serin

Your Baby Sister

You don't remember anything about this; it's all stories: How when your mother comes home from the hospital, your grandmother brings you carnations. You give one to everyone there—father, grandfather, grandmother—except your mother. Now you can imagine your stern look; your stomach sticking out as you stand solemnly, concentrating on separating the stems; your sturdy careful steps—flower held out—toward each guest. You do not look at your mother or the bundle in her arms.

A later story: The neighbor girl is found standing over the crib, dropping safety pins into the mouth of her infant sister. When your parents tell this, you wonder if they are suggesting that you weren't that bad or that you would have done the same if you'd thought of it.

All you have to go on are the photographs of that time—your permanent scowl.

Sharing a Room with Your Sister

When you're little, she's scared of the dark and must have the door cracked open. The L of light that comforts her keeps you awake. You wait until she falls asleep, then quietly close the door. Now you are wrapped in darkness and dreams. Colored grates slide open and you fall gently from one to the next, slipping at last into water filled with familiar fish. One night you are awake when you dream the fish and point them out to your sister. To your surprise she starts to cry, scared because she can't see them.

She has nightmares about the atom bomb and wakes up screaming. Your nightmares take place in bright rooms where caped villains or mysterious, incurable diseases overtake you. The two narrow beds are like boats, and when one starts to sink, you scramble to the other, two sisters whispering while night laps around you full of fish and dreams.

When you are older, she is messy and you are neat. You draw an imaginary diagonal through the room—this is yours; that is hers—and push her things across it. You paint your bureau Chinese red with black trim and get ready to become a teenager with your own room, your solitary nights.

You Chase Your Sister

She's squeamish. You chase her with earthworms, running after her in the field, the drying grasses snapping at your knees. You are gleeful when the cats produce segments of tapeworm and also discover that you can substitute a grain of rice in a tissue, pretend it's a tapeworm, and chase her with that. One time she's so scared she locks herself in the bathroom. You wait by the door; she'll have to come out sometime. She screams, threatens to climb out the window. You know she can't; it's high and narrow. Then silence. She did it.

Another time she screams in the bathroom and calls you to rescue her from an ant. "It's at least three inches long," she shouts.

Even when you're older, she's still squeamish. She's taken over much of the cooking and, while your parents go into the city to see a play, she makes an omelet. The bottom is burnt. You tell her it looks like a fluke-infested liver. You are surprised when she throws away her portion and goes without dinner.

How You Are a Big Sister

You tell her stories—in the car, in bed at night: There is a spoon, Spoony, who lives in the little house on the other side of the road you aren't allowed to cross.

You wake her while your parents are still sleeping, and the two of you climb onto the table, eat sugar out of the bowl with the sugar spoon, a delicious entertainment that combines three things you aren't allowed to do. Later you will have a game at restaurants, seeing how many sugar cubes you each can sneak out of the bowl without your parents noticing.

You can often read each other's minds. Your family has a ritual: When two of you say something simultaneously, you cross pinkies and make a wish. Then you can't talk until someone asks you a question. You and your sister start the same words so often that your parents tease you by refusing to ask questions, joking that now they can finally shut you up.

How You Are Not a Big Sister

You're shorter. When strangers see you in the matching outfits your grandparents buy—flowered dresses with puffed sleeves, pink for you, blue for her—they ask if you are twins and you vehemently insist that you are older.

When you are twelve, your parents build an addition to the house, and you and your sister each get rooms. Now you have your own closet. Before, clothes weren't important, except for your list of things you hated—puffy sleeves, blouses that button down the front, pink. Now they are, and the closet is so powerful that it persists in your dreams for years: That frantic dream in which you are dressing for school, trying on outfit after outfit, and none of them look good. A pattern starts. Your sister comes into your room and asks to borrow a skirt. You don't want to lend it but say yes. A couple of days later you ask to borrow a sweater. She says no. It happens again and again but you never refuse her.

When you're in eighth grade and she's in seventh, a classmate asks her to go steady. He's shorter than most of the girls but at ease with them in a way the other boys aren't. She wears his chunky school ring on a chain around her neck, hidden under her blouse. You're furious. You tell your parents, who make her return the ring. At the school bus that afternoon you think all her friends are pointing you out—the jealous girl who ruined her sister's romance.

Inheritance: Irons

Sharon Anderson Lewis

>*for Willie Cole and Bruce Robbins*

In a misty memory of a June-time
she stands cocoa legs vaseline gleaming
stockstill on the sidewalk
connecting the wood screen door
to the channel-coast thoroughfare
somewhat segregated perhaps.

It is nineteen sixty
two years after her grandmother's house
a musty rose-shingled tax-ridden
boathouse become cottage
hunkered down shamefaced
on a sandy lot on a homely street
in that softly affluent seaside town.

Bruised pears loaf about the stickerberried yard
somebody—no doubt an ossified uncle or cousin—
has moved the corroded swinging bench
out by the curb just under the shade
where she, her sister and cousin
play marbles, tea, make mud pies
worry to death each of the three cats
their gracious grandmother has given them.

Facing east and cracked vinyl cushions
delphinium sky and tender lolling dunes
she hears the sheet-wrapped board screech up
scorched so often by the iron's bottom
imprints offering the various shades of her people
she waits for someone grown
to take her by the hand
to take her to the beach
she comes to know she is in the world.

Miss Dorothy hum-sings "Come, Ye Disconsolate"
a hymn she plays Sundays on a decrepit piano
four doors down at a seafarer's church Bethel U.A.M.E.

The Sunbeam hisses
she dips, finger-flicks cool water
thrusts the iron over a tinctured rag
over the collar of a severe white shirt
earning her living standing, stooped
pressing her perspiring mind down
through flaccid, cramping arms
through arthritic hands
down into a body full of incurable sickness.

"Exquisitely fine work, Mrs. Hall"
Local summer-season laundress

"She was liked well, paid and tipped well, too."

Three grandgirls renounced domesticity
don't iron cook or clean for anybody
even for themselves for that matter
all stripes of dirt other than sand insult.

Nevertheless
traced with forbearing dispositions
they remain subservient
to their charmed-life occupations of the interior
the font of their foremost lessons and assumptions:
being good girls both liberates and traps
the inequitable good fortune of their birth
having unshackled and sat them down.

Hair Inspection

Dahlma Llanos-Figueroa

M iss Bacon, our gym teacher, made the announcement at the end of class that we would not have to change into our green gym suits the following day. We let out a collective "yeah!" and were excited about the news until she finished her little speech. The following morning she would check our scalps for lice. We were to wash our hair and have it squeaky clean for the inspection.

All the girls were still celebrating their anticipated freedom from the dreaded uniform. But slowly, the black girls went quiet as the news sunk in. We marched silently out of the gym but all hell broke loose when we hit the locker room.

"Ain't that some shit?"

"Is she crazy? On a Wednesday night?"

"*Lice*, what she trying to say?"

"Ain't nobody got no cooties around here!"

Miss Bacon had short shiny black hair that swung around her head every time she moved. She was of the I-wash-my-hair-every-morning school of beauty. In fact, she often walked into first period class with still-wet hair plastered across her forehead.

This woman had no idea what it took for most black women to do their hair in those pre-Afro days. My hair was pressed with a hot comb because my mother didn't want me putting those strong chemicals in it to relax the natural curl. So, "just wash your hair tonight" translated into hours of grooming. Washing, air drying (no money for a hairdryer back then), pressing and curling—not the kind of thing you asked your mother to do for you on a weekday night after a long day of work. So I knew what the answer would be.

I was doing my homework that evening when Mom came home from work. In one motion, she dropped her bags on the kitchen table and looked in the pot to see what I had made for dinner.

"*Bendicion*, Mami."

"Good bless you, *M'ija*. Smells good. I'm starving too."

She kissed my forehead and headed for her favorite chair. She let her weight down slowly and began removing her white shoes and stockings. I brought in her soft slippers and sat down by her. She massaged her wrinkled toes to get the cold out and the comfort in. I could see the weariness in her face as she arched her back and settled into the cushions.

"I've been waiting for this all day," she let out a sigh of relief.

"How was school, *Mamita*?" Even in her weariness, I could hear the honeysweet when she called me that. She reached down again to massage her swollen feet and was still rubbing her instep when I broke the news.

"Mom, can you do my hair tonight?"

"*Como que* do your . . .? Tonight? What's gotten into you? I just got home. It's *Wednesday*. You know better than . . ."

"I know, I know, but Miss Bacon is doing hair inspection tomorrow and she says we *have* to wash our hair tonight."

She looked at me like I had grown another head. I braced myself.

"I don't care what *she's* going to do. Has she lost her mind? You have homework to do and I just got home from work. We don't have time and I certainly don't have the energy for all that. No way. Not tonight!"

I tried to explain but her hand whipped up, palm out, in a stop motion. I knew to shut up.

"I'm not doing your hair tonight and that's that. She can check another day. The day she comes home from working a sixteen-hour shift, on her feet almost the whole time, that's the day when she can tell me when and what to do with your hair."

"But Mom . . ."

"We're not discussing this anymore, *Nena*. I'll press your hair over the weekend. We'll curl it and style it and make it *real* pretty. But, she'll have to wait till Monday to do her inspection. And that's final."

The next day, attendance was way down in the gym. A number of girls stayed home or were very late for school. I noticed most of the absentees were black girls and I kicked myself for not having thought of the same solution to the problem. But I knew I didn't have the guts to cut out. My mom would *kill* me if she ever found out.

Miss Bacon stood in front of the room behind a wooden chair, a little table and a trash can beside her. She wore surgical gloves and had a box of Popsicle sticks nearby.

The girls who had come to class stood in fifteen rows, in their assigned places facing her. I stood near the back and looked around. Those rows reminded me of prison movies when the inmates are taken out to the yard for supervised exercise. I had never noticed that before. I stood near the back of the room trying to blend into the wall.

As she called each girl up, you were supposed to sit on the chair, with your back to her as she parted your hair with the sticks. The white girls and the Hispanic girls with straight hair did fine. She smiled at each and moved on to the next. But as each black girl sat in front of her, Miss Bacon made a face. Some girls had chosen styles with neat parts that didn't require separating the hair into sections for inspection. But for the rest, it took a little more effort to part hair that had been freshly oiled and curled. I knew it had taken hours of work. But Miss Bacon was not pleased.

Finally, it was my turn and I sat down face burning. I could feel the stick on my scalp. I knew she would find two weeks' worth of normal scalp secretions: dandruff, oil and perspiration. I imagined the look on her face and couldn't wait to get it over with. The sooner I got up, the better.

I felt the first tug all the way down the back of my head to my neck.

"WHAT'S WRONG WITH YOU PEOPLE?" The words bounced off the tiled walls and seemed to reverberate all around me.

She punctuated each word with another tug at my hair. "Didn't I tell you yesterday to wash your nappy head?" She was talking directly to me. Her words fell like acid over my head and shoulders and sank into me.

"Yes, but I . . ." My words came out small and finally just disappeared into the charged air.

I could feel all the girls' eyes on me. The black girls had a look of recognition when they saw the shame on my face. It wasn't my hair but the public humiliation that shamed me. I tried to control the tears of anger that pushed up against my eyes and were threatening to gush out. I closed my eyes but tears of frustration burned my lids. In my mind's eye I saw myself getting up on the chair and slapping that woman until her face broke open and everyone could see her ugliness oozing out of her. Time stretched out in the silence of the gym. The black girls fumed but held their tongues. In the back, a group of white girls laughed out loud pointing at me as they whispered. The black girls in the front turned to stare them down. I closed my eyes to them all, knowing the girls in the back would be taken care of later.

Miss Bacon's barrage continued.

I tried again. "But my mother works and . . ."

"Aren't you old enough to wash your own hair? Can't you manage even that?"

"Yes, but . . ." The words choked me.

"Just get away from me," she said as she pushed my head away from her. She flung the stick in the basket, making a great show of disgust as she snapped off her gloves.

"I don't care what happens to any of you. Class dismissed!"

I sat in the chair, on fire, ears, throat, eyes burning. I sat with my dignity in pieces on the floor around me. Girls walked all about me picking up their books and clothing. Then they were all gone and I was the last person left in the world. I just couldn't move. My mouth was straw dry. Time was gone.

I must have been sitting there for a long time because the light in the windows had changed when I finally felt two arms and then four wrapping around my shoulders. I looked into the familiar faces of my friends Marjorie and Dawn. I didn't know when they had come into the gym. I never knew how they had heard about the incident. But they kneeled on either side of me and held me—tight. I let out all my misery in a river of tears that they absorbed into their sweaters as they rocked me. Neither of them said a single word the whole time. They didn't need to.

My Cousin Olivia

Cleo Fellers Kocol

My cousin Olivia died last week. Uncle Dan's son, the passer-on of gossipy information, enjoyed waiting until a story grew legs and our memories of the deceased caught up to the present before he called. Olivia's life and death needed no extension. As soon as I heard the name, years fell away like the family ties that dissolved once our grandparents died.

A child again, in memory I lolled through a long, lazy Midwestern summer afternoon waiting for Olivia to appear. Twenty-some years older than me, the focus of flattering family gossip, she was my idol. My parents almost named me in honor of her, but at the last minute decided on Christine, and called me Tina.

During those halcyon summers at our grandparents'—the homestead with its main house and assorted buildings housing us all—we kids vied for sleepovers with Aunt Em at the guesthouse so we could be near Olivia. Our crush on her exceeded understanding, but everyone knew Olivia shone above the crowd.

Mother explained the family adulation this way: "Olivia's kind." She set up committees to feed the poor, funded summer camps for orphans, and gave expensive gifts bought from a trust fund started by Uncle Carl before he died. Her gifts to family exceeded expectations. One year I received a doll bigger than me, another a whole family of dolls.

When I pushed Father for explanations, he said Olivia was intelligent as well as good-looking and friendly.

It was Uncle Dan who breathed the words that came to be the ultimate accolade. Using his movie-star good looks and voice, he spoke in ways that sent ripples running through his sentences, ripples that moved like a tide to engulf the listener. Head tipped to the side, fingers stroking his mustache, eyes half-closed, he said, "Olivia's sophisticated."

Olivia was different. At a time when women held low-paying temporary jobs and seldom were divorced, Olivia headed an office full of girls and had shed a husband. During her short-lived marriage, she'd had to hide candy bars and other tasty tidbits throughout the house so he could "find" them. Uncle Dan mused that Olivia should have been tasty enough on her own, an allusion I didn't understand, but remembered. Others said her husband had a limp wrist, another reference that flew past me like the quail in our fields.

Grandma's and Grandpa's house sprawled on a knoll surrounded by green lawn going a quarter mile down to the driveway entrance. The guesthouse, where Aunt Em held sway, sat among stately oaks and maples nearby. Listening for Olivia's car that day, I squirmed around in a kitchen chair but agreed to settle down when Aunt Em held Olivia up as an example to follow.

Finally Olivia burst through the outside door, bringing energy and life into the summer cottage. Swathed in city clothes, she cried to me, "Aren't you the one, getting prettier every day." Inhaling her heady, exotic fragrance, I took her in like a poor relative grabbing a food basket. Taller and slimmer than her mother, she wore a black and white dress that skimmed her body while never quite hiding it. Her auburn hair was in an upswept do when hardly anyone in the family had taken to the style yet, and her face glowed with the proper amount of makeup. Seeing her, I thought exotic places: nightclubs and penthouses, airplanes and ocean beaches. Grown-ups said Olivia wasn't beautiful, but when she got herself together, everyone took notice. I thought she was gorgeous.

She handed Aunt Em packages of strawberries and asparagus

and asked me questions I didn't know how to answer. Why had I grown so fast when she was just getting used to the old me? What right did I have being so pretty I'd drive men mad and my parents to distraction? Pushing me gently to begin planning my future, she tossed off asides to her mother and hugged me several times, her smile large as she told me how much I'd grown.

While Aunt Em put the produce away, Olivia shed her high-heeled pumps and padded toward the stairs in her stocking feet, drawing me along with her. "I want to hear all about you."

"Hot in the city?" Aunt Em asked, folding the brown paper bags and twisting the twine into a ball.

"Beastly," Olivia murmured, answering her mother but keeping sparkling eyes on me as if letting me in on a secret. "Rodney's picking me up, and Tina's going to help me get ready." Her brilliant smile bathed me.

Change hung in the air, new thoughts crowding against old ones in my mind. I felt nervy and different, as if on the brink of discovery.

"So tell me," she prodded as we entered the room she used on visits, a room with sheer tailored curtains, a plain satin bedspread, no ruffles anywhere, just shiny surfaces and gold-framed mirrors. "Do you think marriage is a girl's only option?" Olivia's glance met mine briefly in the dressing-table mirror. "Is there a mandatory rule saying double harness should be more than a *divertissement?*"

"I don't know," I muttered, not really understanding, only knowing her eyes got that challenging, teasing look that said she wasn't buying it. Proceeding to undress, she spoke in an oblique fashion about needing something to fall back on in case a girl didn't find the "right" person the first time. "Like me."

She'd never talked *personal* to me before. Late afternoon sun was flooding the room with light and heat, and as she sat on the dressing table bench shedding stockings, she had me push open the window to catch lingering breezes. I looked up to the main house, but the view was blocked by foliage.

Olivia paused to look at me. "You're getting so pretty. Got a boyfriend?"

I blushed and shook my head. I'd only begun reading those books where boys kissed girls and did things that were never quite clear.

"You will. Believe me, you will. It's all part of life, kind of wonderful and treacherous at the same time. It's like a waltz. A box step, maybe." She winked at me in the mirror. "And you don't understand a word I'm saying. But you will. Believe me." She studied her face a minute. "Tonight I think we might go to that place where they play gypsy violins. Recently I met this person who certainly has that look." Free of her stockings, she wiggled her toes and inspected each one. "You certainly must like some boys better than others."

"I guess." I knew I did. All the girls liked Billie, but we never admitted it to grown-ups. His mother had died, and his father put him in foster care, something not quite nice. I wasn't sure why.

Olivia was pushing her linen dress over her head, and I turned aside so she wouldn't catch me looking. Neither my mother nor any of the aunts undressed in front of me. Once I'd glimpsed Aunt Em without her clothes, and she'd slammed the door in my face with an indignant harrumph. Trying not to appear embarrassed, I took the gown Olivia handed me and hung it in the closet. When I returned, she was taking off a lace-trimmed brassiere. "Brassieres keep one from jiggling," she said shrugging. "I'm told a lady never jiggles. Funny, isn't it?" She laughed as she said it.

Not knowing whether she considered jiggling good or bad, I said nothing. She added, "Run the bath water, will you, sweetie? And don't skimp with the bubble bath. I like to smell nice. Did you know women have a better sense of smell than men?"

I shook my head and raced to do her bidding, testing the water so it didn't burn or freeze her. When she came in and slipped off the robe, her breasts all rosy-tipped and almost touching me, I didn't know quite where to look. She was what Uncle Dan called well-endowed, and as she crawled into the tub I saw the marks her bra left on her back and shoulders. I wondered if they were like stigmata. I'd been reading about religions, too.

Steam rose and the air grew heavy with the fragrance of Olivia's special soap, a musky odor that filled me with unknown longings. "I need you to help," she murmured, paying no attention to my discomfort. "Here, take my rings." She slipped sparkling wedding and engagement diamonds from her fingers. "They keep away the unwanted."

It was the second time I'd heard her say something similar. The other time Uncle Dan had narrowed his eyes, and that half-smile had tickled his lips. My mother had kept her gaze on the floor, and Aunt Em's frown had deepened.

I put the sparkly pair on the back of the toilet.

"Now, please do my back, and I'll tell you about this gypsy place." She held out a sponge.

I took it reluctantly but a little excited, too. Olivia had pinned her hair to the top of her head, wispy strands falling around her face. Eager to please, I followed Olivia's instructions and rubbed the sponge up and down her back.

"Ummm, that's great." She smiled, a faraway look on her face. "Let me tell you about the restaurant. It's dark and smoky with a kind of sweetish flavor in the air. Or maybe a fragrance like rich meat and dank wine." A contemplative look passed over her face, and for clock-ticking moments, she said nothing. Then she shrugged and stretched, her breasts popping above the surface of the water. "Sit down. I want to hear all about school. I understand you won the English prize."

Distracted, I put the toilet lid down and sat. I ran off my list of accomplishments while she added water until the suds rose and threatened to spill onto the floor. But they never did; I expect they wouldn't dare. "Tell me about the restaurant some more," I suggested when she finished murmuring her congratulations for my spelling and literary A's.

"It's not cave dark in there but gray dark, so you can see the outlines of things, the edge of other tables, the gleam of the dance floor, the flirt of a skirt. And you don't know who is who, who's a man, who's a woman until people light cigarettes. Sometimes foreign brands. Then you can almost see their faces." She chuckled, and her voice went from airy to flat. "Clear enough anyway."

For a while she said nothing, and after a long silence while I tried to think of something to say, she stepped from the tub, a towel held strategically. With only a flash of long legs, she padded into the bedroom. Although the aunts dissected her appearance often, proclaiming that she was too high-waisted, not slender enough around the middle, too heavy on top, and with an absolutely flat rear, they agreed she was extremely attractive. Her smoky gray eyes were thickly lashed and usually shone with some inner excitement as she held forth on the latest place she'd been, a show she'd seen, a restaurant where she'd dined. The aunts approximated recipes from her descriptions of foods she'd eaten, found knockoffs of the designer clothes she wore, learned the latest dances from her.

I often quoted Olivia's maxims like a mantra: quality before style, name brands before bargains, the right accessories, hang the expense.

Now, I attempted to ignore her nudity as she patted and rubbed herself dry, murmuring with pleasure as she discarded the towel and held a terry-cloth robe loosely in place as she talked to me. Her date was new. "Someone to take me places, if that makes any sense to you. Men give women entrée. Remember that, *mon amie*."

She laid filmy stockings, underwear all matching in texture and color, on the bed. Everything in her room mimicked the subtle shades of shuttered sun, matching the colors in the chaise lounge and the thick, spongy carpet. She'd designed the room herself.

Absorbed with my thoughts, I never noticed the moment Olivia reversed her robe, putting the back in front and the opening in the back. Sitting down at the dressing table, she smiled at me and held out a huge powder puff.

"Here," she said. "Cover my back and don't skimp. With dusting powder, toilet water and cologne you can't be subtle. Perfume is a different matter. A little goes a long way."

Reluctantly, a bit timidly, I smacked her back with the puff while she fussed with her hair and face and murmured, "Lower, and more to the right" until I completely covered her spine, shoulders and upper buttocks with cream-colored powder, the same heady aroma as the soap and bubble bath. Words stuck in my throat, and my arms felt stiff as sticks. Clumsily, I dropped the puff and retrieved it, red-faced. I had speculated about girls becoming women, wondering what really happened, but when I broached the subject, Mother's mouth got tight, and I'd have died before I'd ask Aunt Em. I eye-balled Olivia's spine and the indentation into her buttocks. Should I ask her? The whole procedure had to be naughty, otherwise why didn't somebody tell me? And why was I feeling so guilt-ridden just thinking about it, and just doing this?

Putting down an atomizer, Olivia said, "I'll impress with fragrance if nothing else!" Her throaty laughter followed, and with a lightning movement she whipped the robe off and put it on properly. Still, I had a flash of woman. Both relieved and uncomfortable—no hair from belly button to knees like a girl in school had said—I fidgeted, saved from total embarrassment by Aunt Em calling us for supper, having fixed the asparagus crisp like Olivia said was the way it was served in the better restaurants.

I fell asleep thinking of Olivia in that smoky gypsy place, her voice so mellow and sweet, some man like Uncle Dan lighting her cigarettes, she flirting her skirts on the dance floor.

It had to be late when she returned, her voice stinging the air, harsh whispers startling me awake. "Dang no-good," she muttered, her voice remaining in the room and sending shock waves into me.

"What happened?" I whispered in turn.

"Stupid stockbroker down on his luck, *he said*." She put her beaded bag on the dressing table. "Stiffed me. Which wouldn't have been so bad if he hadn't clung to me like a leech. Luckily I had more than a comb and lipstick in my purse. You understand?"

I shook my head.

"I paid for the evening's entertainment. And had to put up with him to boot."

Sitting on the dressing table stool, she kicked off her shoes and spoke oblique sentences about beautiful women and rotten men, details lost in mumbled words. Through a fringe of eyelashes, I watched her mouth move, heard her voice, the sense of the words zooming by me. I decided she'd been drinking. Teachers taught about the evils of alcohol, the pastor railed against it in church, and once the village drunk reeled around Grandma's yard and shouted about people who thought they were god almighty. Olivia's amused, lilting voice held the anger I'd heard in his.

"Don't trust them," she muttered, focusing slightly past me. "I gave the gentleman—a term I use loosely—his walking papers."

I must have looked blank.

"The boot," she hissed.

I jerked back, but she never noticed. Emboldened, I said, "Like kicking off your shoes?" One of hers had landed near the chaise lounge.

"You got it, kiddo. Promise me, Tina, don't trust men who misunderstand pure unadulterated friendship."

"I won't," I muttered, hunkering down in the bed I shared with her.

"They're phonies, not worth the time you spend getting ready." Without ceremony she tossed her dress toward the chaise.

I struggled to stay awake as she fought the lid off a cold cream jar. "Damn nobody," she cried, slathering cream over her fading makeup. "I should have left him washing dishes. Shit! Stupid slobbery kisses to boot. Not one redeeming anything. Nothing." Her voice cracked, and then she started to cry, her shoulders heaving, her hands covering her face.

Frightened now, I held the sheet tight to my chin. I'd never seen an adult cry, and certainly it shouldn't be Olivia. In a way I didn't understand, she'd let me down. "You woke me," I said, using Aunt Em's scolding tone.

Struggling to gain control, she dabbed at her eyes with tissue. "Sorry I woke you. Go back to sleep."

But my eyes had been pried wide open by thoughts colliding in my head. My world had been secure in its sameness. Now, the familiar was foreign, Olivia a stranger, her words a puzzle, her actions not the actions of the superior being she'd been. A summer wind was rattling the blinds, and from somewhere far off a car motor whined, and a train whistle sounded. Shivering, I willed myself to forget it all, but I couldn't. When I was younger and bad dreams frightened me, Olivia had rocked me, whispered that it was all right. Now I needed reassurance, but instead I heard a loud, inelegant snore that finally lulled me to sleep.

In the morning, sunshine blazing a trail across the bed, Olivia was already up and dressed when I knuckled my eyes. "Hey, sleepyhead," she called in her usual soft, cultured tones, but the memory of her tears lingered like stagnant water between us. Not knowing what to say, I didn't get up until her sports coupe roared down the drive.

Today, a half century later, the memory of those years resurrected by the call, I said, "Tell me about her."

"A heart attack most likely. I heard she was playing piano in some hotel in the Middle East, pop tunes from the '40s and '50s, like 'Ebb Tide' and 'Sweet Leilani.'"

Sunday afternoons she'd chorded songs on the old upright, we kids surrounding her and trying to sing along, she playing by ear.

"Someone else said she did photographic stuff for art magazines.

That kind of thing. But I remembered her on the other side of the camera. She was in most of the old pictures."

"Yes, people always had her posing," I agreed.

"Remember that time she dove from the pier into the lake? Perfect swan dive, Dad said."

"I remember."

Clearing his throat, Dan Junior added, "I also heard she was in some high-class bordello in Hong Kong after she left the States. Or maybe Singapore." He chuckled and I heard a resemblance to his father in tone. "Wouldn't have surprised me."

"I'm not so sure," I said, bits and pieces coming together. That long-ago summer, immersed in a boy-kisses-girl story no one wanted me to read, I hadn't heard the uncles approach until Uncle Dan spoke. "What Olivia needs is a real man." A snicker rode his voice, and I could picture if not actually see his narrowed eyes, his mouth in its half-smile. He never knew I heard.

For a while, as the memory caught me mid-chest, neither Daniel Junior nor I said a word, the past floating like a kite with a string I needed to wind. I asked him about his family and he asked about mine. Then there was nothing else to say.

"Thanks for letting me know," I said, and an image of Olivia crying, her shoulders shaking, the sound sadder than anything I've heard since, rose once again and filled the room with sound.

Her Benevolent Concern

Dody Williams

> *A very small degree of hope is sufficient to cause the birth of love.*
> —*Stendhal*

My mom left in the middle of the night when I was six years old. I haven't seen her since. Sometimes, she's all I dream about. Fits and starts, like. It gets me to thinking, but I have to admit my memories get jumbled up with the dreams. Last night I woke up like you do after a particularly loud dream. That's what I call them: loud. You know—a busy sort of dream; where you're jolted awake kind of sudden like and then try to go back to sleep just to finish the dream to find out how it all ends. Last night my loud dream was about her dressing table again. She was walking out the door and I was sitting at her dressing table with my dictionary, looking up words as fast as I could trying to find the right word to make her stay. It's because of my mom that I look words up in the dictionary; even the easy ones that everyone thinks they know. It's the best way to find out the truest meanings. Webster's says this about love: *maternal love for a child; unselfish loyal and benevolent concern for the good of another.* I can't tell you how relieved I was when I found that in the dictionary. That is what I remember about my mother—her benevolent concern.

When the loud dreams happen to me I try to latch on to what Webster's says about memory: *the power of recalling what has been learned and retained especially through associative mechanisms.* There's something soothing about looking up the meaning of words. I know more that way. It helps me understand. The memory of her dressing table is my truest, my best associative mechanism. It shines in my head like I figure angels must shine when they appear, so it's easy to think about. I suppose that's why I dream about it all the time.

That pretty little dressing table had been hers from the time she was a little girl. It was the best piece of furniture we had in the trailer. She always told me that someday the dressing table would be mine. It was glossy white with dainty little legs that turned up at the edges like elf feet. Three slim drawers across the top were lined with sweet smelly paper, and it opened with green crystal knobs. What I remember best is the time when I was three or four. She pulled me up to sit on her lap. She leaned in and sniffed my just washed hair and it made me shiver, it felt so good. She said, "You pick out my lipstick, Reenie." So I pulled open the drawer full of pretty colored tubes and handed her one. I watched carefully as she put it on and then I said like a prayer, "You are so pretty, Mama." In the dark it is easy to remember her. The dream helps me.

She was so pretty, with long blond hair, sleek like my cat Mary Rose's fur, and the sweetest face. I thought she looked even prettier than my one and only Barbie. I remember feeling shy and privileged to be on her lap. I wished we would sit there forever. I wished that in the morning I could sit in her lap all over again instead of me having to pour my own cereal into the bowl and eat it dry because the milk was too heavy for me to carry or because we just didn't have any milk. I wished that she would be awake before I had to walk to the bus stop myself. Every morning when I woke up I ran to her room and waited until I saw her chest moving up and down. Or I would lean over, turn my head, and put my ear on her chest to listen for her heart. I couldn't pour the cereal until I knew she was just sleeping. I would pretend to myself that she couldn't walk with me to the bus because she was really Sleeping Beauty and had another few hours to go before the hundred years was up. I imagined my dad kissing her, breaking the spell sometime while I was at school, only I knew that was silly. It really wasn't a spell at all.

My dad was usually out in the building behind our trailer sleep-ing on the couch. He slept out there most of the time. He called it the office. It was nicer than the trailer because Dad said his clients deserved only the best surroundings while they were playing cards or pool. The office was a real building, brick and everything with new carpet and a bar, a new refrigerator and sink that didn't drip. It had a beautiful, big TV and there were six tables covered in green felt for poker and blackjack. There were three pool tables and framed pictures of my dad winning trophies in places like New Orleans and Atlanta. He was so young and handsome in the trophy-winning pictures. One time I heard my mom say he had reminded her of Rhett Butler, but then she would snort like it was the stupidest thing she'd ever been reminded of.

I used to ask my Aunt Abby where she thought my mom could be. "I just don't know, Reenie." She always answers the same way. Worn-out sounding. Sometimes I think my mom might be dead. Other times I just think she wasn't up to being a mom. I'm fourteen now, so that was eight years ago, but when I was small, her leaving me was the thing I worried about the most. Probably because I wasn't the first kid she had left behind. I have a half brother named Quint who is five years older than me. Quint lived with my mom and dad and me for about a year when I was in kindergarten. I haven't seen him in a while. Sometimes I ask Aunt Abby about Quint.

"Do you think we should call Quint?" I say. Each time I ask, I know the answer.

"Oh, Reenie, I don't know where Quint is." Aunt Abby will say, "He dropped out of school and his dad hasn't seen him in over a year."

Secretly, I keep hoping Quint will call me but he never does. In the dark, when I'm remembering, I think about how he taught me to get cereal for myself in the morning so my stomach wouldn't growl until Mom and Dad woke up. We walked to the bus together and I was proud to have a big brother, even if he was only half related. His other grandma and grandpa had given him a Game Boy for his birthday and he shared it with me. God! Those Super Mario

Brothers cracked me up!

Quint was the person who told me about all the other cousins I had. He told me stories when we walked to the school bus about when Mom and his dad had been married and lived in Savannah, in a real house, not a trailer. "Mom had a job back then," he told me. "She worked doing secretary stuff at the college where her dad was a professor or something."

"What's a professor?" I asked.

"It's like a teacher, only in college," Quint answered.

"So my grandpa is a teacher? At a school?" That seemed funny to me; a teacher being a man. "What is my grandma like?"

"Goddamn, Reenie!" Quint used swearwords when he was sore. "That's all I know, okay? They're old people, nothing much to tell, okay?"

I knew when to shut up. I had learned that Quint couldn't be forced to tell me things. Instead, it had to come out of him all of a sudden, like when the wind switches on a humid summer day. As we walked along I could tell he was considering something and he finally started talking like he was remembering from a long time ago, "Mom has sisters too, Aunt Abby is my favorite. She is a lot older. I guess Mom was the baby or a mistake or something." He said, "Aunt Abby has some kids, two are older and the younger ones are close to my age; there's even one your age. But they are just girls, like you."

As we were walking to the bus he was picking up rocks and throwing them across the road. One rock was shaped exactly like an egg. It made him stop and think. "You know," he confided, "every year there is an Easter egg hunt in Aunt Abby's garden. She lives in a big ol' house on probably an acre or something. They always invite me even though they haven't heard shit from Mom in years."

I was hanging on his every word. This story was too good to miss simply because I couldn't be patient enough for Quint to tell it in his own way. It was coming out in fits and starts, so I didn't talk anymore. I just started humming "Here Comes Peter Cottontail" to help him along, hoping he would say more about the Easter egg hunt. It worked.

"I usually find *all* the eggs, since I'm the only boy," he boasted, "but Abby goes ahead and gives everyone a prize anyway." I could tell by the way he said her name, kind of soft and shy, that he had a soft spot for Aunt Abby and it made me like her too. I tried to imagine the big old house Quint told me about and my mom's sister Abby. When I was supposed to be resting during kindergarten, I pretended I was at the Easter egg hunt, winning one of the prizes that Aunt Abby bought for all the kids. I loved having Quint live with us. He knew so much about my mom.

My dad didn't want him around, though. He said Quint was a "wisecracker" and didn't show any respect for my mom. One time my mom told Quint that if he was late coming home from school again, she would have to punish him. Quint answered back, "Being late must run in our goddamn family."

"I don't like your tone, young man," Mom said, not sounding real sure of herself.

Quint would look over at me and roll his eyes and then say the same thing, only in a higher voice. I would always giggle. Quint did talk back a lot but I think he was just showing off for me.

"If you don't stop your swearing and being such a smart aleck, I'm going to have to call your dad," Mom warned him. Her voice sounded squeaky like. But Quint, he just couldn't help himself. There was a mad spot balled up inside of him. When my mom finally did call Quint's dad she screamed into the phone, "You come here and get this boy, he's just too much for me to handle!" I begged her to hang up. I was crying and holding on to her leg and her cigarette ashes were floating down in my face. I told her that it was my fault he was smart-alecky. "*Please*, Mama," I cried. My mind was racing. So I latched onto the first thing I could think of, but I only made it worse, "I was *scared* like shit in the middle of the night," I told her, "you weren't home, and he was just talking back to you 'cuz he was mad at *me* 'cuz I got into bed with him. Please, Mama, please!" I screamed. "Don't make Quint go back to his dad!" I suppose swearing and reminding her that she'd been late again didn't help.

I knew the Game Boy and all the cousin stories would go with him, but really, it was more than that. Quint was a super good reader. He never minded reading me *Hop on Pop* a million times. We would laugh and laugh at Mr. Brown and Mrs. Brown, they were such doofuses! Plus, I liked having someone to watch TV with. He would steal the keys to the office from Dad's pants and we would grab our pillows and sneak out to lay on one of the pool tables and watch the Power Rangers on the TV out there. It had cable and worked better than the one in the trailer. One time, I spilled my Lucky Charms all over the green felt of the pool table. When my dad found out, Quint told him that he had done it. My dad whopped Quint with his belt and made me watch, but right then and there I knew he was like a whole brother to me.

Sometimes when I try to figure out why my mom left, I just tell myself she was kidnapped. I have a kind of cloudy memory of Griffin, the creepy guy who was staying at our trailer the night she left me. He had become one of my dad's clients right after Quint was sent away. I started having nightmares about being left alone in the trailer, so my mom took Quint's cot and made a bed for me in the storage closet of the office. I would crack the door and watch my mom deal blackjack, sitting on a stool with her legs crossed. She looked beautiful. Her hair was so blonde and shiny, and she had the tiniest feet. I imagined they were just as small as Cinderella's. When Griffin started coming, he always sat next to my mom and sometimes I would see him cover her hand when she laid the cards down in front of him. It seemed to me like he was trying to hold her hand and I didn't like it. He was handsome in a wicked way and kind of looked like my dad used to look in the trophy-winning pictures.

Not long after Griffin started coming to the office, my dad had to leave for a pool tournament in New Orleans. That same night my mom told me that Griffin would be spending the night at our trailer. I pinched myself all night to stay awake and peek out my door down the hall to the sofa where I could watch Griffin and my mom. When I saw Griffin giving my mom a shot with a big ol' doctor needle, I screamed. I hated shots and knew they hurt. Mom came into my room to hush me up.

"Why was Griffin giving you a shot, Mama?" I asked her, afraid somewhere in my stomach that she was sick and had to have one or she would die.

"Oh, sweetie," Mom said to me, "we're just playing hospital, like you do with your little doctor kit." And she giggled in a silly way that embarrassed me and her eyes were sleepy looking and barely open. I hated Griffin and wished my dad would come home from the tournament and make him leave.

"Mom," I asked, "don't you miss Dad? When's he coming home?" Her sleepy eyes became narrow like slits and I thought she was going to say something. But then she thought better of it and said instead, "Go to sleep now, Reenie, it's late and I am tired." Then she got up off my bed and stumbled out of the room.

When I woke up the next morning, I got up to check to see if Mom was sleeping in her bed like I usually did. She wasn't. There was no sign of Griffin either. I went out to the office to see if she was out there and the door was swinging open. It looked like raccoons had gotten in behind the bar. My feet were damp from running across the dewy ground since it was early spring. I started to shiver in my thin Little Mermaid nightgown, but the shivering felt worse than just cold. It took hold of me and I felt like a giant was shaking me around. I knew my dad would be angry about the raccoon mess when he got home, so I tried my best to pick it up but the shivering was so bad I cut my thumb on some broken glass that was scattered all around and it started to bleed. It wasn't too deep but seeing my own blood made me shiver even harder. While I was sucking on it almost gagging on the taste, I remembered that Santa had put some Hello Kitty Band-Aids in my stocking at Christmas, so I ran back to the trailer to look under my bed where my stocking had been shoved since Christmas Day. Sure enough, I found them, but not before I had made a pretty big mess of my favorite nightgown and all. I put about five Hello Kitty Band-Aids around my thumb and just started to cry.

It's funny, I wasn't mad at my mom. I wasn't even crying because I was surprised that she was gone. I was crying because it had finally happened. I always knew somewhere deep down in the pit of my stomach that she was going to go. When Quint had lived with us, I remembered him telling me about the night she had gone away when he was five.

"She left in the middle of the night," Quint told me. "When I woke up my dad told me I wouldn't be seeing her much anymore and that he was taking me to my grandma's house to live."

"Do you know where she went, Quint?" I had asked him. "Did she tell you she was going away? Did she dress up or put on lipstick?" I was trying to find out what the signs were, to be on the lookout for them.

"Nope," Quint answered. "She just put me to bed like regular and then after that, I didn't see her much, only sometimes on Saturdays. She would come get me with your dad when you were a baby and we would go get some ice cream or something. And then one day, they came and told me to pack some stuff. My dad was dating someone new and my grandma was having an operation and couldn't take as good care of me. So Mom showed up and said I was going to live with them, and that's why I am here now." Quint seemed to be thinking hard about the possible signs before he finally said, "No, when she goes away, she just leaves without any fricking warning."

I had always known this day was coming. I wished that Quint was there with me right then. I felt for sure he would know what to do. I was still shaking, so I got myself dressed in my pink Sleeping Beauty sweatshirt and purple pants. I looked down at Sleeping Beauty's picture on my shirt. She was lying on her pillow with her long blond hair spread out and her arm up over her head, waiting to be kissed, and I felt a little better. I started to pretend that Mom had finally been kissed by the prince and was just off on like a honeymoon or something. When my thumb began to throb a little I started to pretend that I was the next Sleeping Beauty and I had just pricked my finger on the spindle.

My stomach was in a nervous state that whole damn day. I sat on the couch feeling that gross, I'm-going-to-throw-up feeling, waiting for something to happen. I couldn't pour my cereal. I couldn't move. Mary Rose, my cat, stayed close by curled up like she understood why she didn't get her cereal either that day. Finally, I heard the gravel on the driveway crunch and my dad drove up and got out of his car and went out back to the office. I heard him cussing and kicking the door, and then he came in and found me sitting in the dark on the couch.

I must have looked pitiful or something sitting there with my hair all messed up and puffy-faced from crying so long. It must have made him forget all about the raccoon mess because he looked at me so tender with a look like I had never seen before and said, "She's gone away, ain't she, Reenie, honey?"

I was so glad I wasn't alone anymore. I knew my dad didn't know much about taking care of little girls. But something inside of me told me I just needed to take care of myself, and so I said to him, "Hi, Daddy. Do you want me to pour you some cereal for dinner? I bet you're hungry after your trip."

It's funny, but in the dark you can remember things that aren't so clear in the daytime. You can see the colors and smell the smells. I do my best thinking in pitch-black. The nights when there's no moon work best. I start thinking about the trailer my dad still lives in even though I don't live there anymore. I see him sometimes, even though I can tell he never knows what to do with me. But that old trailer; it's always a mess. We lived in a little run-down town about twenty miles from Savannah called Beulah. The highway that led to Beulah wasn't traveled much, so along the sides of the road all you saw were lots of old, gray, tired sharecroppers' houses or beat-up trailers next to tiny little cotton fields. The town was mostly just a street with a Twistee Treat and Oinkie's Barbeque. The businesses had been closed up for a long time ever since Walmart came and parked itself between Beulah and the town next door, Wendell. Our trailer sat off the highway way down a dirt path marked by car treads. My dad liked to brag about how he had won the land in a poker game, and he told the story about coming to claim his winnings with the trailer right behind him, brought by a trucker fella who owed him money. It was secondhand, probably another payment for a lost bet.

My mom told me we moved here when I was about three. Before that, she said, we had lived on the road. Dad was a top pool champion, traveling the South, winning tournaments and eating fancy meals and staying in hotels like Holiday Inn and Marriott. He met my mom at one of these tournaments in Savannah. She'd been sitting at the bar and he asked her to chalk his pool cue for good luck. He won about a thousand dollars and invited my mom to help him spend it. That was back when he looked like Rhett Butler, and she said he made her feel like a lady. She didn't think much of the trailer, she used to say to my dad, "When are you going to haul this *hovel* away and build me a house like you promised?"

"I like this *hovel*," he would answer her smiling. He just loved it when she said words that he had never heard before. But the smile would disappear, and he would sneer, "When are you going to remember how to act like a wife, darlin'? Remember who feeds you. When you do that, I'll consider building you a house."

After my mom left, the trailer seemed to sag even more. The screen door broke off in the wind and my dad just threw it out behind the office on a garbage heap. The office wasn't the same after that night either. The raccoon had messed up some of the felt card tables and without my mom to clean, it just got dirtier and dirtier. Because my mom used to deal blackjack, my dad had to do it himself. The customers weren't coming as often. Business was bad. To make matters worse, Dad never bought milk and I had to eat my cereal dry all the time.

Every morning it got harder and harder to get out of bed. I gave myself baths when I could remember to do it, but about a week after Mom left, I ran out of shampoo. My hair had knots in it, so when Crystal Lumpkin offered to comb it out during recess one day, I let her. Even though it hurt a lot at first, eventually she got most of the knots out and she even told me my hair reminded her of a princess. I thought about how my mom had looked like a princess.

I appreciated Crystal for saying that, but my dad said the Lumpkins were a bad bunch. "You stay away from that family," he scolded me when I told him about Crystal helping with my hair knots. "They got way too many kids down there. I hear they support themselves with foster kid money and I don't want them thinking just because your mama is gone off that you're some sort of orphan. Plus, they talk like rednecks and I don't want you to lose talkin' like your mama did, you hear what I am saying? It will give you an edge someday."

Mom was what my dad called educated. She had been as far as college once and he told me that was what had made him notice her at first. "I had never met a woman like that," he said, like he was talking about a long-ago memory: "Someone who looked so good and didn't say *ain't* ever. She talked like she had been born into money, or education, or somethin'. Yes sir, she was pretty darn polished, that's for sure. Clients loved her. She attracted the very best." Dad really missed Mom.

I am not sure when I noticed that my head was itching real bad. I was playing with Crystal Lumpkin at recess every day. Crystal told me to bring all of my Barbies so we could pretend that they were two different families. "I only have one Barbie," I told Crystal. "You got more than one?"

Crystal looked at me wide-eyed. "Everyone has more than one Barbie," she told me.

"Well, I only got one, but she looks exactly like Sleeping Beauty," I added hopefully.

"Bring her anyway," Crystal sighed. "I will try to think up a story. She could maybe be like an *orphan* or somethin'." Crystal glanced up at me to see if I had heard her say orphan, but I still had a dad so I just pretended I didn't notice.

It was while we were at recess scratching our heads and playing Barbie the next day that the teacher, Ms. Conway, and the school nurse, Ms. Rench, came over and asked us if we could come with them to the office. At first I thought I was in trouble but when we got there the nurse put me up on a stool and took out a comb and gently parted my hair in the back. I was embarrassed up to my eyeballs because I hadn't brushed my hair real good in a couple of days. "I'm sorry, Ms. Rench. My mom broke her hairbrush and we don't got a new one yet, but thanks so much for brushing my hair . . ."

Crystal was sitting on another stool opposite of me while our teacher Ms. Conway was parting the back of her hair. Suddenly she blurted out, "Unh-unh! Reenie's mom took off with some man that hangs out down at her dad's place. It's not legal, you know, his place, that's what my mom says. Gamblin's a sin. But her mom, she's been gone a *long* time. That's what my mom says."

I felt the butterflies start up in my stomach. It was that gross feeling that tastes like sour milk, and I was afraid that I would throw up all over Ms. Rench's white nurse shoes. My eyes boiled with fat, hot tears and my throat felt croaky. Ms. Conway and Ms. Rench looked at each other and didn't blink. The tears bubbled over and dropped down my cheeks. I tried to wipe them away, but my head was itching so bad I just had to scratch instead and I knocked the comb out of Ms. Rench's hand. "Damn! I'm sorry! I didn't mean to . . ." I scrambled off the stool and crouched on the floor alternately scratching my head and wiping my eyes.

Ms. Conway finally spoke: "Crystal, you can go back to recess now. Reenie will be out in a minute."

I could tell that Crystal didn't want to leave. "I'll wait for Reenie outside the door. Okay, Reenie?" She was bending over, trying to see my face. I knew what she wanted. She wanted me to give her a look that said I wasn't mad at her. But I was.

"No. Crystal, please go back to the playground." Ms. Conway was firm.

When Crystal had gone, Ms. Conway asked me to sit down next to her on Ms. Rench's little couch. Ms. Rench left the room and I turned to Ms. Conway and said, "I know my hair is messed up. My mom is coming home real soon and my dad isn't a good hair brusher."

"Reenie, I don't want you to think that you have done anything wrong. Please don't worry about brushing your hair. But you do have a little problem with your hair. You have head lice and we will need to let your dad know so that he can treat it and get rid of them."

I remembered that one time in kindergarten the teacher had talked about lice. She had put a letter in our backpacks and told us to show it to our parents. They told us it wasn't anyone's fault and you could get it real easy. Ms. Conway went on, "Crystal has them too. I remember seeing Crystal sharing her comb with you at recess. That's probably where you got them. But your dad can get rid of them in a jiffy."

"Are you going to send my dad a letter?" I asked her. I was feeling gross again because my dad never looked in my backpack to read all the fliers and things. When there was a field trip notice the week before, I had tried to get him to sign it but he told me he had bigger stuff to worry about than an old field trip. So far, I hadn't brought back the permission slip and I was worried that I would have to stay behind like Austin Beamer had to do every time there was a field trip because his foster dad never filled out his slips on time.

"Yes, we are going to send everyone's parents a notice about the lice today. You be sure to tell him, okay?" Ms. Conway had her arm around me and I could tell she wanted to help me out. She was a pretty lady with a powdery smell and I wished that I could hug her and tell her about my mom but something just made me stop. I was sure that if I did something like hug her, my mom would find out about it wherever she was and never come back. So I just sat there stiff as a bunny rabbit who thinks you won't see him if he holds still enough. Finally, Ms. Conway let out a big sigh and said I should go back to recess.

My dad told me that night that he was a busy man and that having lice wouldn't hurt me none. "Reenie, I got problems with the office and with your mom gone off, I got to make some fast money. So we are going to go off to a pool tournament. You're going to have to be a real good girl because we're going to have to sleep in the car until I win some money—you understand, Reenie?"

"But, Daddy, what about Mary Rose, who will feed her?" I was frantic. "And what about my field trip, I just got to go on my field trip, we're going to a petting zoo!"

My dad looked old. I could tell his heart just was not in dragging a little girl around to pool tournaments. The wheels were turning in his head, just like I'd seen them turn in the head of some silly cat in an old cartoon once. Finally, he started to think out loud: "Reenie honey, do you think you can manage on your own here for a few days? I'll put some macaroni in the freezer and you can use the microwave in the office. Are you ready to look out for yourself a bit?"

"Oh sure, Daddy," I screamed in relief. I saw my opportunity and ran to my book bag and pulled out the dog-eared permission slip for the field trip. "If you could only sign this, everything will be fine. I can take care of myself. I already feed Mary Rose and all. And get my own cereal every morning." As he signed my permission slip I hugged him around the neck, I was so glad I wouldn't have to be left behind like Austin Beamer.

Some of my dreams are nightmares. The dreams slide in suddenly like a violent summer storm, dark clouds over my sleep, gray and rumbling. In those nightmares I am alone, and I never get to go on the field trip, which is exactly what happened. My dad left for his trip two days later without waking me up. I decided that I better stay home that day. I was afraid Ms. Conway would worry me again about the lice and ask if my dad had bought the special shampoo. I told her he was getting it, but knew that I couldn't keep lying about it. I figured if I could just stay home for the three days that were left until the field trip, everything would eventually work out. It was scary being alone. I stayed in my room with the door shut until Mary Rose scratched at the door begging to get out. I put my macaroni out and let it thaw, but I ate it cold because I was just too scared to go out to the office by myself in the dark. I colored some and played with my Barbie, but mostly I stayed in bed, waiting for two nights to go by. It is hard to be alone when you are six. It's just hard.

After the second night passed, I heard tires rolling over the gravel on our road. The feeling I got hearing those tires was my purest moment of joy. I ran out of my room and threw open the door to greet my dad. Instead, I found Ms. Conway and two strangers.

"Ms. Conway, my dad is still trying to find the special shampoo . . ." But I could tell by the looks on their faces that things were about to change for good. Ms. Conway came in. When she saw the inside of the trailer she made a small noise like a mouse in a trap makes when it dies. Embarrassment made my knees wobbly. She took my hand and sat down with me on the couch. "Reenie," she began, "these two ladies are going to take you with them tonight. They are from

Social Services." The two ladies that had come with Ms. Conway looked exactly like Mr. Brown and Mrs. Brown from *Hop on Pop*. I started to think about Quint and thinking about him made me get a lump in my throat. The lady that looked like Mr. Brown squatted down and said, "We know you have been here by yourself, and as grownups . . . well, we can't allow that to happen anymore. Do you understand?" I nodded my head yes.

The other lady stayed standing, but she patted my shoulder and said, "Don't you worry, honey. It will only be for a night or two, because Ms. Conway has something to tell you."

Ms. Conway handed me a little piece of paper. "Reenie, before your mama went away she sent me a note." Ms. Conway looked at me with the most hopeful face I have ever seen. I remembered how she had tried to hug me in the nurse's office and how I had pretended like I didn't want any hugs. I couldn't read the note because it was written in cursive and I hadn't learned that yet, but I ran my fingers over Mom's writing, hoping to feel something. The hot tears started to boil in my eyes again.

"At first I was confused when I received this, but then, well," Ms. Conway said, "let me read it to you:

Dear Ms. Conway,

In case of an emergency, please call my sister, Abby Linger.

She is in the phone book, under Harold Linger, 23 Kings Way Road.

She will take care of Reenie. She will know what to do.

Sincerely,

Ellie Banisher, Reenie's mom

"Would you like to go and stay with your aunt?" Ms. Conway asked after she finished reading my mother's note.

I needed to be sure of something before I decided: "Ms. Conway, is this an emergency?"

Yes, Reenie, I think it is," Ms. Conway answered. The two social worker ladies who looked like Mr. Brown and Mrs. Brown nodded their heads in agreement.

I thought for a minute. I thought about how old my dad was looking and then I thought about the note for a minute. I remembered what Quint had told me about Mom's sister Abby and I almost heard his voice telling me, "Abby goes ahead and gives everyone a prize . . ." and then I asked, "Is it almost Easter?"

Ms. Conway looked at me kind of puzzled. "Well, yes, Reenie, it is almost Easter, it's next week, why do you ask?"

"Just wondering . . ." I had made up my mind, but in my heart somehow I knew my mom had remembered Aunt Abby's Easter egg hunt.

I looked up at Ms. Conway and said, "I think I *would* like to stay with Aunt Abby." Mrs. Conway nodded and offered me her hand to hold. I looked at her for what felt like a real long time. Finally, she smiled just about the sweetest smile anyone ever gave me, so I decided to take her hand. It was soft and cushiony just like I'd imagined Mom's hand would be if she'd walked me to the school bus all those times I imagined it. Mrs. Conway squeezed and my tummy jumped. I squeezed back and we went outside to her car. Before I got in I yelled out to the hole in the underpinning, "Mary Rose, I'm going to Aunt Abby's now, I'll ask her if you can live there too." And I left feeling pretty certain the answer would be yes.

Creamed Peas on Tuesday

E. Lynne Wright

I was a young college graduate with a great new job, my own closet-sized apartment not far from my family home, and a brand new Chevrolet, which would be all mine after just thirty-five more payments. With the boldness of youth, I could hardly wait to get started setting the world on fire. I would never have been so arrogant as to say I was going to actually change the planet, but I did have it in mind to rearrange things a bit, for the better, of course. I planned to begin with my parents, whom I thought so bored with life they verged on being brain-dead. I was convinced they needed my help.

I tried persuading my mother to develop outside interests, get a job maybe, stop imitating a doormat. It amazed me that she continued to pick up socks from the floor where my father dropped them.

As for Daddy, obviously he needed to get in touch with his feminine side. Which was like telling Mr. Spock to send flowers to Lt. Uhuru on Valentine's Day.

I had barely begun planning a campaign to improve their lives when Mom called to tell me she was scheduled to undergo major surgery, nothing life-threatening, but scary just the same. In her usual self-effacing way, she seemed more concerned with my father's welfare than with her own postoperative care. She had arranged with a neighbor, Mrs. Halsey, to help out at home during her brief hospital stay.

Shortly before her planned admission, she phoned me, frantic with the news that Mrs. Halsey had broken her ankle and a replacement for her couldn't be found at that late date. Would I be responsible for getting my father's dinner while she was in the hospital?

"Mom," I said. "He's a grown man. Can't he feed himself?"

Sepulchral silence. Then, in her best Bette Davis voice, "He works very hard."

"Mother," I said, gently. "I work, too."

The silence was exquisite.

"Oh, all right," I said. "I'll do it to relieve your mind, not because Daddy needs a nanny."

Reluctantly, I put my campaign to rehabilitate my parents' lives on hold and agreed to go to their house each day after work and prepare dinner for my father and me. Mom seemed satisfied.

On the morning of Mother's surgery, my father, the former stoic, the man who taught me to laugh at the boogeyman, who explained long division, the intricacies of the T-formation and the internal combustion engine, looked as lost as an Easter egg. The desolation on his face when they wheeled Mom away nearly broke my heart.

After an interminable, nerve-wracking wait, Mother's surgeon came strolling down the hall, patted my father's shoulder and reassured us that all was well. I was astonished to see tears in Daddy's eyes. I couldn't have been more surprised had I seen the faces on Mount Rushmore weep.

The rest of that day was a tedious blur. When Daddy and I finally kissed Mom goodnight, we were both exhausted, so exhausted, I managed to suppress my guilt about not cooking as we picked up a pizza on the way home.

In spite of Mother's continued progress next day, my father was still pale and haggard with worry. At home that evening, I thought he deserved some special consideration.

"Relax, Daddy," I said. "I'll make dinner."

"You've learned to cook, honey?" he said, already behind a newspaper.

"Like a pro," I said, proceeding to prepare his Tuesday night dinner.

I said "Tuesday night dinner," because, like so many other things in our house, meals were, in effect, ordained according to my father's wishes. He was a man who never liked surprises. On Sunday, our family dined on roast beef and mashed potatoes, on Mondays, it was meat loaf and buttered beets. On Tuesdays, we had hash and creamed peas. Etc., etc.

Touched as I was by my father's obvious concern for Mother, I wanted to do something comforting for him. All my infertile imagination could come up with was to prepare his regular Tuesday night dinner, sort of a gesture of stability.

I tried to make the hash exactly as Mom did the countless times I had watched her over the years, heavy on the onions, crusty on the outside.

When we sat down to eat, I noted the pleasure on my father's face until he saw the creamed peas. He sat, staring at his dish, seeming to struggle for words. Then he cleared his throat.

"Honey," he said. "I hate creamed peas."

Now, Jack Nicklaus could hate golf. Paul Newman could hate Joanne. But my father, hate creamed peas?

"You've been eating them every Tuesday for twenty-six years," I said.

"I've been hating them for twenty-six years, too," he said. "I can't eat them tonight."

I was dumbfounded. "Why didn't you say something about it a long time ago?"

"Because I didn't want to hurt your mother's feelings. She made them the first week we were married," he said. "She didn't know much about cooking then, but she tried so hard."

"Why didn't you tell her later on?"

"After I made such a fuss the first time, she wanted to please me, so she made them again the next week."

"And you complimented her again?"

"Well, I couldn't stop," he said defensively. "You're not to mention this to her, of course."

"For twenty-six years?" I said. "You ate creamed peas for twenty-six years and hated every one of them?"

"You have a lot to learn, sweetheart," he said. "Just because you're married to someone doesn't mean you stop considering their feelings. Of course you can't expect candlelight and concertos every day either, but now, take your generation . . ."

I felt a lecture coming on. According to my father, nothing good has occurred on this planet since 1960.

"Your generation is so busy doing their own thing, feeling good about themselves, they've lost sight of the joy there is in making someone else happy," he said. "And when you love that someone, well, that's just about as good as life gets."

I thought about my mother picking up dirty socks and my father eating creamed peas for twenty-six years. I wondered, too, if my seemingly uncomplicated, unsophisticated mother might have foreseen a father/daughter-bonding experience like this when she made her arrangements. She would deny it, I knew. And yet . . .

"There's much you don't know yet, daughter of mine," he said, chewing thoughtfully on his hash. "Yes, in spite of that fancy college degree, you still have a great deal to learn."

He was right, of course. I am still learning and I expect I will be for a long time.

TWO

WHAT THEY GAVE ME

Current Events

Frances Saunders

On my fifteenth birthday, FDR won the presidency. From the joy and reverence my mother showered on this man, you would have thought the Messiah had appeared.

The moment the news broke, a jubilant crowd collected on our street, the likes of which had not been seen since the Sharkey-Schmeling fight. Neighbors who were accustomed to snubbing each other forgot their ancient grudges. Women embraced, men pounded one another on the back for the pure joy of having something to agree on. Our janitor Fred, who on an ordinary day guzzled schnapps and chased his wife down the alley, opened his basement window, filling the air with the umpteenth radio rendition of "Happy Days Are Here Again."

My mom, sitting on the stoop of our building, called to me with a fervor reserved to denounce the murdered Tsar. "From now on we'll buy apples in the market, and everybody will have a job. Pop will get his raise and next summer, God willing, we'll vacation in the Catskills."

How a president, even one so exalted, had the power to soften my father's boss's heart made as much sense as my mother's tireless struggle to force-feed me a last dose of farina for the sake of starving Armenians.

At the time this rare celebration took place, my family lived on the second floor of an apartment building in the East Bronx, on

Manida, a short street starting at Hunt's Point, and dead-ending into a wooded area where boys smoked cigarette butts and puked on pilfered grappa. All day, and far into the night, frenzied mothers shrieked at their children in a stew of tongues, as if their kids were hard of hearing.

Our upstairs neighbor, Mrs. Schoenberg, who had needed a strong arm to navigate the three flights to her apartment for some time, had moved out shortly before the election. According to Fred, who considered himself the official newscaster in the building, Mrs. Schoenberg had sublet to a relative who looked to buy a house.

At night, I would lie awake and weave dreams. A young man, movie-star handsome, would rent upstairs to brighten my long, cheerless winter.

A few days after the election, when the sky resembled curdled milk and the sun had traveled south, I waited on the landing for fur-niture movers to maneuver an ornate desk up our narrow staircase. Partially concealed behind the desk, a tall, stocky boy I guessed to be close to my age held a long-haired wiener dog under his arm. I tried to recall what mitzvah I had performed that deserved this unexpected gift. When he removed his tweed cap a tumble of lank blond hair fell over his pale forehead. Dumbfounded, I squeezed past him, blood rushing to my face. Tongue-tied, I ran down the stairs and out the door.

After school I dashed home, hung around the vestibule, hoping by chance he might reappear. The door opened, but it was only Mrs. Klein, bringing a blast of cold air and her nosey self inside.

"Florrie, you're okay?"

"Just stopped to tighten my shoelaces, Mrs. Klein."

A day or so later, my mother could hardly wait for my coat to come off. She sat me down at the kitchen table in front of a bottle of milk and a sugar bun. Mom didn't miss a thing, and I could tell from the confidential way she leaned toward me the subject on her mind was boys. Her mouth had the same tight-lipped expression as when my body began to change and I had turned to my friends for what they might know of such matters, only to become more confused.

"Stay away from boys. They're like cigarettes. Once you start, you can't stop."

Start what? Vague, mysterious. Another question for my friends.

"You remember Aunt Dora?" Mom went on.

"You mean the relative we don't talk about?"

"What's to talk about? A fallen woman."

I pictured Aunt Dora bent over like a sapling in a hailstorm.

"Used goods no decent man wanted to marry. When she was your age, she skipped school, rouged her cheeks, and chased after every pair of pants. And that foolishness finished her. For the rest of her life she scrubbed other people's toilets for a living. For your own good, think about what I'm saying, unless you want to end up like Aunt Dora."

I said I didn't and licked the icing on my bun, washing down the sweetness with milk. When I caught Mom's eyes probing mine, I looked away for a sin I hadn't committed.

In class I concealed my inattention by riveting my eyes on the teacher's face while thinking about the golden-headed neighbor. I composed a scintillating dialogue to go with the romantic scenes in my head. But when Miss Stubbs began to talk about FDR in homeroom one day, she pulled all our eyes toward her.

"Girls," she began, in the somber tone a rabbi might use to deliver a eulogy, "it's worth noting how blessed we are to be living in a country where every citizen has an equal opportunity. Whether you are sturdy or infirm, our nation's highest office is available to one and all." She paused for her profound words to sink in.

"Sez who?" someone in the back of the room dared to mock.

For a moment, Miss Stubbs looked as if she might cry. "There is a lesson in all this if you care to listen. Without perseverance and a good education, nothing will be handed to you."

I glanced sideways to stare at Maggie, who wore leg braces. She covered her face with her hands. I tried to feel what it must be like never to dance. The unbearable thought forced me to look away.

Veronica, the stammerer, also caught my attention. On rare occasions when a teacher had to call on her at least once, my stomach knotted. I would watch her neck cords swell, listen to her choke as if dislodging a fishbone. I held my breath praying for the struggle to end.

My friend Phyllis, who was known to speak her mind, waved her arm urgently.

Miss Stubbs couldn't deny an honor student. "Yes, Phyllis?" she sighed.

"Miss Stubbs, would you please define the word *infirm*? And, also, is that the reason women don't run for public office?"

Phyllis's needling brought on a blast of laughter. The algebra teacher poked his head inside the room, tapping his pocket watch. We formed lines to change classes and, to my amazement, Miss Stubbs ignored Phyllis's insolence. Having given up on us and visibly agitated, she charged out without patrolling the hall.

FDR's fireside chats were a sacred ritual in our house. To miss an event of such gravity could be compared to a violation of the Sabbath. On the night the President was scheduled to speak, my mother expected me to cancel meetings, come home after school, eat supper, and get the dishes cleared early. Then, at the appointed hour, I was to take my place in front of the radio. I had no interest in an alphabet soup of regulations, PWA, TVA, delivered in rolling cadences that impressed my mother. Maybe the President's polished diction made her aware of her own deficiency and that's why she pushed college and teaching for me.

I grew twitchy at his speechifying, my mind on the elusive Erwin.

(I had learned his name sleuthing around school.) *Tap your foot, Erwin, if you're listening to FDR. Harder if you're thinking of me.*

One morning when I was late for school, Mom stopped me at the door. "Don't forget tonight."

"I know all about the New Deal. We had a discussion on the subject yesterday during Current Events. I promised Phyllis I would come over and study, stay for supper, and help with her baby brother Buster. Her mother works for Lofts and the Christmas candy rush is on. Don't worry, Mom," I threw over my shoulder, a little too fast. "I won't be late."

"Shame on you." Mom shouted down the stairwell. "Someday you'll be sorry you missed hearing this great man."

What I had said wasn't quite true. I would be at Phyl's, but not to study. She had bribed her older brother Frank. If he taught us to dance the jitterbug, she would write his report on "The Power of the Presidency." That settled, she asked him to invite Erwin to be my partner.

It had started to rain before I reached the subway. I welcomed the sting of wet needles on my lying face. The train roared into the station, blowing grit in my eyes. I wiggled into a small space. Overcome with the smell of damp wool and garlic that hung in the air, I breathed through my hanky and opened *Les Misérables*. I tried to read but the letters crawled across the page like a parade of black ants. I closed the book and stared at the strange string of ads above the seats. Castoria, Doan's Liver Pills, trusses, and a box of sanitary napkins without an explanation of what they sanitized.

Up from the underground, I saw that the rain had turned to a flurry of snowflakes. Delighted, I ran all the way up the three flights to Phyllis's apartment, tingling with anticipation. I removed my wool hat and finger combed my straight brown hair. Phyllis answered my knock, threw her head back, and rolled her eyes toward Myron and Sammy, who were shadowboxing like two halfwits. If I knew Frank, he hadn't exerted himself to find Erwin, and he'd substituted two losers to make himself look good.

Phyllis started the music. The needle skipped on the worn record, distorting the beat. Frank clasped his girlfriend Kitty's hand, flung her out, reeled her in, flung, reeled as if he were possessed.

"Stop!" Phyllis clapped her hands. "Stop showing off, Frank. I know you can dance. Slow down so we can follow or else. Do I have to spell it out?"

"Okay, Phyl, don't get hot under the collar." He bowed with a flourish. "Ladies and gentlemen, grab your partners and let's do-si-do."

A moment later, he turned up the volume, twisted and turned his partner with demonic abandon. Suddenly Myron grabbed my hand with his clammy palm, jerked my arm up and down, up and down, like a pump handle at the well. His crazy gyrations and pimply outcroppings convulsed my stomach. I stopped short. Wham! He stomped on my foot, crushing my toes and pinching my heart.

"What's with you? Got two left feet?"

I hobbled to get my coat, apologized to Phyllis, and left. Gray slush covered the sidewalks. I jumped puddles. Adding to my discomfort, I had to invent a lie to cover the first one I had told Mom earlier.

I needn't have bothered. My parents were too absorbed in the newspaper to notice my arrival. My mother's eyes were red and I heard my father read "Germany, Palestine," and someone named "Hitler." Absentmindedly, Mom held a platter of roast chicken aloft, forgetting to put it down. I had no appetite, picked at my food out of guilt, concerned that perhaps my deception had in some way contributed to Mom's misery. That night I listened closely to what FDR had to say.

During the long gray winter, I found any excuse to spend more time at school, where I scoured the school halls like Javert running through the sewers of Paris. Mom grew increasingly suspicious that this had something to do with Erwin and not volunteer tutoring.

She took off on the Heisers. "Who ever heard of running a business in an apartment? Did you see their mailbox? Elsa Heiser, Masseuse, Rolf Heiser, Bookkeeper. Who do they think they are, Count and Countess Petrofsky? Tell me who in this building has enough money to hire a bookkeeper or afford the luxury of a massage. It's to show off, if you ask me." Mom's voice had spiraled, her fair skin blotched crimson.

Mom had left Odessa after the Great War to escape a harsh life and had worked in a sweatshop, sewing linings inside heavy winter coats, where she learned to stitch without pause and keep her discontents to herself. After marriage, her circumstances didn't budge. That's why the New Deal was a sign of hope. Separated in Russia by class, education, and status, she resented the comfortable Germans who arrived before her and looked down on those they considered less worthy. Mom judged them arrogant. Germans first, Jews of a different sort.

I felt sad for her, but at fifteen all I cared about was a peek into Erwin's apartment, his furniture, his world, to study at his desk, our heads touching. I had questions. Why did he leave Germany? Had he ever visited Odessa or Paris?

One morning while Mom puttered in the kitchen preparing hot cocoa, I opened our living room window, thinking Erwin might leave early for some special reason. Much to my surprise, he sprinted down the stoop behind a black-coated figure wearing a homburg.

A hand circled my waist, pulled me inside, and slammed the window shut.

"What am I going to do with you? Come eat." Mom leaned against the sink watching me stab at my bowl of cereal. "You're looking for trouble. That Elsa passed me on the steps and looked right through me. Even a Rothschild smiles at a peasant. Like I've always said, the apple doesn't fall far from the tree."

As days went by, I became more obsessed with the idea of Erwin than the real boy. Had he ever existed, or had I seen an apparition on the staircase? I wondered whether I had invented him.

I had despaired of seeing Erwin again when we collided on the staircase. Seeing him so suddenly, my heart bumped against my chest. He held the vestibule door open, a shy grin on his face. He was dressed as if he had stepped from the pages of a Dickens novel, tweed Norfolk jacket over a heavy knit sweater, knickers, and oxfords. The script I had prepared was gone. The sound of his w's replacing his v's, a charming keepsake.

The subway sped. I had the worrisome thought that we'd part without my seeing him again. Aboveground the wind took my breath away. Exhilarated, I grabbed his arm and together we ran.

At the school entrance, I said, as casually as I could, "Erwin, how about meeting in the library during study period?"

We compared schedules and then I discovered why we missed each other. He left home early and stayed late to work on a project for admission to the prestigious Bronx High School of Science.

"Frank says the boys call you the professor. Do you mind?"

"No, everyone has me figured for an Einstein. I'm good in science, but that's my father's wish. What I would like to do is visit the West and climb mountains."

Before I met Erwin in the library, I rehearsed the most important question of my life. "Erwin, do you suppose it would be okay if I came to your apartment for help with questions for an upcoming history test?"

For a moment he looked uncertain, rested his book bag on a table next to a card catalogue, and tightened the straps. When he reached for a book that caught his interest, I swallowed hard.

"Erwin, did you hear me?"

"Sure, sure, fine. When?"

My father had surprised my mother with theatre tickets for *Where Is My Child?* starring Stella Adler at the Second Avenue Playhouse. Given the after-show tea and strudel, they would be home late.

"Wednesday is good. How's seven?"

Later, I worried if I had been a little too pushy.

The evening of the play, we ate early. I helped Mom with the clasp on her pearls and closed the snaps on her corselette.

"Don't open the door unless you know who it is. Mrs. Katz is home for emergencies."

As soon as my parents were out the door, I put on my good brown dress with the lace collar. Standing on tiptoe to see in the mirror, I pinched my sallow cheeks. Would Erwin like me better with a light application of Mom's Tangee lipstick? I decided against it. In the excitement of the moment, I forgot that one of the knobs on the dresser had fallen off. My dress caught on the nail and I yanked, knowing before I looked that the cloth had ripped. My second best dress had a stain. I rummaged in Mom's chiffarobe, found a paisley scarf and tied it around my middle to cover the hole. Remembering that Mom had taught me a guest didn't come empty-handed, I filled an empty bakery bag with chunks of her peanut brittle, grabbed my notebook, and peered into the hallway.

At Erwin's door, I took a deep breath, fluffed my hair, and pulled in my stomach. I tapped. Their wiener dog Hanzi barked. The door opened a smidgeon. A tall mannish woman in a starched white butcher apron over a blue forget-me-not print dress raised her eyebrows.

"Yes?"

"Erwin offered to help me with history questions."

The door opened wider. She commanded Hanzi to sit. I saw Erwin at the end of the dimly lit hall.

"Erwin, go in your room. This is none of your business."

She looked at me. "Are you living downstairs?"

I nodded extending the bag of candy. "This is for you."

She looked inside the bag, handing it back. "We don't eat that."

She presented me with a frosty smile. "Young lady, where we come from, girls don't visit boys. Erwin knows better. I'm sorry. Go home."

I didn't think she was a bit sorry. The door closed. I stared at the black apartment numbers through a watery haze, ran downstairs, threw my clothes on the floor and hopped into bed.

Sometime before midnight, I tiptoed into the living room and opened the window, the same one where I had looked out with such longing. The streets were silent, as if they had died. I watched snowflakes dissipate on my windowsill and saw what Mom disliked in me and what had led to my humiliation. Impulsiveness, arrogance, a Miss Know-It-All.

Back in bed, I gazed up at our cracked ceiling and winced at the sound of heavy footsteps from the Heisers' apartment overhead as if my heart were being crushed. When Mom came home, I pretended sleep. She turned up the radiator and smoothed my comforter. "Handsome is as handsome does" cut through my tattered thoughts.

It would take years before I understood what my mother meant. That night I couldn't be consoled.

Briolette

Sheryl L. Nelms

excavating a corner
of my mind

I unearth this memory
of my father

dusted off
it sparkles

iridescent:

I wait
polished

in pink dotted Swiss
and black patent
for him to come
home from
the War

then he's here

opening the green
screen door
to hug

me

War Was a Game

Gretchen Fletcher

I remember when war was a game
we played in backyards. We girls,
the nurses, treated wounds
of neighbor boys who entered
mildew-redolent pup tents
to be bandaged with leaves.
We girls never went into combat—
a job for boys—who ran around,
fingers cocked, shooting each other,
shouting those words
we had learned from our parents—
Krauts and Japs—from yards,
making the sound effects of war—
whooshes of bazookas,
whistle and whine of falling bombs,
exhalation of explosions
that brought more boys into our tent
to show us their bare chests
we smeared with ketchup stolen
from mothers' kitchens
when war was just a game
we played in backyards.

FICTION

The Untimely Demise of the Other Frank Sinatra

Dan Seiters

Whenever I was present, at least, my mother was always sane, practical to a fault. No matter how much fun something might be, if it'd get her labeled as a nut, she just wouldn't do it. The extreme opposite, my father seldom worried about anything, certainly not his image. He liked to sing, dance, play cards, shoot craps. And tell stories. Aesop would have taken one peek at my parents and proclaimed my mother an ant, my old man a grasshopper. Opposites may have attracted, but in the case of Roke and Maxine Owen, lusty love quickly turned to something else.

I saw how it'd play out early in life. When I was about three, Dad carved this man out of an orange peel. Two arms, two legs, a head, and a cock. Dad and me, we both giggled like geese when Dad left this long skinny stem of a cock on the peel man. Mom, though, didn't find the cock one bit funny. She got monumentally riled, and the argument escalated. I remember cowering as the ironing board sailed across the room. I don't remember who threw it, but I decidedly recall my old man stomping out, slamming the door so hard our family portrait crashed from the wall. Once more he was storming toward Amanda's Salty Dog Tavern. That man knew how to exit. He was like Zeus raging through the door, trailing a shower of sparks and streams of lightning.

Amanda's Salty Dog. About once a month on a Saturday afternoon, the old man'd let me tag along to the Dog, a wondrous tavern of worldly delights. Smoke made splendid weird shapes, fierce monsters in the blue light. I loved the smell of the beer, the pretzels, the peanuts. Although I didn't know the word then, that mixture was my ambrosia. Looking back, I see that it was a simple neighborhood tavern, deep, narrow, with a straight bar running the entire length of the place. The wooden floor looked old, its black paint fading to gray. The regulars ranged from reeking bum to business honcho, but most, like my old man, were either railroaders or steelworkers. I found the men grand, the women exotic. The sparkling bottles on glass shelves before mirrors promised forbidden thrills. Except for those songs that told stories, the country music was kind of boring, but of course what kind of kid can wrap his soul around the plight of some love-wounded cowboy?

I had this fine cloth crow that served as airplane, diving eagle, sparring partner, and wrestling bear until its back ripped open and its foam-rubber guts spewed all over the apartment. I paraded up and down the bar, filling the empty carcass of my crow with loose change people gave me and occasionally sipping the dregs out of a beer bottle. I thought I was possibly the slickest, slyest child on the planet, yet looking back, I suspect the adults could have detected and prevented my petty larceny any time they chose.

To Dad and me, the Salty Dog was heaven. Mom saw it as the other place entirely.

So divorce, I suppose, was inevitable. Harmony's hard for the ant and the grasshopper. There was no peace, certainly no prosperity in the Owen apartment.

About a year before the divorce, though, my mother did something so utterly and flagrantly out of character that it still astounds me. Legislatures and humane societies have long since banned the practice, but years ago, baby chicks and bunnies dyed a variety of pastels were big sellers during Easter. Few survived, and many, I suspect, met horrible ends, mauled by hot little hands. But my mother didn't consider this. The Easter after I turned four, she bought me a fuzzy pink chicken. Thinking it a most splendid gift, I named him Frank Sinatra after a guy I often heard singing on my mother's records and on the radio. I had seen a picture of Mr. Sinatra once and, like me, he was a skinny little guy.

Now a baby chicken—even a pink one—for a farm kid might make a lot of sense. Even for a kid with the merest patch of yard, a pink chicken wouldn't be insane. Or a rooftop where a cage might nestle. But in a three-room apartment in Gary, Indiana, a fuzzy pink baby destined to evolve into a huge white Frank Sinatra bordered on madness.

As a wee fuzzy pink chick, Frank Sinatra was barely an ounce of trouble. Even when he hopped around the apartment and left "gifts," they were tiny and wiped up in a whisk. He babbled incessantly, but the cheerful peep, peep, peep seemed more endearing than chafing. Of course even the nastiest tempered, scraggliest old alley cat was cuddly as a kitten. Jasper, the rottenest bully on the block, was probably tolerable as an infant. It's possible that as babies kicking and cooing in cribs, even some future serial killers were cute. But they all grow up: the alley cat, the bully, the serial killer. And of course my chicken. Loveable, happy Frank Sinatra grew into an enormous—and beautiful—grouchy white rooster with a faint pink tinge to the tips of his feathers.

From the beginning, Frankie was eccentric, maybe even bizarre. We kept him in a shoebox, and to get him to shut up at night, we had to cover him with the lid. He would go to sleep when we put the lid on and wake up when we took it off in the morning. But Frankie grew, got to be the biggest chicken anybody ever saw. The shoebox didn't grow. No matter how big he got, when bedtime rolled around, Frankie considered a shoebox his birthright. He didn't mind looking absurd, this giant chicken who ended each day by wriggling and scrunching around until he had the lower quarter of his body in the box. Dad said Frankie looked like a woman squeezing into a dress three sizes too small. Sometimes it took him a half-hour to get comfortable. Then, with his head lowered, he'd sit there and cluck and howl and bitch until someone balanced the box top on his back. In the loosest possible sense, then, he'd be in the box, and he'd finally go to sleep.

Unfortunately we no longer had to remove the box top for that idiot rooster to wake up. At the first slit of sun, Frank Sinatra would shake the box top from his back and crow like a maniac. A lifelong insomniac, sometimes I hadn't even fallen asleep when that dumb rooster announced a new day.

Now, chickens, I later learned when I observed a few of Frankie's kinfolk, seem to live by a code of their own. Even on a farm, they dart around aimlessly, chatter incessantly, get into stupid fights, fly with no particular destination, and get up too early. But even among chickens, most of whom were born to look dumb and act weird, Frank Sinatra was crazy. Even I, at four and a half, could see it. Frank Sinatra was clearly a lunatic.

Maybe it was because big Frank never had room to be a real chicken, never had the space to stretch out and run and always lived with such a short runway that about half of his flights ended in crashes against a wall. Sometimes he even hit the window, which could have been fatal because we lived on the second floor. As he grew bigger, we finally had to keep the shade pulled. I see now that the loss of the light from that window probably increased our isolation, added to the tension in the house.

But as I said, even among chickens, Frankie was a ditz-bomb. If he didn't hit the wall when he flew, he was likely to come down on someone's head.

"You dumb cluck!" Dad used to shout at Frankie, batting the big airborne bird away. Dad was a Golden Gloves champ, a boxer and barroom brawler, so I was not surprised when he took a few swings at my chicken. Mom, though, was as peaceful a woman as you'd find outside a Quaker meeting, but even she had to instinctively swat Frankie away when he landed in her hair.

Any cat, even one that's daft, clumsy, and addled by dog fear, can leap up onto a cluttered dresser fifteen times its height and not disturb a single thing. Chickens can't do that. At least Frank Sinatra couldn't. He'd land on a table and stuff started flying. Glass things shattered, and round things rolled into deep hiding. What he missed with his wings and his initial landing, he kicked behind him as a sort of second effort. Then that idiot would hop down, and where he should have skulked humbly in shame, he strutted. Actually clucked and strutted—as if he'd found the cure for cancer or something.

"Cluck alert! Cluck alert!" Dad taught me to shout when Frank Sinatra'd take to the air. I'd see that enormous chicken start to fly and shout "Cluck alert! Cluck alert!" and dive for safety under the table. It seldom worked. Frankie loved to find me and peck me. I couldn't let anyone know how often that foul bird nipped me or Frankie surely would have been executed. It got to the point where I was afraid of my own chicken. Chicken of my chicken. Really, it was almost impossible to avoid the conclusion that Frank Sinatra was a menace, although at the time, I don't think I knew the word menace. I did know the word asshole, though, and if ever a chicken were an asshole, Frank Sinatra filled the bill.

As I mentioned, insomnia has cursed me all my days. When bedtime rolled around, however, I'd lie down without putting up much of a fight because there was too much strife in the apartment without my adding to it. So I'd lie down and close my eyes, even though I knew I was in for a long slow night of pretending to be asleep. With me supposedly unconscious and unaware, the fights escalated. I'd lie there in the next room saying, "Please don't get pissed off and leave, please don't leave." I'd spend most of the night praying: "Please, God, if we're all still here in the morning and if the hatchet man hasn't split any of our skulls, I'll become a better human being. I'll even stop swearing the very day I turn twenty-two." I didn't see how I could go out and play with my friends if I kept that promise. Still, I figured life was pretty well over by twenty-two. You were probably too old to have any really good friends, anyhow.

So I worried about being deserted in my sleep. Then, after Frank Sinatra moved in, my parents also began to talk about how we'd all be better off in a chickenless apartment. How many sentences did I hear that started off with: "If Frank Sinatra were frying in a skillet . . ." Those words always made me weep as if I were being dragged out to be publicly hanged. Despite my fears, Frankie escaped each night with his feathers intact.

Although I was afraid of Frankie, and I don't think I liked him very much because you couldn't pet him or anything, I nevertheless thought I loved him. He was, after all, mine, and Mom gave him to me. So I worried about whether or not my evil chicken would be alive and clucking when I got up each morning. I started feeling sorry for myself. Having a nasty, unlikable chicken as my first pet seemed to be just one more instance of how my life would never quite work out. It was like the magnificent spy code ring I ordered and waited for for two weeks. When the mailman delivered it, it turned out to be a big clunky thing that no kid would ever wear. That's the way it turned out with everything I ordered. I would have cried had I not dedicated myself to being tough.

Speaking of being tough, I intuitively understood that Danny was not an adequate name for Gary's fierce gray streets. When they named me Danny, I'll bet my parents never once thought of the fact that I'd have to go outside the apartment every day. We lived in a city of steel mills and smog, of concrete streets and alleys and almost no grass. It was a city where gangs roamed and where if you survived, even as a tiny kid, you had to be tough. If your name were Zeke or Rex, no one would mess with you, but nobody'd call me Zeke or Rex. So I thought maybe I could survive, even prosper, with a tough name like Charlie. When I suggested Charlie, my family and friends acquiesced. Sort of. They called me Chuck. Chuck! Who quivers upon hearing the name Chuck? But Chuck became my name. Just one more thing that didn't quite work out.

One evening after Dad got home from work on the railroad, he and Mom called me into the living room. "Oh, no!" I thought as I trudged in to meet them. "This is it. This is where Dad splits forever. This is what divorce is." I tried to look fierce, but tears seeped out as I took my seat in a chair five times too big for me.

"Chuck," Dad said to me, "how would you rate our lives since Frank Sinatra moved in with us?"

I might have said a thousand things, many of them meaningful. I wanted to explain that my life resembled nothing so much as a reeking chicken turd since he and Mom declared war on one another. Frankie, they needed to know, wasn't the main problem. That was the plain truth, and I should have laid it out flat on the table. But I opted for choice number 1,001, the pitifully ineffectual "I don't know." Little, puny, whiney voice. I heard myself utter those three despicable words and turned away from the mirror. Who could look at a spineless, quaking coward dwarfed in a gigantic chair?

Then Mom and Dad united for the first time in months. Even though I was sure they planned to sentence Frankie to death, it was at least nice to hear them agree on something. Finally Dad ended with a flourish: "You've got to admit, Chuck, that since Frank Sinatra joined our family, our lives have turned to chickenshit."

I tried to keep from crying, attempted to brace myself, to accept Frankie's execution order from on high. But I couldn't. Tears rolled, and I could barely get out the words: "Please don't kill Frank Sinatra."

Mom and Dad looked at each other and laughed. Actually laughed. Together.

"We aren't going to kill him, honey," Mom said, still laughing.

Oh, no, I thought. They're going to evict Frank Sinatra, cast my gentle chicken out into the gray, surly streets. The streets where the hatchet man roams. Where the devil emerges at night and scopes out the city from his fire escape landing two apartment houses down. When Edmund, Jenny, Heather, Tom, and I climbed up his fire escape and knocked on his back door last Halloween, he burst upon us all red and horned with pitchfork poised. He caught us before we jumped off the balcony, caught us and tried to buy us off with candy. Said he wasn't the real devil.

Across the street, the little redheaded girl lurks in her own aura of evil, waiting to hit Frankie in the head with a brick, the way she did me. That little brat! She probably grew up to be Tabitha, cackling and stirring dead things in a caldron, soaring across the night skies on a broom. Wouldn't that little brick-throwing hag just love to capture a nice fat chicken for her pot?

And on these very streets, Frankie might meet Jasper, a bully six years older than I was, a punk who used to catch me and punch me and squeeze my balls until my old man found out. Dad called Lee Bob Hampton, Jasper's old man, out into the street. Much bigger than Dad, Lee Bob snorted with laughter as he emerged for the fight. But Dad hit him hard and hit him often, cut him so deep that about a gallon of his blood splashed out.

"Lee Bob," Dad said to the bloody, crumpled mess in the street, "if that whore's melt you spawned ever touches my boy again, I'll be back. And I won't leave so soon next time."

Jasper was afraid to touch me anymore, but he'd surely take it out on Frank. Better to murder Frank Sinatra in the living room than send him out into the streets.

"We wouldn't kill your chicken, Chuck," Dad said. "But we can't live with him, either. So tomorrow evening your Uncle Russ is gonna come through Gary."

"We're going to put Frankie in a box," Mom said. "Then tomorrow Uncle Russ'll take him out to the farm to live with Grandpa and Grandma McBride."

I cried, of course, at the thought of life without Frank Sinatra, but what could I really say? I had expected divorce, then Frankie's execution, then his eviction, which would lead to certain death. Exile and relocation was about a thousand times better than anything I had expected when I heard about this family meeting.

The truce failed. Hitler and FDR were as likely to remain friends as Roke and Maxine Owen. Without Frank Sinatra there to unite them, they could concentrate on their own personal war, on hurling mental stones small and huge. Through a microscope of hate, the smallest slight loomed monstrous.

Frank Sinatra got exiled to the farm in May. By August I had joined him. The divorce—quick, fierce, final—was sealed by October. With Frank and me stashed safely on a flat Illinois farm, Mom went off to find work—and possibly a replacement for Roke. I was deeply into my fifth year. Frank Sinatra approached a distant two.

I can't remember if I missed Roke very much, or if at all after a month or two. Mom's negative PR campaign against him was so harsh and effective that two years later, when I heard he might come and visit me, I was filled with dread. I didn't hear anything more about him until my Uncle Chet told me that my half-brother had been born.

"When Moon Mullins walked into Amanda's Salty Dog and told your old man he had another son," Uncle Chet said, "Roke threw down his cards and said, 'Gentlemen, read 'em and weep. That's a straight diamond flush and I thank you for the pot. Best hand I ever held. We'll be calling the wee lad Diamond Douglas.'"

Mom couldn't have expressed greater disdain if Uncle Chet had reported that Roke had taken to swallowing horse turds in exchange for drinks, but secretly I thought—and still think—it was way cool. I wished Diamond Douglas were my name, actually. I didn't hear anything else until my second half-brother was born. Roke and his wife called him Chuckie, possibly named after me. Probably not.

So like, damn, Shazam! Life transformed me utterly, ripping me from the belly of a city slum and planting me on a farm. I don't know whether I changed at all, but I do know Frank Sinatra didn't alter his weird ways one bit. I can't believe my grandparents actually did this, but these unsentimental farm folks put that moron chicken to bed each night in his shoebox. Balanced the lid on his back so he could sleep.

It never occurred to Frankie that he was alive only because my grandparents loved and indulged me. He was no great chicken of gratitude, that Frank Sinatra, and he refused to acknowledge his debt to me. Strutting on the rim of the frying pan, he remained forever an arrogant asshole. A giant among chickens, he terrorized the other roosters, molested the hens constantly, and flew at and pecked me and Grandpa and Grandma so incessantly, it seemed that he was on a divine mission to peck. Grandma and Grandpa felt sorry for me, so they didn't fry his feathery ass, but it was only me and nothing more standing between him and the fiery pan.

That my grandparents allowed him live was astounding, especially Grandpa, who was enormous—about 6' 3"—and weighed over 300 pounds. Big, powerful, profane, that was Howard McBride. He talked—mostly swore, mostly shouted—in his sleep. Often I was jolted from sleep in the next room by a voice so loud and deep it seemed to come from the core of the earth. "You son of a bitch!" he'd rumble, low and loud as thunder. "I'm gonna kick your ass." Most folks called him Big'un, and though he was always exceptionally gentle with me, I saw in him a volcanic capacity for destruction.

These farm folks who put Frankie in a shoebox for a good night's rest each evening, of course, were more accustomed to killing and eating chickens than coddling them. The front yard was perpetually spattered with blood where Grandma tied chickens to the clothesline by the feet and lopped off their heads with a butcher knife. It was better, I think, to be killed by Grandpa. Death came very quick because he just grabbed the chicken by the head, flicked his powerful wrist the way you'd snap a bull whip, and the body would crack loose from the neck. Or if he happened to catch the feet first, he'd just step on the head and pull. Headless, the chicken would dash around in insane patterns for a while, pumping blood and spatter-painting the grass.

How Frankie survived Grandpa for three or four months, I don't know. But I survived. Frank Sinatra survived. Still, farms are quiet, not like Gary. I wandered around a lot and nobody beat me up like they did in Gary. I didn't miss getting stomped, but I did miss the action. The city noise. I was glad to be forever rid of Jasper and that little brick-throwing bitch across the street and the mad hatchet man and the devil on his fire escape. But I sorely missed all the other kids. Frankie was a poor substitute for real friends. For Amanda's Salty Dog. For the kids on the block. You can talk to a dog, even a cat, but you feel silly reciting a litany of the wrongs you've suffered to a chicken. Not even the noblest of chickens would listen as I explained that I was so bored I sometimes feared my heart would stop. I didn't fear that it might break, just that it would stop for lack of interest.

Then, from deep funk to elation. World War II ended and my Uncle Chet was coming home. Not only was Chet a big, handsome soldier who laughed a lot and paid attention to kids. Me. But some of my relatives said that he was going to try to bring home a monkey from the South Pacific. The mere possibility that a wonderful monkey might enter my life sent me into ecstasy. My nights were flooded with monkey dreams and during waking hours I thought of little but my uncle's monkey. I smiled constantly, sometimes indulging the mean-spirited notion that my friendship with the good monkey would certainly put that ungrateful Frank Sinatra in his place. I'd teach that feathered crud to peck me. I envisioned the monkey just slapping the hell out of that rotten Sinatra and teaching him some manners.

My ecstasy sometimes was shattered by harsh reality. "Now remember, Chuck," my grandmother said, "until we actually see the monkey, we won't know for sure Uncle Chet's gonna be able to bring him."

I tried to prepare myself for disappointment but found a monkeyless life just too barren to contemplate. I also wondered what a monkey might eat, what he might find on this farm. Monkeys like bananas, I knew, but bananas were rationed because of World

War II. I couldn't remember the last time I saw one. But surely, I decided, if a family were lucky enough to entertain a monkey, God or the government or something would provide bananas. Absurdly, I thought maybe if you could find out who your senator was and phoned him up in the morning to tell him your monkey was perishing from lack of food, a truck packed with bananas would roll in by afternoon.

Never sleeping much, I slept less and less as the time approached for my uncle's monkey to join us. The night before he was to arrive, I didn't even bother to go to bed. I divided the night between prayer—"Please, God, let him arrive safely"—and staring out my second-story bedroom window. To keep Grandma and Grandpa from finding out how excited I was, however, I stayed in my room until after the sun came up. Then I bounded down the stairs, ate a morsel or two, and climbed the tree in the front yard to stand watch. Noon came and nothing yet. No one drove down the dirt road, not even a tractor. At noon I ate a little more, then back up into the tree.

It was nearly five in the afternoon before I noticed a gigantic tail of dust coming down our road. Soon I heard a horn honking to announce the return of the conquering hero. Uncle Russ was driving, honking his way down the gravel road. In the car with him were all three children of Howard and Lily McBride—Uncle Chester, Aunt Wanda, and Mom. And my cousin Russell Jr., who was eight years older than I was and seemed to have everything figured out. As far as I was concerned, Junior really knew how to be.

When they all piled, laughing, from the car, I leapt from the tree. Uncle Chet pulled his duffel bag out of the trunk and heaved it into the front yard. Then he and Uncle Russ hefted a wooden box out of the trunk. "The poor monkey," I thought. "That's a mighty small box for a monkey." With some regret, I guessed the monkey must not be bringing a friend.

Then, to my horror, I noticed that there were no holes in the top of the box. When Frank Sinatra was small enough for the shoebox lid to cover him entirely, we poked holes in top so he could breathe.

"He's dead," I screeched, shoving my way through the crowd of embracing, celebrating friends and relatives. "He's dead for lack of air!"

How, I wondered, could any relative of mine be so utterly stupid as to kill his monkey? How could we all be looking up to Uncle Chet as a hero? He looked like a warrior god, splendid, sturdy, and tall in his uniform and medals, handsome in a smile that banished gloom. Perfect as he looked, he was an idiot, nothing but a monkey-murdering moron.

"Who's dead?" Mom asked.

"Uncle Chet's monkey. Stupid Uncle Chet brought him all the way home from overseas in a box with no air holes. He couldn't breathe and now he's dead."

It took everybody about a minute to figure out what I was raving about. Then Uncle Chet said, "Chuck, there's not a monkey in that box. Here, I'll show you."

Uncle Russ got a claw hammer out of his trunk and they opened the box. Inside were four big shiny brown things, sort of round.

"What are those?" I asked, almost afraid of them.

"Coconuts," Uncle Chet explained. "I had them shellacked and brought one back for Grandma, one for your mother, and one for Aunt Wanda. And I'm gonna keep one for myself. And there's an army jacket for Junior and one for you."

What a grave falling off was this. I plummeted from the towering hope of a monkey to the reality of four stupid brown lumps. A vulture ate my heart.

Don't show nothing, I snarled to myself. Nothing. Don't cry. Don't run away and hide in the barn. Don't let them see how much they hurt you. Never let them know they even have the power to hurt you. Laugh. Laugh with them. Pretend you knew all along there wouldn't be a monkey in that box.

"I was joking," I said. "I knew there wasn't no monkey in there. I wouldn't want no stupid monkey anyhow, 'cause I got my chicken. My own chicken!" I tried to laugh, laughed too hard, too loud. Hysteria. And, gravest betrayal of all, my eyes were leaking all over my face and my nose was running and my spit was getting thick. I wasn't crying, refused to cry, would not cry if tears would call forth ten thousand monkeys. But in front of all those people, I looked like I was crying, so it was almost the same as shedding actual tears. It was almost the same as if I'd been weak, as if they'd been capable of inflicting pain on me. Damn my tears and damn that monkeyless box!

Mom ran to me and hugged me, and Uncle Chet picked me up. "I'm sorry about the monkey, Chuck. I had him for a couple of months before my discharge, but customs inspectors wouldn't let me bring him home. I'm sorry nobody told you." Then he hugged me tightly.

It was small comfort. I didn't even know what a customs inspector was and what the son of a bitch might have against monkeys. How could any living creature hate a monkey? I did know, though, that I would enjoy putting that customs guy and Uncle Chet together in the manure spreader.

But who could stay mad at Uncle Chet? He hung around the farm for about two weeks after everybody went back to their lives, and spent most of his days with me. He went to town in the evenings, coming home just after Frank Sinatra heralded each morning. He'd sleep a few hours, and then the rest of the day was mine. He told me stories, endless stories about Mom and Aunt Wanda as kids, stories about Grandma and Grandpa. Stories about Roke. He liked Roke and actually seemed to be a lot like him. And most of all, he kept me laughing as he told me about his life as a soldier. I now know that he left out the bad parts, that there was really nothing funny about World War II. He told me he won his Purple Heart because he got drunk and sprained his ankle when he fell off a truck. I later learned he'd been wounded in battle. And he told me they gave him his Bronze Stars and the other medals to make him feel better about the pain in his ankle.

Uncle Chet had been on the farm about a week when he said, "Chuck, Grandma and Grandpa are dirt poor. I'm afraid you're gonna have to make a sacrifice and help them out. Like the soldiers I served with, you're gonna have to sacrifice a friend."

"Sure," I said, "they've been really nice to me. What do they need?"

"I'm afraid if you don't let them eat Frank Sinatra, they might starve."

"Eat Frank Sinatra! Oh, no!" What was Uncle Chet saying? You don't just eat somebody's chicken. Besides, there were other animals my grandparents could eat. Who cared about the cow? Why not eat the pig? The pig stunk and nobody liked her. Not really. That pig had no friends. Who would miss that fat old reeking sow? Or maybe we could eat hay like the cow does. Boil it in water.

We talked for a long time, with Uncle Chet laying out the requirements of a pet. "A pet, first of all," he said, "is cute. Is Frank Sinatra cute?"

"No, but he's big and strong and brave."

"So is a lion, Chuck, but you wouldn't want to sit down and talk to a lion. Also, a pet's loyal and loving. Has Frank Sinatra shown you one scrap of loyalty? Of love?"

And so it went, with me finally admitting that Frank Sinatra was an asshole and that really, he was about as popular as the pig. But I hated the thought of Frankie in a frying pan. Asshole or not, he was my chicken. He attacked me and pecked me and kept me half afraid all the time, but he was my pet. I never had an abusive parent, but I knew kids who got kicked around hard. They hated to say they didn't like their folks. And I, with my asshole pet, just didn't want to admit I didn't like my rooster.

Finally, Uncle Chet said, "I'll tell you what, Chuck. Let's fix it so you can make a profit out of this deal. What if I give you a $100.00 check plus a one-dollar bill for Frank Sinatra?"

"A hundred dollars plus a dollar?" I said. I didn't know exactly how much money there was in the world, but I didn't think it could be much more than that. And Frankie was, after all, an asshole. With $101 in my pocket, I began to see that clearly Frank Sinatra was the worst chicken that ever crowed.

So I had my money and Uncle Chet had my chicken. Then he said, "Now it's time for you to learn to play poker."

I turned out not to be a natural poker player. Before the sun went down, I had lost $100.00 back to uncle Chet. He took the check and put it in his pocket. Then he said, "We've got to quit playing now while you still have a dollar. Besides, after this day's work, I need to go to town and get a drink."

The next day Grandma, Grandpa, and Uncle Chet ate Frank Sinatra. I wasn't hungry.

It was only decades later at a reunion of the McBride cousins that I learned why Uncle Chet had to talk me out of Frank Sinatra. When Aunt Wanda, our family historian, told the story of Frank Sinatra and the shoebox, my cousin Lois asked why we had cooked Frankie when we had other chickens.

Aunt Wanda astounded me when she said, "Because Dad killed him. Frank Sinatra flew up in his face, and Dad kicked him. Frankie was dead by the time he hit the ground."

I didn't say anything, but I was stunned. Suddenly I understood something wonderful about my uncle. Frank Sinatra was already dead when Uncle Chet was trying to talk me into letting the family turn him into dinner. He paid me and played poker with me all afternoon just to keep me from learning that Grandpa had killed my chicken with a single kick. He must have understood that because of the divorce and loneliness and other uncertainties in my life at that time, I was too strung out and confused to handle the news that Grandpa had booted my chicken straight to hell.

I'd always loved Uncle Chet, but that day my love blossomed into something sublime. In civilian life you don't get Purple Hearts and Bronze Stars for quiet acts of kindness and heroism. But I'm sorry my uncle isn't still alive, so I could bestow some sort of honor on him. A Medal of Life. Of course he'd have laughed at it, even if he might have cherished it. He joked about his Purple Heart and his Bronze Stars. But he earned them. I'd give him an award anyhow. We'd share one last laugh together and drink top-shelf whiskey till sunrise.

Wrong Color, Right Size

Charles Henry Lynch

In the '40s and '50s at finer stores
like Hutzler's, May Company, and O'Neill's
even when we walked through the door
staff gave the once-over real real slow.
Couldn't try on bras, girdles, or underwear.
No law against it, but saleswomen knew the code.
No returns. All receipts were stamped FINAL.

I did day's work for a lady had oodles of money
and dressed to the nines.
Got waited upon hand and foot when shopping.
But if she was busy or left Baltimore,
I was the stand-in for her head.

Stewart's was the absolute worse.
One move to lift a hat, they'd scurry over.
 "I'm sorry. That's not for you."

I'd pretend to be startled, then calmly reply,
"Oh? The Missus did notify this department
her help would be coming this week
to make purchases. We're the same size,
and she very much trusts my selections."

Clerks would fluster. The floor manager
flip through a registry, then nod, steely-eyed.
A few stood close enough to pressure me,
arms folded. Well, then you *know*
I just had to take my own sweet time.

Plunk on every damn size seven.

Pull gently to check if a feather or bow was tight.

Run my hand round the lining.

Brim up. Brim down. Tilt. Pushed back.

Study sequins, beadwork, braiding.

Turn this-a-way and that in counter mirrors.
Then stroll the aisle to the floor length one,
staring over my shoulders and to all sides.

I'd make no telling gesture or give opinions
'til I chose what Mrs. what's-'er-name should like.

Even tallying her account and boxing
merchandise, they'd still be frowning.
Stiff. Never say "Thank you" or "Goodbye"
or "Have a nice day." But I'd look 'em
dead in the face. And smile. Always smile.

Draper and the Dragon

James E. Stanton

Specialist Seventh Class Don Draper held the title of "super lingy" at Ramasun Station in Non Sung, Thailand, in January 1969. It was a title specifically created for him. When he left six months later none of the lesser lingies of the Seventh Radio Research Field Station was judged worthy to hold it. The title itself was retired a few years later, still unoccupied.

There was nothing physically remarkable in Draper's appearance. He was about thirty, of average height and rather slender build. Neither handsome nor ugly. A long, narrow face. A long, narrow, and rather large nose. Ears that stuck out a bit from the sides of his head. Still, most who met him came away feeling that he both looked, and acted, somewhat unusually, even strangely—at least for an American—especially for an American GI.

He was also surrounded by an aura of mystery. *Some* said that at least part, if not most of that mystery was of his own deliberate invention. He lived in the village of Non Sung not far from the front gate of Ramasun Station, a U.S. military post dedicated to "signal intelligence," a fancy euphemism for electronic eavesdropping, or radio spying if you will.

This spying required a staff of translators for several Asian languages. Draper translated Lao and Thai to English. He had been doing it for seven years and nobody was better at it. Nobody even came close. He lived in Non Sung with his "Thai wife." Her name was Viendara, shortened to "Dara" by his American associates. They had two children. All this was unknown to, or at least officially unrecognized by, the authorities at Ramasun Station.

They lived in a house atop a small hill. Really not more than a slight rise of ground, behind the Buddhist temple in Non Sung. It was an old teak house, surrounded by other old teak houses, in what had once been the "best" neighborhood of Non Sung. The other teak houses were dilapidated and crumbling. There were even some vacant lots where houses had been pulled down and taken apart for their salvageable lumber.

But Draper's house was in good repair. It had even been restored to its former glory. A very singular thing in rural Thailand in 1969, long before the renovation of old teak houses became trendy. Draper's house had no electricity, though electric power had been available in Non Sung for nearly ten years. It also had, in keeping with Thai tradition, no furniture other than some storage chests and low, portable rattan tables. Draper sat and slept on the floor like a native-born Thai, which he had come, over the years, to closely resemble. It was even rumored that, like a true prosperous Thai, he had a *mia noi*, a "small wife," in a remote village who he occasionally lived with, and who had borne him two additional children.

As with all things concerning Draper, fact could not be easily or reliably separated from fiction. For instance, his gorgeous wife, Dara, was said to be either a Thai princess, a Lao princess, or a Vientiane bar-girl who was an extremely convincing actress. It didn't really matter what she actually was. She was beautiful, gracious, and highly intelligent.

As for Draper himself, it was said that he had dropped out of college after one year and been drafted. Had ended up a company clerk because he could type. Had seen a notice for the Army's Language Aptitude Test. Had taken it and scored high. Had been sent to the U.S. Foreign Service Institute's first ever course in Lao in 1961. Had passed the course with flying colors. Had been sent to Bangkok in 1962, and had been in either Thailand or Laos ever since.

Just the fact that he had been continuously in Southeast Asia for seven years set him apart from every other GI at Ramasun Station. The standard tour of duty in Thailand was eighteen months. A one-year extension was routinely available to those who wanted it. Any additional requests for extensions were almost always denied. A few of the lingies and radio operators had been back and forth to Thailand several times, but none had ever served anything close to a seven-year stint. It was said that Draper had friends in the CIA across the river in Vientiane who kept him firmly planted in Northeast Thailand for various "special projects" which involved his high-level translating skills. It was said that the "Puzzle Palace" at Ft. Meade, Maryland, (aka the National Security Agency) had him secretly on their payroll to ride herd over our translating operation at Ramasun. These were only some of the more plausible explanations for his unusually long tenure.

Draper worked the 4 p.m. to midnight shift at Ramasun. That is, he worked it some of the time. He often disappeared for extended periods and then, just as everyone thought he was gone for good, he calmly and silently walked back in the Operations Building and sat down at his old desk as if nothing had happened. Though he told none of his colleagues what he had been up to, a few days later two or three different stories would be circulating around the base regarding Draper's latest exploits.

While he was revered by his fellow lingies, others were less keen on him. Some of the mostly drunken lifer sergeants who shuffled papers, made up schedules, and pretended to be in charge of things at Ops hated his guts for the same reasons that the lingies admired him. Draper ignored sergeants. He didn't talk back to them. They could have handled that. He didn't talk to them at all. He didn't even deign to recognize their existence. That infuriated them. While some of the lifer sergeants merely hated him, others both hated and feared him.

Now, there is no earthly reason why anyone should fear a person holding the relatively rare and decidedly oddball rank of Specialist Seventh Class in the Army. It was a rank that had no rank. The Army's technical term for this was a "non-command" rank. In other words, a person who is paid the same as a Sergeant First Class for his specialized expertise, not for commanding or supervising any troops. Draper didn't even qualify to be admitted to the NCO (non-commissioned officers) Club. Not that he would ever have wanted to go there. In fact, that was probably the last place he would ever have wanted to go.

Still, he was feared by many sergeants and even a few lieutenants. Stories circulated of run-ins between Draper and various officers, both commissioned and noncommissioned. Draper always won these head-butting contests working in ways that were both mysterious and Machiavellian. The fate of the losers was eagerly recounted in all its gory detail among the enlisted men who saw him as a sort of olive-drab Robin Hood. If all these stories were to be believed, Draper had sent at least two lieutenants to the deadly rice paddies of Vietnam. He also had engineered the "lateral transfer" of one particularly obnoxious 2nd Lieutenant from officer in charge of the Lao Translation Section to officer in charge of voter registration and absentee ballots for the 1968 election.

Sergeants fared even worse at his hands. He was credited with putting one into a mental institution and getting two others cashiered for habitual drunkenness and neglect of duty—a feat which seems hardly possible in the booze-sodden conscript Army of the Vietnam War era. Even fans of "Draper stories" could not agree on the exact number of sergeants he managed to get busted to private.

Given Draper's track record, it came as a great shock to his fellow lingies one day in June of 1969 to hear the latest rumor. "Draper's in trouble. He's pissed off the Colonel. Something bad is going to happen to him." As usual there was a flood of wildly contradictory details concerning this "trouble." Just the night before Draper had been working away in his usual quiet and unruffled fashion. Now he had disappeared—apparently for good. It took several of the best lingies months of spying (after all, that's what they were trained to do!) and comparing notes, to assemble a rough and partial picture of what happened to him.

Dragons were at the crux of it. Or rather, a single specific dragon—the dragon whose egg is interred in one of the large stone jars from which the Plain of Jars in Laos takes its name. This dragon, which most Lao people believe to be real rather than mythical, springs to life every few centuries to drive the bothersome foreigners out of Laos. In 1969, Laos was crawling with bothersome foreigners, and most of them were well-armed. Americans, Vietnamese, Chinese, Russians, Thais, a few leftover Frenchmen, a smattering of Corsican Mafia opium exporters, some Korean and Filipino mercenaries, and other groups too numerous to mention. So the dragon had his work cut out for him.

One man, however, was confident that the dragon could get the job done. He was Colonel Kong Le, a half-Lao, half-Hmong former captain of the Royal Laotian Army. Kong Le had started a coup in Vientiane in 1960 that, though it initially had almost no backing, ended up overthrowing the Lao government of General Phoumi Nosavan, which had been so carefully put into place by the CIA just three years before. He was able to do this only because all the notables and aristocrats of Laos were in the royal capital of Luang Prabang attending the funeral of King Sri Savang Vong, who had actually died a year before but was just then being buried based on the advice of the court astrologers.

Luang Prabang was an isolated place at that time, the more so as it was completely surrounded by Communist troops and reachable only by air (and even then only when the North Vietnamese were not within mortar range of the airport). So all the notables and aristocrats had to stay put, while Kong Le and his ragtag band of co-conspirators slowly and incompletely took over the country.

He was finally able to form a new government by bringing

back Prince Souvanna Phouma as head of state. The portly prince was the guy the CIA overthrew in 1957. Well, to make a very long story short, there was a little civil-war type fighting, a lot of diplomatic jawing, and eventually the CIA decided that Prince Souvanna Phouma wasn't such a bad guy after all.

They never warmed to Kong Le, however, even though they had trained him a few years earlier. So the deal was that the portly prince was a keeper, but Kong Le had to go. And after a lot more jawing about the fine print and details, he did finally go, to France, in 1964. He stayed there in comfortable exile until 1969, when he came back to check on dragon eggs. When he publicly announced his findings, all hell broke loose both in Laos and at Ramasun Station.

Draper had taken Kong Le's message on the evening shift. It was definitely a translation only he could do, as it involved literary, mythological, and astrological allusions that no other lingy would have been able to handle properly. The result was a masterpiece of linguistic art, a sacred copy of which was maintained in the Lao Translation Section for many years in a secret spot in the files known only to a select circle of the initiated.

Draper scanned his masterpiece with justifiable pride and then hand-carried it to the communications center to be sent out to the waiting world corporately known as the "intelligence community." Some members of that "community" were not that happy to see it. Some even thought it was a hoax. They quickly and vociferously contacted the Colonel who was supposed to be commanding Ramasun Station. Well, maybe he actually was commanding Ramasun Station, but he was doing it from a considerable distance—300 miles to be exact.

You see, the eavesdropping done at Ramasun Station in 1969 had only a few years before been done on a smaller scale at a facility just north of Don Muang Airport near Bangkok. Then most of the operation moved northeast, except the Colonel. They say the Colonel's wife had taken one look at the city of Udorn and then caught the next available plane back to Bangkok. Whatever the reason, we seldom saw him at Ramasun. So seldom, in fact, that some even doubted his very existence.

But he did exist and he arrived red-faced and apoplectic at the Lao Translation Section one evening. Those few who were there at the time say that he grabbed Draper by the shoulder and dragged him into the Ops Commander's office. Once inside, he started shouting at Draper. This was to be expected. Then Draper started shouting at the Colonel! Everyone held their breath. Then Draper stalked out of the office with the Colonel still shouting at him from the background.

Within twenty-four hours Draper had left Southeast Asia for the first time in seven and a half years. As he got on the plane to leave, he would have been able to pick up a copy of any one of the Bangkok newspapers that carried the "dragon story" as their front-page headline. It was just as he had reported it—except that his report was much more accurate.

There is some fragmentary information that he ended up at a remote listening station in the California desert called "Two Rivers Ranch." He reportedly stayed there for six months and then left the Army. What happened after that no one knows. Dara and her two children disappeared almost as quickly as he did. It was said only that she "went back to her village," but no one knows where, or even in which country, that village was.

In 1970 and 1971 rumors circulated that Draper had been sighted in either Udorn, Bangkok, or Vientiane—but those rumors were unconfirmed.

Coteau, 1969

Ann Olson

"I'm cold. It's dark. I don't know where the hell we're going. And now you're telling me I gotta take my shoes off and walk barefoot through the woods?"

That was Steve's cousin's voice from the backseat. His "California" cousin.

"It's the best way to *feel* the spirits," I answered. Defensive and not liking it, wishing I hadn't said it.

Seventeen miles from nowhere, we were just getting out of our cars in the empty parking area of Sica Hollow State Park, a deep dent in the ridge of the *Coteau des Prairies* in northeast South Dakota. Our trunk held cases of 3.2 Grain Belt beer, two bucks a case. And we'd all just dropped mescaline—supposed to be the most natural cactus high, milder than peyote. Three cars, ten teenagers. Just about midnight.

Darkness swallowed the first of us to step our bare feet into it. We hovered just outside the cars, not daring to step farther, allowing eyes to adjust, watching the soft explosions of electrified sound as the others got out too, their dome lights and tape decks blaring briefly. From one car, Edwin Starr's "War! . . . Ugh!" seemed to answer Country Joe's tinkly question from the other car: "One . . . two . . . three . . . what're we fightin' for? Don't ask me, I don't give a . . . ." Slam. Car doors and the night itself cut them off.

We stood in the black listening to the ticks of the cooling car engines. The stark contrast of the eight-track music to the too-sudden night silence disoriented us, complicated our hearing with blood rushes in our ears that echoed our heartbeats. The sweet-dank night smells came alive and curious, invasive as the darkness, seeking every pore, pressing against eyelids and probing earwells and mouths. Nostrils were afterthoughts to these night smells. Eyes open, all we saw were moving windshield shapes in retinal neons on black. So we tried closing our eyes to feel more natural and watched the soft colors pulsate on the backs of our eyelids. Senses exchanged functions: Ears pricked on smells; eyes felt waves of sound; and feet tasted things in the dark earth that eyes could not see in daylight. Our senses melded and our bodies dissolved into night. Then we were gone. Our voices became us. We were our sounds. We entered the spirit world of Sica Hollow.

We were stoned.

Going on sixteen, I was a veteran of this prairie town rite of passage. I'd helped to induct others maybe four times since my first time, usually in the fall or summer, but spring was good too, like now. Steve—we've been together over thirty years now—brought me here our first night out the summer before, when we stood in the bowl of the hollow and looked past the tree-dark hills that circled us. Our faces tilted toward the sky, its dome just a shade less black than the horizon line of forest. Then we saw, both of us at the same time, the stars falling, streaking, arching across the moonless expanse. A meteor shower, probably the Persiads, though we had no clue at the time. Giddy, we tried to count the comets, eight, nine, ten . . . twelve . . . fifteen, sixteen . . . thirty . . . thirty-two . . . until we could only laugh, hold hands, and kiss.

This night Steve was trying to initiate his cousin from California, well, at least trying to keep him entertained. But the cousin was a year or two older and accustomed to the night light of the urban West Coast, with the easy choices a city offers. We were country mice with nothing but stars for night life. California broke the spell of the darkness: "Can't we just go back to town and get drunk in some nefarious bar?"

"So what kind of a spirit do you think you're going to meet in Abby's Tav? Maybe the ghost of the drunk who pissed in the corner in 1953," Steve answered.

California retorted, "How about an 80-proof spirit? This three-two beer's like water." Steve didn't answer, but I thought, He's wishing this relative would go home to California.

And what else could we flatlanders of South Dakota do for entertainment in those days? There was TV to watch. "The Monkees" or "My Mother, the Car," right after supper and the daily body count from Vietnam and color footage of our generation getting smeared on the evening news. Or we could drink and drive, play music and get high. There weren't that many options. Our town of 2,500 had a Tastee Freeze stand and an A&W. One movie theatre on Main Street opened on Friday and Saturday nights during the winter, showing Hollywood hits two months after their release. A drive-in movie on the edge of town opened every summer, and we'd get dropped off on the highway and sneak under the fence to find friends who'd paid and had cars to sit in. Beer to share out of the trunk.

We had one thing to be proud of. The one geographical deviation in thousands of miles of plains—the *coteau*. Where the prairie folded and rose and rolled west for twenty-thirty miles before it leveled. There wasn't another elevation like it across the whole state until the Black Hills of Mt. Rushmore fame. The *coteau* was our mecca. Where our spirits gravitated toward the sky and toward each other. Where we went to get away and above the pull and politics of the real world.

We'd beer up and carpool to Sica Hollow, the deepest ravine near the highest point in those hills. Perhaps some past high schooler discovered the haunting thrill of the ancient hollows, the forest so dense that, literally, the sun don't shine. And that began our rite of passage. We always got drunk first or high or both. And we had to be barefoot. Sometimes, we'd get psyched up, as we called it, by telling ghost stories at the lower spring. Then finally, hand in hand, we'd follow a leader along winding dirt paths through oak and maple, ash and birch, about a mile and a half up the hollow to the bald top of the highest hill. Midnight and moonless was best.

Barefoot, with mescaline coursing through our nervous systems and beers in our pockets, we shuffled and shoulder-bumped, laughing our way to the lower spring, just a hundred yards or so from the parking lot through the picnic area. Sica Hollow was famous for this spring that historically, even during the worst drought years, kept its burble of pure water surfacing from cold groundwells that pooled and fell in myriad tiny waterfalls from a rocky slope. Years earlier, someone had fixed a pipe in the spring where we could fill bottles or just cup up the water to drink from our hands. The spring made our starting place. Sometimes we'd light a fire, but tonight the dark was so powerful that no one thought to insult it with firelight.

We felt our way to the picnic area, and some of us struggled to pull two wooden park tables together. Then someone's voice began with the oldest story, one from the Dakota Sioux Indians who lived here before our ancestors arrived and still live here, mostly out at Old Agency, though Sica Hollow had once been all theirs. "Sica," she began, pronouncing it shee-cha, "means bad in Lakota, and their stories tell why. . . ."

She continued telling what most of us had heard before. How some early Sioux tribesman saw a deer go down in the quickmud of the upper spring, about three hundred yards above us on the path. This upper spring was deeper and older, with no friendly waterfalls or drinking spouts. An ancient hole of primordial mud where ground water mixed deep with topsoil and minerals for eons, made swamplike and fecund with overgrowth. The Indian heard the deer's mule-like death bray and watched it struggle, give up, and sink down. When he returned the next day, he saw nothing, but the spring water had turned red. It looked like blood, and a sure sign that the earth demands sacrifice.

So the place became Bad Hollow, Sica. Some thought the Indians made up the stories to keep outsiders away from a precious water source. But we wanted the sacrifice, the romance of the killer quickmud. We wanted to believe.

Anyone who'd ever been to Sica could relate a scary or weird experience. So we took turns telling. One said he'd heard bodiless voices among the trees speaking in strange tongues. One claimed he saw a "monster" up on the ridge; he said it looked like a deer with a dog's face, thick legs, and a long tail. Another saw moving man-sized shapes of lights in the trees that moved away from him when he tried to approach.

We all knew natural reasons to account for the supernatural. We knew about the high iron content that tinged the water red and stained overexposed rocks and plant life to rusty "blood." We knew about the nocturnal movings of skunk and raccoon and the too-human calls of coyotes. We knew about the natural phosphorescence in the moss on the north face of tree trunks that made them glow and shimmy in the dark. And we knew about campers who wake in the middle of the night to see heavy shapes lumbering toward them in the trees, but the broad light of day shows them only cows behind solid fencing. But none among us wanted reasonable explanations now.

Another's voice spoke his turn.

"We walked this path one time in the middle of the day," it said. "You know, where it ends down that way." We could hear the swish of his arm in his nylon jacket as it moved to point the direction that no one could see but we all knew.

"There was this whole group of Indians drinking down there by the other picnic tables. We had to pass through them to get to the road out, but I wasn't scared. One old guy came over to us and started talking. Pretty soon we got to telling 'bad hollow' stories. The old guy said his whole family was out here once in the very spot where we were standing. They were taking a family photograph. You know, four-five generations. He said later when they saw the developed picture, they also saw these extra people along the back edge, standing behind their family. About a dozen of them. The guy's mother recognized the extra people as her dead parents and grandparents, two aunts and an uncle. There were cousins who'd died as children—and more that she couldn't name."

Another voice, a girl's, had a friend the Indian spirits spoke to. "What about the Windigo that Ed Slocum heard?" she said. Ed was older than us, a musician-poet, thought to be more perceptive, perhaps psychic. He said one night he'd walked the hollow alone and was sitting at the top just grooving on the stars. Then he heard a voice out of the trees say, *Manito ta hoya hey.* That's all. Nothing else happened. But later he looked up the word *Manito* and learned it wasn't even Lakota, but Algonquin from the older northeast coastal Narragansett word, *Manitto'wock.* He said it meant a supernatural force or spirit that takes over other living things—humans, animals, even trees. And it spoke to him.

About this time, one of us tried the oldest scary-story-in-the-dark joke, saying, "Wait a minute. Did you hear that?"

And a few seconds later, "No. Wait. I'm serious. Listen."

And when we had all strained our ears for a while, mouths open in concentration, the joker grabbed the person nearest and yelled *Shey-na-a-ah!* That was a local Indian idiom meaning, in this case, something like "Gotcha!" or "Fool!" Then we all pushed the joker off the bench. Someone else, it sounded like the California cousin, must've gotten bruised in the scuffle because I thought I heard him mutter, "This is so stupid."

The joke was our signal to begin the barefoot walk. Steve was the leader. I came next, then California, then the seven others—all putting a hand in the hand of the person before and after in single file. The path was level at first as it crossed the bridge over the creek and curved gently around the swamp of the lower spring. Then it climbed a gradual slope. Thick oak trees held up their arms and touched over our heads, making what felt like a shady lane in day seem more like a tunneling cave at night. Alice's white rabbit would have felt right at home. Shrubs and grasses bordered the bare path, only a couple of feet wide in places, and though we were blind, our bare feet easily distinguished the smooth-packed dirt of the path from the rough weeds along the sides.

The cave-dark and the earth itself were our mutual allies by then, our countrymen, our comrades. Our fellow revelers in the moonless end of May. With this dark, you could shut your eyes and open them and forget which was which. Our bare feet grasped the worn-smooth path like primates' palms. All our sense of direction and placement in the world centered in the arches of our feet that relayed directly to the nerve center in our groins, then traveled up our spines, enveloped our hearts, and moved, delayed, to our brains. Smells of dewed plant life at night, the black-dirt scents of the earth itself, are richer than in daytime—but it was strange: The smell itself seemed to come unexpected, not through our nostrils but through the nerve-work in the soles of our feet. We became plantlike, rooted to the soil but able to move and re-root with each step. We became grounded to the living force in the earth, the force that demands and draws down surface heat and moisture in return for seeds and roots that send life up to the light—reciprocal.

Suddenly my left hand jerked back and down. A jumble of voices and scuffling sounds seemed to be pulling our whole hand-linked group down and over the path's edge. A voice from the back of the line spoke up, sounding too loud and not a little scared, maybe a little angry, a harsh violation of the sacred, "Well, we just about lost John—and he tried to take us all with him."

Another anxious voice said, "What did you say back there about quickmud and the Indian and the . . . *dead deer*?"

California, at the end of my left hand, echoed, "Yeah, what about that quickmud?"

Steve, at the end of my right hand, said, "The path horseshoes just up here. That's where we have to be careful."

Someone else, oblivious, asked about poison ivy. Another answered, with just a touch of ridicule, like an older sibling, "If you don't see the poison ivy, it doesn't have the power to hurt you."

We felt the path taking a turn then, slow and uneven, a serpentine rippling beneath our bare feet. A neglected wooden pole fence, more like a rough railing about hip-high, bordered the path as it curved around the quickmud spring. That fence was rotten, and sometimes it slid right into the pit it was supposed to guard us from. Steve halted just before it, his free hand stretched out to find the sliver-ridden wood before he ran into it. And we dominoed behind him. He reminded us that the spring was directly below us now, the mud hole that sucked down a living deer of legend and spat back its red-iron blood. He described the twelve-foot downslide into the mud like a cutbank on a river—straight down and eroding, with protruding roots and avalanching gravel. How difficult it would be to get back up that crumbling bank if one of us should take the slide.

He slowed his pace then, moving one bare foot forward about twelve inches, sweeping it from side to side to mark the solid edge on the right and the disintegrating edge on the left which suddenly fell off into nothingness. Then he stepped and swept with the other foot the same way. Walking point—like the grunt who puts his life first-forward to search the earth by inches for boobytraps. We sidestepped behind him, trying to stay within the narrowest line, like subsequent soldiers in a minefield. We advanced for about a hundred yards until we passed the danger of the spring. Soon our bare toes stubbed up against the log steps dug into the hillside, our final ascent.

We'd been subdued somewhat by the threat of quickmud, but still exhilarated and laughing, making jokes—still high. But we hushed again as we left the trees and came out under the open sky at the top of the *coteau*. We felt the awe, and then we saw it. The lighter black of the sky stood out against the utter black of the surrounding trees. Myriad patterned stars pricked out as if switched on. Silhouettes of single trees and sumac in the meadow grew distinct and seemed to move toward us in their clarity. Looking back, we could see the cave mouth of the path we came from, but were we seeing with our eyes now? Or still using the earth vision imparted to us by the soles of our feet? And we felt the spirit, not individual, not ghost-scary, but as part of the god-ness of the pattern of the stars. We were the stuff of those stars, minute facets of the great jewel of the earth that hangs like a pendant among shining globes against a velvet universe.

We sat in the clearing, pilgrims at our holy shrine, in reverence and awestruck, tired and satisfied, mellow as yellow. Some lay back full length and stared up at the sky. A single owl echoed himself. Someone lit a joint, and we traced its small red spot as it brightened before pursed and smiling lips then lowered in a descending arc, bobbed and hesitated as fingers of one negotiated the passing to fingers of another and then arched up to the next person's lips. Minutes passed in silence. Each of us eased into our own personal darkness. Then someone's soft voice, barely audible, said, "My cousin Gabe was killed in Da Nang last week." Another answered that his big brother, just eighteen, got his "Greetings" from Uncle Sam that very day. No one spoke for a while.

Then someone began to sing like a ritual mourner, a young woman's high sweet voice that could have been emanating from the North Star, that my now hypersensitive ears understood to be coming from the North Star. It was a Crosby, Stills, Nash & Young song with their trademark harmony, a capella, but that single voice took on a wailing timbre that embodied and blended all four parts in one. She sang:

Find the cost of freedom,
*   buried in the ground*
Mother Earth will swallow you,
*   lay your body down.*

We sang some more and smoked some more and talked and drank our beer. We stayed until the first blue of dawn made us too cold.

When we rose to leave, it was with quiet respect, like people leaving a church service or maybe a funeral. The earth-and-sky's hold over us, undeniable as magnetic north, was weakening. Talking in low voices we took hands again and shuffled behind the leader in reverse, down the dark path to our cars, to our tape decks, our shoes and socks, to our homes and the day-to-day of TV war—the one that sent California home nine months later in a box.

We were tired of knowing the earth, its beauty and its burden. But once, on the way back down, I'm pretty sure I heard Steve's cousin say, "God. This was the best thing I've *ever* done."

What They Gave Me

Beverly Cottman

I am from Black women who took what the world offered and
    NEVER let it break them.
Poppin' their fingers to jazz AND
                Hummin' gospel tunes.
Kept right on steppin' during Jim Crow—'Cause they
". . . didn't want to go in that place anyway."
When it came time to march, protest, boycott—they said
"You go on baby; stand tall; do it for the race.
Get your education.
Get yourself a piece of land. But don't get so high you forget where
    you came from!"

Doc Mittermeyer

Thomas R. Smith

The last of the old-fashioned GPs in our town,
he still made house calls, delivered
babies, pulled the occasional tooth.
Maybe it's because his hands lifted me
into life that I've never entirely shaken
a secret fantasy that I belong
among the many he fathered. I often
played with his real children in the cedar-
shaded alley behind their large house. As a teen,
I'd see him, rheumy-eyed, owlish, dressed
in a long tweed topcoat on winter nights
cheering his sons on the basketball court.

The last time I encountered the great old
doctor, I was strolling with my mother
on an unhappy visit home in the Seventies.
He looked frailer, his white brushcut a little
overgrown. My mother asked him, "Well,
are you proud of your big boy now?"
She meant his eldest, Frank, recent college
graduate already making a career
for himself in medicine. But for the rest
of that evening I savagely berated
myself for my idiot grin, having for a
split second assumed she referred to me.

Ice: A Memoir

Carla J. Hagen

You reflected me skating on the rink under the neighbor's yard light, blades scratching your surface. You creaked occasionally but did not complain.

You sustained my drunken friends and me, along with a quarter-ton of 1960s metal driving the road plowed across the Rainy River to Canada, land of dances with live bands from Winnipeg and bars that didn't card. We were fools and you were merciful, letting us cross back and forth without ever cracking and sending us to frigid, watery death.

You froze my wet hair into rigid dreadlocks, terrifying my grandmother, who evoked her Norwegian God, *Gud i himmelen!*, swore I would catch a cold, get frostbitten, contract pneumonia, die. But I was walking from house to car, not fjord to fjord, and I never got sick.

You were treacherous, and all of us in that tiny border town knew it. If we slipped, we could break wrists, legs, feet, ankles, backs, hips, even skulls. If you cracked on the river or lake, immersing us in glacial water, we would expire in minutes if someone didn't extend a hockey stick or branch to pull us out. Parents and teachers schooled us in ice rescue the way people teach desert children to survive heat and sand.

At the same time we feared, we prayed for your long life, so we could keep playing hockey under blue January skies or by moonlight. You gave us glass-covered trees, icicles to suck, a firm base for dog sleds to fly us down the river.

For a mass of frozen matter, you were noisy and restless. First silence as you skimmed creeks and ponds, then tinkling bells as waves on Lake of the Woods smashed sheet after sheet of water against rocks. You persisted and triumphed, spreading across the inland sea, creaking and shifting, sprouting fault lines that cracked, heaved, and swallowed reckless people who ventured out too soon. You grew thick and ponderous with responsibility: home to colonies of colorful ice shanties little bigger than large outhouses, trucks, cars, snowmobiles, skaters, skiers, people large and small, deer and moose.

But we were fickle. After waiting for you, measuring thickness, using you for fun, we got bored. We longed for the thaw, strained toward it like a hard-to-reach orgasm. For two days you melted. The beater car someone always drove onto the Rainy River foundered. *Almost there.* We held outdoor parties, shivering in cutoffs, clutching cans of Molson Canadian with numb hands, looking down at the free-flowing rapids and winter's detritus: waterlogged moles, saturated stocking caps, lost gloves, the eternal beer bottles. Then you froze up again. Not quite, not quite.

No wonder you tired. No wonder you grew dull, gray, pock-marked, thin as an old person's bones. Water gurgled beneath your surface. You developed fissures, sighed, became cranky and unreliable. Finally you gave up, shattering bit by bit, a relief to finally surrender after months of weight and expectations. Bells sounded again as you splintered into crystal shards and nose-dived into the waiting water, taking along neglected icehouses, cars, and dead animals.

Petting

Donna Emerson

When Ricky felt me up lying down, I got mixed up. I was used to kissing and hugging because we'd done that all our lives. Even tongue kissing, though that wasn't as exciting as the boys acted when they talked to each other in Mrs. Foreman's physics class behind the Bunsen burners. So slimy, especially after Ricky smoked cigarettes.

But lying down meant we touched toes and thighs and higher. Then something else happened. Our bodies started moving all on their own. The way Coach Wilson told us to move our hips when we learned the butterfly. I liked the dreamy feeling at first, but then Ricky started breathing so hard he scared me and I began wondering if this were petting.

I knew necking was all right when you were fifteen, but Dear Abby said necking was only from the waist up. This was definitely from the waist down. I felt mushy in the head and wished Mom would call me upstairs.

Later that week I even asked her to give me a 12:30 curfew. Like all the other girls. She laughed and said okay, so at least I could say that to Ricky and the rolling thing didn't happen so much, for so long. I wasn't sure, but thought it could lead to going all the way.

When Ricky went to college, I dated other guys I met at Canteen. Jimmy Preston was twenty-five, which I liked when he first asked me to dance. He looked like the Morrisville boys. I didn't know where he lived. He kept trying to put his hands down my skirt.

Reaching under the waistband when we were sitting up. I wished Dad would ask me how old he was or say he couldn't stay, but he didn't seem to notice. He and Mom were usually asleep by the time I got home. Those every-night martinis smelled up their room. They never woke up.

When I pushed Jerry's hands away from my thighs or skirt zipper, you know what he did? Put his hand right on my crotch on top of all my clothes. Acted like people in church after the Introit when Reverend Palmer told us to shake hands with all the people around us. Squeeze-pat-pat. People we never had seen before. So I said I had to go to the bathroom.

When I came back, I walked to the front door, opened it, and told him my mom said he had to go.

Remembering Margie:
Thirtieth Year Class Reunion

Ann Struthers

Everyone remembers Margie. How could we forget
the girl famous for her escapades
in the backseat of Herb Mazvinski's Chevy.
He bragged about her gymnastics,
whether it was truth or lies
and everybody knew she drank beer with the boys.

Margie tells us everything:
she's divorced thrice,
has joined AA, lives in public housing
in Portland.

We old girls sip our strawberry wine coolers
while Margie relates that she's taken up
quilting, bought a puppy, studies the Bible
with a circle of born-again ladies.

What can we say—
strangely disappointed—
she who was rebel for us all,
come finally to sobriety and piety
while we have been struggling all these years
toward Margie's wild nights.

THREE

VOWS

SWAK after 55

Georgia A. Greeley

Kissing is still fun,
it's just not quite as important.
I might kiss his elbow
or belly or knee,
because it's in front of me,
and easier.

Vegas Wedding

Susan Peters

When a woman past sixty receives a marriage proposal from an attractive, prosperous, intelligent gentleman, her inclination is to throw maidenly decorum aside in favor of an exultant "Yes!" In my case, however, there was some hesitancy. This was not due to any lack of affection on my part, or any glaring flaw in my prospective groom; no, it was the prospect of planning the damn thing that made me want to continue—as my mother would have said—simply "living in sin." For one thing, Norm and I were living and working in Europe. His family was scattered from Florida to Michigan, mine from New York to California. He was hinting at a ceremony at his summer place, on an island off the coast of Nova Scotia; I was adamant that guests not be required to bring a passport and seasickness pills. My mother had died a few months earlier, and I was not sure of the etiquette: Was there a standard waiting period? And finally, I simply did not want to deal with all the details: flowers, minister, music, limo, dinner, and most of all, The Location. Neither Norm nor I was a churchgoer, but I wanted to be married in something church-*like*, if not an actual place of worship.

And then my sister sent me an e-mail about Las Vegas, along with some Web sites of wedding chapels. What a revelation! There were package deals that included all the fiddly stuff I'd been dreading: flowers, minister, music, limo. All my siblings could get to Vegas easily—some could even drive—and I could use my frequent-flier miles to get my daughter and her family there as well. Hotel rooms were amazingly cheap if you reserved ahead of time. There would be tons of choices for the wedding dinner. Best of all, the ceremony would be videotaped, and could be viewed online by our friends around the globe. Before you could say "Visa or MasterCard," I'd booked Package C at the Little Chapel of the Flowers on June 28.

Hey, I was going to be a June bride!

My fiancé took the news of a Vegas wedding in stride, probably because it was low cost. (His last venture into matrimony, ten years previously, had cost him a bundle.) He also liked the idea of the wedding being on the Internet, and started e-mailing our friends overseas with the details. "Two p.m. in Vegas—that's mountain time, right?—would be what, 10 p.m. in Paris? What about daylight savings, is that earlier or later?" However, he did need some reassurance that Elvis would not be performing the ceremony. We found out later that the wedding immediately preceding ours did indeed have an Elvis, which caused much excited comment among the Internet viewing groups in various foreign countries.

The night before the wedding, we gathered for dinner at the hotel. Not a rehearsal dinner, because there was no need to rehearse. The limo was coming at 1:30, we'd picked up the wedding license earlier, I'd pressed my dress, and all systems were go. I probably should have made an appointment at the beauty shop for the works—hair, makeup, waxing of various body parts—but Cheyenne, my thirteen-year-old granddaughter, wanted to do my hair. She's a veteran of cheerleading, dance, and theater performances, so I figured I'd be in good hands.

The next morning, I realized I'd need to book a place for the wedding dinner, so I was reading various brochures while Chey worked on my hair. In other words, not paying attention. Finally I looked up.

"Chey," I said, "*what is this?*"

She considered. "Well . . . it does look a little like George Washington."

Or, I thought, panicky, a badly groomed Cape buffalo. I took the brush and with the help of more hair products than I had dreamed existed, managed to get back to "human," if not exactly "blushing bride." On with the dress, on with the heels. I was practicing non-wobbly walking when there was a knock on the door.

It was my three sisters, but what were they wearing? The clothes looked vaguely familiar, but not in a good way.

"Since Mom couldn't be here," Jill said, "we thought her wardrobe should be here instead." She had on a brown jungle print dress with funny sleeves. It looked hot—not sexy-hot, make-you-sweat hot. I remembered Mom's wardrobe: where polyester went to die.

"I got first choice," said Wendy. She had on a navy pantsuit with red and white flowers.

"I had to get *special underwear*," said Penny. She was wearing a pale blue dress with a pleated skirt. I remembered Mom had worn it to Jill's wedding. Penny is considerably larger than Mom ever was, and the pleats looked stretched to their limit.

My daughter came in just then, very chic in a turquoise sheath. "Hey, didn't you guys bring me something to wear too?" As it happened, they had, a blue-and-white-and-green print. She pulled it on over her dress and tied the sash belt around her head, hippie-style.

So this is what you see when we show the wedding video: the bride's sisters, perspiring gently in various vintage outfits; the bride's daughter, the maid of honor, tall, blonde, and gorgeous, a girl from an Austin Powers movie; the bride's granddaughter, giggling in the front pew. Here's the groom, very handsome—after all, he had no grandson messing with his hair. And here comes the bride, walking slowly down the aisle on the arm of her brother. She's looking happy, or at least relieved; she's not wobbling, she's got the bouquet firmly in hand, and there's not a hair out of place.

These Easier Wants

Bonnie Louise Barrett

These easier wants, these fading
powers
shall more do in the lopped
hours left
than crying need
in abler youth did.

These
pressed drops
shall more drink make
than the jet that gushed
from gashes
of bliss and bane
long agone.

If never
to feast again,
well, then, the fitter
for fasting,
I work and pray.

Middle Solutions

Susan Pepper Robbins

"I told him, 'I'm not dead yet. You can have them all then, but not now. Not before then.'"

Mary turns her head to me, who is not dead yet either, although almost. This year I have lost twenty pounds and gained back thirty, so I am ten ahead. I do not know if people can really die of broken hearts, or sudden weight loss and gain, but I do know that breaking up is hard to do when you've been married thirty-two years and do not want a divorce but need one or something in between divorce and death, a middle something.

Richard and I had driven three hours to this New Year's Day party at Eleanor and Stan's new home just outside Washington, and Mary was the first person we met. We had not seen Eleanor and Stan, our oldest friends, for a year, but we were trying to live a new life since I had learned about Richard's suicide attempts: more people, more parties, more day trips, more anything. We agreed with Mary, though we had never put it so clearly—we were not dead yet.

This middle solution/situation is not all that uncommon. I know a girl—she is sixty-six—who is dating her husband who has not lived with her for fifteen years. He is now in chemo. After their dates, he goes home to his girlfriend, who is fifty-five. Yes, Harry Lassiter goes home to the house he bought for his girlfriend Estelle, not back to the house he built with Joyce, where their two daughters grew up. Joyce and Harry have their dates, never overnights though, and Joyce calls to tell me where they went to lunch, what they had, and how Harry's doing on this series of treatments.

Mary does not lower her voice even though we have, with the slight shift in her weight when she looks at me, sunk deeper down into a V in the soft, white sofa and are very close to each other, her left upper arm glued to my right. I am sure that I have bad breath, so I don't breathe and wouldn't want to anyway because of what she is saying: She was telling her son about her not being dead, and about the rings that weren't his until then.

There is only one person who talks like this Mary in the America I live in—rural, New South, Virginia, Bush country, family values, Walmarts, Support the Troops bumper stickers—and that is Irene Washburn. She is going to tell Harry, the dater-husband, our mutual friend and her classmate all through school, how he can leave the girlfriend and come back home to Joyce, his true love, his wife. Irene has laid it out for him, and now all Harry has to do is follow her plan, which is simple and ends with Harry's walking into Joyce's arms, and then locking the doors behind him, the doors of the house he and Joyce built forty years ago. Yes, Estelle will have a gun when she comes looking for Harry, but she won't shoot through the locked door because she won't want to kill him. It's Joyce she wants to kill. Estelle and Joyce both think that they have ruined and are ruining each other's lives. Neither one blames Harry. He is innocent and now that he has cancer, he is very innocent. Irene herself has cancer and is here to tell us that it isn't as bad as everyone claims.

Irene can say anything to any of us because her son is in Iraq and her daughter is protesting the war, so she knows a whole range of feelings, and she herself has a rare liver disease, but not from drinking, and she has found a lump in her breast. Harry will have to listen to Irene as we all do because of her greathearted son, who may object to the war in principle, but not to going himself if ordered to, as he has been. Whatever war it would be, he would never refuse to serve, but his sister, who loves to laugh, has organized all-night vigils to protest the war. Irene is on her son's side and stays furious with her daughter. This split in her feelings also elevates her in ours. We feel that she is qualified to speak on all matters of the heart.

Deep down, Irene says—and we all listen to her diagnosis— Harry wants to come home to Joyce. She always adds, "But the fool simply does not know how to do it. He doesn't have sense enough to leave Estelle."

I take a page from this story that Irene tells me in chapters on the phone: Richard may want to live but does not know how, in spite of being sixty-seven. I am the fool, the Harry, in the story, in spite of the shrink's telling me that I must not take it personally.

Irene might have some plan for me to get my life back on track, one that will have all the benefits of a divorce without the pain of grieving that Richard's death would bring—an ocean for me to tread water in toward eternity, where he would be impatiently waiting. The benefits of an Irene-plan would, I was sure, offer an alternative to this middle solution that Richard and I were jerry-rigging for ourselves.

Now, Mary is talking in a chilled-vodka way that is making me vicariously drunk. I am in my kind of heaven. I was close to my kind of heaven last week, too, when I spilled red paint down the refrigerator onto the floor from the top of the ladder as I was painting the cabinets, which I had thought I would stain a plain green, the color of oak leaves in the drought we were having, but, on impulse, had switched to red. The splatter of a gallon of China Red #75180 opened up a whole new vista of possibilities, a crime scene. Forget about divorcing. I was shocked and a little thrilled with criminal thoughts. Then Richard stuck his head in the door, saw the thrown gobbets of the bloody mess and smiled. Maybe he understood my view of our lives better with it all spelled out on the kitchen floor and walls.

It was clear at that moment that we had needed something like a murder long ago, years before I met Richard, one that would have taken his mother away from him when he was born and certainly before he was three. A murder would have helped Richard, removed him from his mother's frozen perfections. His father, as a widower, would not have mattered because he was away in the war, and the grandmother would have taken over. Richard should have taken care of his mother problem long before I met her when she was a gentle old lady, but younger than I am now. I don't mean that he should have shot his Rose Kennedy-type mother as soon as he could have held one of the guns from his grandfather's gun cabinet, but he should at least have screamed at her a few times.

Dream on, Nell, I tell myself. It never happened. And worse, according to the doctor, Richard never knew until last year that there was anything to scream about.

Richard and his Nell, me, are celebrating New Year's Day, many years after Richard was a toddler. I could see again how much good it would have done him to have killed his mother or to have lost her in some violent event, and it would have saved me years of what the shrink calls our "compensatory fantasy." No blood running down the walls as the red paint had run down our refrigerator and kitchen walls in the house we had built in 1979, and where Richard had always come home to me, not to a girlfriend's house as Harry was doing when he went back to Estelle's, leaving Joyce in their home. I mean that if Richard had only yelled back at his mother, had had one little tantrum, had given her some lip, or had known how to yell, get mad, or cause hurt feelings! As Richard's doctor says, if Richard had only been allowed some autonomy we would not be in the sad place we were here at Eleanor and Stan's party to welcome in the new year, hoping for some distraction, some relief.

How wonderful it was to meet this Mary at this New Year's Day party.

Hearing Mary say that she has recently had to tell her son that she was not dead yet cheered me up and took my mind away from the big rock of a fact that it had been Richard who had tried his hand at suicide this past year and two times before that.

Suicide has more than one victim. The Latin is right. I recall that the genitives singular and plural are the same form. *Sui* means "of himself," or "of themselves." The murder is of several selves. How true, I think, pre-drunkenly on the white sofa. And suicide targets the wrong person. It doesn't kill just one person or even the right person.

Irene has said that it is always the wrong person who gets taken to the mental ward. The least ill person is always the one institutionalized while the most ill ones are left on the outside. Irene speaks from her own experience of being the one taken to the mental ward of the hospital. She has been in treatment for fifteen years, and though she has shot the gun up in the air over people's heads and driven her Lincoln into a tree to make a point, she makes a good case for being the most well-balanced person in her family.

I have learned this year to practice being well and alive by remembering useless facts for my students. For some reason these give me shots of happiness and the will to live. I write on sticky notes: "The Roman Emperor Valerian was killed by the Sassanians in 260 BCE, and in 378 the Emperor Valens was taken prisoner at the Battle of Adrianople. The captures of the emperors happened many years before the official fall of Rome. Rome did not fall in a day." I will try to use these notes in my tenth grade world history class to make the point that if it took a long time for Rome to be built, it took just as long for it to fall. I try to find a use for the facts I collect, and teaching history opens up a huge vault for useful information.

It has taken a long time for Richard and me to fall. I wrote that on a little yellow note and stuck it inside my pocketbook.

One trouble with being a history teacher is I am learning that what I thought were facts, are not. They are just my version of the past, what I thought was going on with us.

Richard, my much loved husband of more than three decades— oh, the long evenings of happiness—who had been trying to kill himself/themselves, which is to say, both of us, was laughing and talking to people across the room. He is a liar on many levels. I now know that he lies about having a good time. He made his mother think she was perfect until she died at ninety-three. He certainly made me think that I was happy with him. I was the entertainment center of his very being, all of those reasons women fall for and need men. But during that time, as he has told me under the light of treatment, he had been choosing a tree on the roads around our home to plow into on a trip to the store for dog food or milk. Suicide, he says, and so does the doctor, does not deny the preceding happiness.

I am trying to get hold of this view, but I feel like the second Mrs. Thomas Hardy, who had to listen to the poems Thomas was writing to his dead first wife. She must have known the poems were great, but she must have also been bleeding all over her kitchen or parlor. I would have burned the poems in the fireplace after the great man had gone to bed. Irene might have lowered her gun and leveled it at her husband if he had tried the suicide way out of their marriage, not that he ever wanted to. He loves/needs Irene's sturm und drang, he says. It's his bourbon, hold the water.

Mary was still going on about the rings, and I was feeling happier than I had felt in a long, long time. She was telling us, "I have my great-grandmother's, my grandmother's, and, of course, my mother's, but not until I'm dead does he get my rings." She was diverting my attention from Richard. A blessing. I take a long drink of my Bloody Mary, the celery tickling my nose.

I had just met this fabulous Mary, but to look at her and me on the sofa, you would think we were best friends, heads almost touching, her talking so loud about her death and her rings, her son's request for one, all very personal matters. Mary turned away from me, just her head, but by now, our arms were even more closely pressed together.

She went back to staring at her son across the room and announced to me as if I were out in an auditorium, not three inches from her head, almost cuddling, "Not dead yet seemed to slow him down some. At least, he did not give her a ring for Christmas. Not one of my rings! Look at her. Can you see her with him? I can't see one of my rings on her hand. Can you?"

I was filled with sadness suddenly, wishing that Richard's mother had been more like this Mary, violently sure of herself, telling Richard what he could have and what he could not. Like Irene, waving a gun at life, being taken all tears and rage to the hospital by her family who were crying so hard, even the son now in Iraq, even the laughing daughter, that the doctors did not know which one should be admitted.

The her and him of the rings' story Mary was telling are tall, beautiful young people: She had floating brown hair and looked like the marketing major she was. This fact Mary reported sadly.

It was clear to me that this young woman Mary and I were looking at did not have much of a chance to use her major, to sell herself in any way—at least, not to Mary. Mary's son was, evidently, so much in love that he had asked his formidable mother for one of her rings.

Here, Eleanor, my friend of fifty-four years, who had heard Mary say from across the room that she wasn't dead yet, laughed and told Mary that she had delivered a wonderful line, and that she had been trying to make her way over to her to tell her how great it was. Mary asked which line, and Eleanor laughed harder, acknowledging evidently that when Mary spoke there was always a great richness of choice in her lines. "That one about not being dead yet."

Mary was not pleased. It was clear that it was painful for her to think of her Kenneth's wanting to give such a marketing major from Florida one of Mary's grandmother's rings or one of the other rings. Eleanor's flattery about Mary's brutal truth-telling was not entirely wasted, but it didn't help Mary's deep wound. I knew the feeling. Richard loved me, but he also wanted to kill himself. It did not compute, as my students say.

Eleanor repeated the line to Stan when they met at the kitchen bar. I could hear her telling him and laughing. He loved it too.

Mary definitely was not the only person who wasn't dead yet; nobody in those rooms full of people in their fifties and sixties, a house filled with books and vases of flowers was, either. We were very much alive and enjoying every minute. It looked easy.

The ringless young couple was, at the most, five feet away from Mary and me on the sofa. She had on spike heels, so she was as tall as he was. Mary was telling us in her un-lowered voice that her name was Tanja. Tanja with a j, the Russian spelling. From Orlando. Tanja hoped to break into television. We heard her saying that Ted Turner might give her an interview. Mary was unimpressed.

Tanja was in an off-shoulder turquoise sweater; her hair fell in shampoo-commercial perfection to the middle of her back. She did not toss her hair but flicked it back, so that it floated away from her. She shot us a wild look as Mary went on talking, obviously, audibly, about Kenneth and the rings. Mary repeated to me and to anyone who was nearby, "I'm not dead yet, so no rings."

I said to Mary in the encouraging way I use with my students, not that she needed it, "I love ring stories." It was way past clear, as my students say, that she did not need any encouragement.

Without looking at me, Mary said, still staring at Tanja and Kenneth, "Then you'll love the ones I tell. I have hundreds, but I'll tell them later."

Richard's and my middle-solution plan to go out into the world and get him recharged so that he would want to live—that was our simple-minded plan—was working so far, and we'd just gotten to the party. I wished that Richard were sitting with us on the sofa, but no such luck, and he looked, as he always had, as if he were having a great time.

Later, Mary told me about her son-in-law, Arthur, who, when he had heard about Kenneth's request for an engagement ring from her cache of rings, had bellyached (Mary's word) that *he* had not been offered a ring to give Mary's daughter two years earlier when he had proposed and had really needed one.

"I told Arthur, '*You* didn't ask for a ring. You have to ask.'" Mary spoke with the finality of a tornado warning from the weather channel, and I was thrilled to be taken into the center of her family's drama. Son-in-law Arthur did not know the rules for getting a ring, and son Kenneth was being refused a ring for two reasons— his mother was not dead and he had Tanja, the wrong girl, in mind to marry. Arthur and Kenneth were idiots! I felt a new kind of happiness.

I might have gotten all these complicated rules about asking for rings wrong, though I felt that I had known Mary and her problems all my life, and that the rules I was learning for the first time were as ancient and inevitable, as natural as the fall of Rome.

We could see the Potomac through the open doors to the patio. Mary was now talking about living in *Firenze*. "Florence to you," she almost said. We were still on the white sofa drinking Bloody Marys and eating scallops wrapped in bacon. Mary was wearing a brown cashmere turtleneck and gray wool slacks with black velvet slippers, a stark contrast in class signifiers to Tanja's Floridian colors. It was a warm sixty-five degrees, with the breezes blowing off the river. It was heaven for many reasons to be there this first day of the rest of our lives.

Eleanor did not know about our brush(es) with suicide, the three that I knew about: two in cars (one totaled, one driven around in for three days as Richard looked for the right bridge or tree), and one with the Demerol he had for his migraines and cluster headaches. Now, six months after that last attempt with pills, we were better, though that word covered a lot of rocky ground. Irene has said that pills aren't serious attempts, not that she knows about Richard's, but she speaks with great authority on all mental illness matters. I have not told her about Richard's years of choosing trees because Irene herself has driven into trees, but not seriously. Her plan in the back of her mind and which she has announced to me several times was to jump from the old Nickel Bridge in Richmond, but now, after treatment and with her son in Iraq, she says she is past that danger. Irene has been a great help, very like having this Mary with me all the time.

Richard's therapist has explained why Richard could not tell me that he was planning to kill himself or that we were secretly much deeper in debt than I knew. This covert planning in various forms had been in place since 1993. The medication the therapist had prescribed, once it was adjusted, would help too. I don't know if these good pills can kill if they are saved for a rainy day. And so, we were not dead yet, even though one of us had been secretly wishing he were for many years.

Eleanor treated us as if we were lost treasures, as we knew she would, and it was very good for us, me sinking into the white sofa with Mary, and Richard strolling onto the deck with a plate of ham and a big saucer of Brunswick stew. We were happy, we were happy. Mary stood up and moved away from me, but not toward Tanja and Kenneth, who looked like movie stars who had dropped in to visit their old neighborhood. Gracious and on duty, except for the glances that Tanja shot across the room at Mary. Desperate and wounded.

Eleanor told me when she took a break from making drinks and platters of good things that Tanja was afraid of Mary. "Who wouldn't be," I murmured, knowing that Eleanor would laugh and that Richard would smile when I repeated my good line.

The suicide attempts did not grow out of a lack of love on Richard's part, the therapist had been at pains to explain to me. I must not take them personally, he said with a straight face.

It was true that Richard had always been very loving and, although Irene has said I do not understand sex, I think in this one area she is mistaken. The attempts grew out of his, oh surprise, his childhood. His mother, lovely and loving, was, like Mary, not completely dead yet either, though we had a moderately elaborate funeral three years ago. It seemed, according to the therapist, that she has remained the problem. As Richard grew up—but, of course, he did not grow healthily, the therapist smiled—there was no crack in the china, no fissure, no place to "gain purchase" so that he could learn how to climb, or how to express his feelings, especially any negative ones. The doctor is a rock climber and uses ropes and equipment and terrain with us to explain what we can't understand.

Richard can't understand his life yet even with these insights. He could and can say only good things to me about his mother. It is true that his mother did speak only of the good in life, never about the irritating, never the sad, never the terrible. And I, coming from a dark, much cracked, many-fissured family, took to Richard's mother like a swimmer who has at last found a cool lake with no other noisy swimmers. So, I hadn't been much of a help there.

And where was Richard's dad? "Absently present," the doctor said. Once he had tossed a football to his sons on Christmas Day. Once, he told Richard that his friend who liked to listen to *My Fair Lady* was "as queer as a three-dollar bill." Richard and his friend were eight years old. Those are the two stories I know from Richard's life with his father. There is one other one that has surfaced in the past month: Once the father tried, but failed, to stop a German shepherd from attacking Richard's puppy. A week later, Richard's grandmother tossed a ball of ground beef with arsenic in it over the killer dog's fence and solved the problem, but too late for Richard's little dog. Still, someone had done something for Richard.

Richard's story of his own life is too simple, the therapist says. It's a child's version of a life, but it's all we have, so I am embracing it, or swallowing it, hook, line, and sinker. I think in clichés, and not ones I have a right to, as the doctor has to his rock climbing ones. I've never been fishing. I am not a swimmer, either. I know about arsenic only from stories, like Richard's dog story. All of my metaphors come from the classroom, from my students who are very helpful in their views of history and current events. They have explained that

Athens deserved to lose to Sparta and that Rome needed to fall.

When I tell my students that their views are helpful, but not exactly in the ways they mean, they cheer. When I tell Irene that she has helped me, she says she knows that she has. I would like to tell Mary what her ring stories would mean to me when she tells them, and especially what her rule about not being dead yet means to me now.

Divorce

Ed Meek

By the time you're fifty if you're in your right mind
you want a divorce from yourself.
You've already tried a trial separation—
a week in the Caribbean, a month in Maine,
a windjammer cruise. You come back and think
you can begin anew
only to find nothing's changed
and that makes it all the worse.
So you join a health club
or hire a personal trainer
to whip you into shape.
You buy natural supplements,
begin a new diet, drink
more water, less booze. Switch
from ice cream to frozen yogurt.
You get a haircut that really fits your face.
You take dance lessons, music lessons, you learn
a new language. At night you return home tired—
older not wiser. How about hormone therapy,
Prozac, plastic surgery?
Forget about it. It's time to file for divorce.
Move to a new city. Leave behind
that fat lazy fool who returns your hopeful gaze
in cruel mirrors every morning
as you brush your caffeine-stained teeth.
He can have the house that needs painting,

the car that needs brakes,
the lousy art in the living room,
the oversized TV in the den.
This is the year to take a train into tomorrow,
one-way ticket in hand,
destination: somewhere new
where no one knows your name
and you can be someone else.

The Making of Lists

Arlene L. Mandell

> *I believe all women, but especially housewives, tend to think in lists.*
> —*Shirley Jackson*

Can list-making keep a housewife
sane: bananas, tomatoes, solitude . . .

Maybe a list of men she has loved?
Or people she detests?
Now *that* has possibilities.

Better return to less perilous
thoughts:
> pomegranates
> kitty litter
> peregrine falcons . . .

Leaving Rolf

Elizabeth Gauffreau

I suppose you think you have a right to know, Terese, but if you were to ask me why I chose today to leave your father for good, I honestly couldn't say. If you were to ask why this day and not another, I would have no answer for you. Why now, you must be wondering, after forty-nine years of marriage? Why now, when he is at long last no stronger than I, his strength and his rage worn down by age and years of drinking, his ability to grab me before I can get away hobbled by knees so badly damaged he can barely walk? Why now, when he hasn't laid a hand on me in ten years?

I simply don't know.

But I suppose you want to know why I didn't leave him for good the time he broke my nose, or when I finally ran out of lies for my blackened eyes. Why didn't I leave when he broke two of my ribs throwing me to the floor? Why didn't I put an end to it one of those times he came home drunk and threw up in the kitchen sink? Or one of those times he didn't make it to the sink in time, spewing stinking vomit all over the floor, so that I found dried bits of it for days afterward in the crevices of the baseboards, no matter how hard I tried to get it all when I cleaned it up. Or the times he forced himself on me, horny from God-knows-what, reeking of beer, fumbling with his pants in the darkness of our bedroom while I lay awake with my eyes squeezed shut, pretending to be asleep, praying—*praying*—that just this once I could fool him into thinking I was asleep and that my sleep was so peaceful he should just leave me be. When that prayer went unheeded, I prayed that it would be over quickly, and I could slide from under his dead weight and curl up on the couch in the living room, clutching the afghan as tight under my chin as I could, as if that alone could keep me safe for the rest of the night.

Even during the worst of it, though, I had no fear for you or your brother. Your father didn't have it in him to harm a child, and I have to give him credit for that, particularly given the fact that it was I who had wanted the second child because I thought that having another baby—specifically a boy—would help our marriage, would settle him down and make him less angry. I thought that if I could just give him a son, he would be happy with me again. Although I told myself that I was willing to keep trying until I had a boy, no matter how many children it took, I felt so relieved when your brother was born that I couldn't stop crying, and I insisted on naming him Gabriel.

For years, I fooled myself into thinking that you and your brother had no idea what was going on and that I was successful in hiding everything from you. I even went so far as to think that I was protecting you. I made myself believe that you and your brother went deaf every time your father came home raging and cursing, that you simply couldn't hear the sickening thud of fist on flesh or the screams I couldn't stop no matter how hard I tried. I honestly believed that you children thought it was normal for a mother to bundle her children into their clothes at three in the morning and wait at the curb down the block for their grandfather to pick them up for a visit, the visits lasting anywhere from several hours to several weeks.

When he had his accident, I thought it would change him, make him kinder, grateful to be alive—but it didn't. It just made him meaner, because he felt he no longer measured up to other men and who better to prove your strength than your wife when you can grab her by the hair and punch her in the face? Then I thought, Well, once he is fully recovered from the accident, he'll go back to the way he was, which wasn't so bad, really.

I hope you and Ronny know how grateful I am that you've taken me in. As much as I don't want to be a burden on either of my children, I couldn't spend another day in the house with that man, and I have nowhere else to go. I suppose until your grandparents passed away, I never thought of needing another place to go. It was just so easy to pack up you kids and go home whenever I needed to. Even after you and your brother were grown, as long as your grandparents were alive, I always had a home to go back to. But they're gone now, and both of my sisters, too, dying of cancer within two years of one another, just like that. And poor Buddy, of course, killed in Korea so long ago it seems I never had a brother. I do have friends, yes, but none I would feel comfortable imposing myself on. How could I, after lying to them for so many years?

I know how hard it must be for you and Ronny, taking in an old woman who wants to make a fresh start when her life is practically over. I saw the expression on your face when I arrived unannounced on your doorstep this morning, with my belongings stuffed into a laundry cart and no means of supporting myself. And after I took off my coat and splashed water on my face, what could you possibly say over coffee and cake to comfort me? *You're still young? Your best years are still ahead of you? You'll find someone else to make a life with?* Even if I could bring myself to speak these words aloud, what could you possibly say to comfort me? I will not ask it of you.

I wish I could tell you how many years I have left, or for how many of those years I will remain healthy. Will I have a stroke next winter and be unable to dress or feed myself? Will I develop Alzheimer's and need to be watched twenty-four hours a day to make sure that I won't decide to walk to school some morning with the other children in the neighborhood, or light the gas oven, or run outside in front of a car? Will I fall and break a hip? I have no way of knowing.

I know I shouldn't say this, Terese, but I feel the Church failed me. I never went to see the priest and ask for help, of course, I wouldn't dream of it, but every week I would sit in the confessional and wonder what I could confess to that would get the priest's attention and make him feel so much compassion that he would find a way to help me.

I confessed to so many sins, mostly venial, it's true, but every once in a while, I had a mortal sin to confess, and I was happy to do it. I confessed to entertaining doubts against the faith. I confessed to failing to accept suffering and giving in to depression and self-pity. I confessed to speaking badly about one's spouse and refusing to forgive another. I confessed to wishing evil upon another. Once I even confessed to despair of God's grace or mercy, adding serious entertainment of suicidal thoughts for good measure.

Every Wednesday, I would sit in that small, dark enclosure, twisting my hands in my lap, wondering what I could say this week to make the priest finally hear me, so close to the priest that I knew which one of them it was before he spoke. Father John gave off an odd smell, like aftershave and dry rot, and his breath whistled through his nose. Father Timothy was much younger, fresh from the seminary; he usually smelled of cookies from keeping Sister Celeste company in the rectory kitchen when she did her weekly baking. It didn't matter which of them it was, though, on the other side of the curtain, Father John or Father Timothy, or what I confessed. I would get the same thoughtless absolution and be sent on my way.

When I decided to leave this morning, I didn't know what to take with me, what in the house I could rightfully call mine. I had no trouble packing my clothes, and I didn't hesitate to put in my hairbrush or my toothbrush. I wavered momentarily about my medications—I take some of the same ones that he does—but then I took them. However, once I had the box packed with my clothes, toilet articles, and medications, the things I could clearly argue were mine, I didn't know what to do next. I set the box on the bed and looked around the bedroom. Could I take my pillow? Did I dare take it from under the neatly folded bedspread and leave the bed with only one pillow, like some poor woman who has lost a breast to cancer? There were framed pictures on the wall that I liked, the still life with yellow roses and the two winter landscapes. I thought that if I took them with me, seeing them in the morning would help ease the homesickness when I woke up in your spare room and realized that I had not slept in my own bedroom and never would again—but I couldn't bring myself to take them off the wall, knowing how clearly it would show on the faded wallpaper that something had once been there that was now gone. Leaning over, I opened the drawer of my nightstand and contemplated my Bible and prayer book, both of which I had received so long ago on the day of my First Communion. I closed the drawer gently and left them there.

I am a coward at heart, it's true. I knew that if I was ever going to leave him, I would have to do it when he was out of the house.

As I sat on the bed next to my belongings, I knew that if I didn't get up and start to move right away, I would still be sitting there two hours later when he got home and began calling for me as soon as he walked through the door and didn't see me in the kitchen. I would sit there on that bed as if in a trance while he trudged up the stairs, slowly, heavily, one step at a time, every footstep landing squarely on my chest, until he crossed the threshold of the bedroom and demanded to know what in Christ's name I thought I was doing.

So I got up from the bed and did a quick survey of the other two rooms upstairs: your old bedroom and your brother's. I was surprised to find nothing belonging to either of you in those two rooms. *Nothing*. I checked every dresser drawer and pulled everything out of those two closets, but could find nothing of yours: no forgotten box of outgrown clothes, no toys, no books, no tattered board games with missing pieces, no ratty stuffed animals, no high school yearbooks or prom mementoes. How could I not have known that the two of you had taken everything of yours out of the house unbeknownst to me, everything, not leaving so much as a wrinkled snapshot or a dusty model airplane behind?

After a while, I could sense the minutes passing, and I roused myself and went downstairs.

In the living room, I scooped up all of the photo albums that had pictures of you and your brother in them. I did not bother to remove any of the pictures that had your father in them. He could be in the picture or not. It didn't matter.

I went into the kitchen last, knowing before I entered the room that every last thing in there was rightfully mine, from the refrigerator to the smallest set of measuring spoons—rightfully mine for no other reason than I was the only one to have used them for almost fifty years, except for the times you helped with dinner under my direction. What use would your father have for them: the slotted spoons and pot holders, the potato ricer and canning jars? None. If he actually lowered himself to cook, all he would need would be the big cast-iron skillet and a spatula that he could wave around as if he knew what he was doing. I took nothing from the kitchen, not even food, even though it would have been a thoughtful gesture to you and Ronny for me to have brought some with me.

I suppose that the hardest thing to leave behind is the house itself. Even though it holds so many bad memories, it has been my home for most of my life, and I will miss it. There were times when you and your brother were small, Terese, that I would put you down for your naps and work on my mending in front of a sunny window and feel perfectly content.

So, you're still wondering, what was there about this morning that made me decide to leave your father once and for all? I think it must have been that he didn't say goodbye when he left the house. I'd made him his usual breakfast of fried eggs and sausage, along with a pot of strong coffee. I sat down at the table with my bowl of cereal to keep him company while he ate. He didn't speak to me, which wasn't unusual; I'd grown accustomed to the silences between us. But then, after he was finished with his breakfast, he stood up and left his dirty dishes on the table, with no thought to how quickly the egg yolk would harden on the plate if it wasn't rinsed right away. Nor did he push in his chair, leaving it where I was sure to run into it as I cleared breakfast dishes from the table. Then he put on his jacket, set his hat on his head, and left the house without saying goodbye. You must know by now that I stopped loving him years ago, but the fact that he refused to give me even that simple human courtesy was simply too much to bear.

I Mean It This Time

Diana Woodcock

I mean it this time:
no more cats, no more lovers.
One dying, the other unable to

keep his promises. Living only
with solitude, my best friend,
I shall take nothing else in.

Oh, there'll be sunrises when I
edge up close to a fisherman
hauling in his night's catch.

And I might sit awhile midday
with the monk playing his ancient
flute in the shade of the gingko trees.

But in the evenings, I shall
let no one but the dew fall
on me, no one but the breeze

play in my hair—tease open
my blouse. I'll let only the blind
man on the corner sing to me

his blues. I'll get all the news
I need from the song of the Persian
nightingale. And only get down

on my knees to the honey
locust trees. I mean it this time.
Believe me, please.

One Morning

Zan Bockes

We sit in the winter-chilled kitchen, my groggy stare following the line of insistent drops plummeting from the faucet into your empty cereal bowl—a plink, plink, plink. And I'm thinking how this would annoy me if I were trying to sleep, the bed too small because of the trough your body makes—how I cling to the side and pull the quilts around me, how I know it will not always be this way, that some night I will lie alone and wish hard that you were still there, as in my dream, where I grasp a wad of high bills that I try to hold on to when I waken—the dread of your absence, my gratitude for the present when you take up the precious two feet on my side of the bed.

"I can give you a twenty—stopped at the bank yesterday. I know you've got ESP about my wallet," you say, and your smile contends that this is okay, even though guilt filters into my head over the small possibility that you resent supporting me. I know the guilt is extraneous, and if I mention it you'll laugh to erase my concern. You're that way, have always been for the thirty-six years that I have been your wife.

"You're right," I say, loving this tease, the way it comes so easily to both of us with no malice attached, like a favorite candy bar equally shared. "I keep track of every penny in your pocket."

The faucet plinks again, a humorous punctuation—how it underscores the silent laughs our eyes exchange. You sip your coffee, tip back your head as though swallowing your Coumadin. You spread the local newspaper across the shiny Formica table, moving your mug beside the ceramic frogs—salt and pepper shakers we picked up years ago at Wall Drug.

I turn my attention to the upside-down newspaper, translating the upside-down headline—PLANS UNVEILED FOR NEW BRIDGE—and I can't picture where the bridge will go or the river it will cross, but decide I'll drive on it one day and notice fresh yellow lines.

Your glasses slide halfway down your nose, and I wish I could push them up for the sake of your comfort and appearance. I wonder how you can read like that, like my father did, his horn rims tilted above his ears to read fine print—and I fear your vision is worsening and that you might be blind within a few years, no longer able to speak to me through your eyes. I watch your crinkled lids, the riff of your brown irises over the long article about the new bridge.

If all goes as planned, the bridge will be five years old when you retire, unless your heart gives out like a tired engine, unless the blood clots in your legs come back. That surgery four years ago—our mortality thrown so close to the surface of our awareness that the hospital waiting room seemed a clear metaphor. We wait for death, reading magazines to pass the time. I search your face, notice the pallor on your cheeks, the creased cheeks, the cheeks I love to trace with my knotted fingers.

"Maybe a ten would do," is what I say next. "We don't need much at the store." I mentally list the items: potatoes, cat food, a loaf of bread for your sandwiches . . . but I feel false about mentioning money when my mind is on the end of things.

"Twenty's no problem. Buy something nice for yourself."

I cannot think of what this might be—some scented lotion? A Salted Nut Roll for us both? I know you'd be happy if I bought something that was not absolutely necessary, if only to show appreciation for your generosity. You slip your wallet out of the back pocket of your overalls and tuck the twenty into my hand with a wink. "I want that all spent before I get home from work."

I feel a shiver, knowing that soon you will begin the long commute to the forklift at Golden's Lumber. I barely look at the same highway when I go to Little Falls for groceries, my focus on the destination, my hands tight on the wheel. I have never been to the lumberyard, but with careful mental construction I can picture it, like a lumberyard I visited once as a child when my father built a doghouse—the stacks of two-by-fours, the sheets of plywood, the high shelves which could collapse any second to crush you.

I see it happen suddenly like that—an accident. A heart attack. The choked calls to Danny and Susie—the best kids in the world. And maybe I should call them now that your paycheck is in—long distance to San Francisco and Seattle—hear the voices of my grandchildren, who always make me laugh.

I should get a job now to pay for a trip out there, go back to the vinyl booths at Big Wally's and carry plates of food all up and down my arms like I did when the kids were little. But the arthritis in my back won't stand it. The faucet plinks as though to say, "That is that."

The cat, Boris, leaps into my lap, the thunder of his purr quivering in his throat as I stroke his narrow black back—poor Boris grown thin and cloudy-eyed—and he climbs onto the table and plunks himself down on your paper, rolling onto his back. Your gentle hands pet his belly and place him back on the floor.

There is a flurry of noises—you turn the pages of the paper, Boris scratches his ear with a vibrating foot, the heat switches on in a soft, warm exhalation. The faucet lets go another drop which is muted by the other sounds. You clear your throat to begin reading to me:

"Safeway has chicken breasts on sale . . ." You are almost talking to yourself, but I feel privileged to listen. "Tomatoes . . . those pears you like . . ." I haven't bought Asian pears since last summer. I relish their sweetness, the soft white flesh with its slightly gritty texture. Such a simple thing.

Another drip from the faucet and I look over at the sink, notice the silver arch glinting in the stark kitchen light. You should fix that leak but I don't want to insist—your days off are precious and I'd rather spend them with you in walks along the river or in a feast of pot roast and mashed potatoes, you slicing the onions so I will not cry. And that's another thing I need at the store.

You look up from the paper to the clock and your eyes pass mine but do not stop. Since it is almost six a.m. you make a small grunt, meaning it's late, but not late enough to elicit a louder response. I know this particular grunt, have felt it move out my own mouth on occasion when something discontents me but is not important enough to form a sentence about. I know how the small bubble of sound moves up your throat, the air blocked by a subtle purse of the lips, a groan truncated by discretion, just to voice a displeasure that has nothing to do with you or with me.

You throw back the last of your coffee and when you get up from your chair I feel the ache in your knees and the weight of an eight-hour shift yet to begin, the long drive, the roads icy along the river . . . . "Be careful," I say, and you look at me quizzically, maybe because you think I'm talking about how you're rising to your feet, not about the drive. "On the way to work. The roads are probably slick."

Your glance crosses to the window above the sink, out that dark square where a hard winter morning crouches behind the reflected light of the kitchen, where I can see you standing with your glasses flashing double for a second, just a second, and you touch the back of your white hair and move to the coat rack with a dull clump of your steel-toed boots.

You shrug your shoulders into the canvas coat and I can smell you in the clothes you wear—that faint gray smell, like a wool blanket slightly damp. These are the clothes you've worn for years. I can see your younger, slimmer body in these clothes, the smoothness of your skin, the full dark hair in waves around your ears, the brown eyes so clear, like the first cup of coffee we shared in the little café with the yellow curtains, the way you touched my hand and said, "I want to know everything about you."

And I think, am I fooling myself? Am I making myself regret the time that has passed?

"Be careful on the roads," I say again with a strain in my voice, because my words might make an accident happen. But maybe they will keep it from happening.

"I'll be fine." And immediately my fear compounds—these words could be your last, said this one morning when everything seems so innocuously the same. You pick up the sandwich I've put in a brown bag.

"I love you," I say.

"I love you too," you say, and I can't decide if your affection is motivated by honest emotion or if you are just saying that because you say it every morning.

"Do you?" I ask.

You utter a small laugh. "Yes. I do. More than you love me."

"I love you more," I say, our mock argument not needing to be continued because we've said these lines before and we both feel the truth in them as well as the humor.

"Glad that's settled," you say, and a quick kiss passes between us.

The cold sweeps in as you go out, closing the door gently behind you, and I can tell your thoughts are already directed to the day ahead as you move carefully towards the black shape of our old Buick with that tight, crabbed way you walk on ice. I watch your figure diminish and disappear, holding this moment tight like the money in the dream—how, if I hold on tight enough, I can keep it when I awaken.

I stand at the door as I do every morning, waiting for you to reach the car, and I tell myself, Never take anything for granted. The faucet plinks in the background. I must wash the cereal bowl.

But your headlights do not go on, though I wait for several

minutes. I wait for what seems like a long time. Too long for you to start the car. Too long for you to come back because you forgot something. I yank open the door, step into the yard in my slippers, the ice crystals breaking beneath their soles like shards of glass, the cold slicing my worn robe.

Overhead, colors ripple across the sky, vibrant rays shifting against the starry backdrop—pink, green, white—like pastel ribbons floating in a breeze, and once I realize these are the northern lights, an ache opens in my heart at their soothing beauty. I stop for a moment. I have never seen this before.

When I peer toward the driveway, the dim shape of the car seems blurred and insignificant. Then I see you standing next to it, the ghost of your face tipped upward, gazing at the same amazing sky.

The Night of the Day

Larry Lefkowitz

The night of the day
We threw away the red sweater
My wife wore the day I met her
Twenty-two years before
I dreamed she did a wild dance
Not at all in keeping with her non-dream persona
Wearing a red dress festooned in scarves of red
And I thought in the dream:
I didn't know you could dance like that
And when she finished
I whispered in her ear:
"I love you," and was filled with desire

Upon wakening I felt a pang
Because I was sixty
And I and my wife
Had been young in the dream

And yet, seeing my wife's
Still pretty face,
The still alluring curve of her lips
I felt a pang of desire
As if the dream
Emerging into the waking
Had left me something of a gift

In which
The she/now
And she/then
Merge
Into she/always

Vows

Barbara Diltz Chandler

He wants another drawer.
He's already taken her body,
laid claim to her soul, her present and future,
her forever and always.
He's reorganized her life and her kitchen
and redefined her time.
Before he moved in she craved his eyes
and lips and hips.
She never got enough of his stories,
his laughter and him.
Before their union she had thirsted for togetherness.
A widow, decades alone, she had dreamt of new marriage,
but now he's always here,
there, everywhere,
for better or worse
in sickness and health
in dearth and wealth,
and he wants another drawer.

Widow: Parts 1 and 2

Lois West Duffy

1. Widow
   What an ugly word
   It has nothing to do with me
   Can't define me any more
   Than wife

2. I'm afraid
   Someone will come along
   And want to marry me
   Before I'm strong enough
   Not to

FOUR

THE PASSAGE OF TIME

Quartet for the Passage of Time: Four Haiku

Philip Dacey

1. Underwood

Rain on the roof. My
mother typed—tap, tap, tap, tap—
all through my childhood.

2. Jettison

Old files. Will it feel
so good, too, on my deathbed?
"Let's pitch this life out!"

3. Upon Publishing His One Thousandth Poem

Here's another crow
descended to join the rest
and pick my bones clean.

4. *Mais où sont*

The horse-drawn wagon's
milkman, who gave us ice-chunks,
long ago melted.

The Wisdom of Fifty

Tom Hansen

I had always supposed that when I turned fifty, I would start to be wise. After all, fifty is early September, the beginning of the last third of the year. Crops are still in the field, but harvest is just around the corner. At fifty, I would have fewer hairs on my head and fewer cells in my brain, but I would begin to make sense of things I had no sense of now.

The day came. Then it went. By the time I woke up the following morning, the truth was obvious: fifty is just another number. Maybe wisdom comes with age, but it didn't come to me—certainly not just because of the Big Five-Oh.

Yet four months later, it bubbled up from below. Signs of mortality began blossoming like precious little death flowers. By itself, each one was innocuous: merely another minor complaint. But taken together, they pointed obscurely to something ominous yet indistinct, something lingering in the shadowy wings just offstage.

First, a lump on my left shoulder burst into glorious bloom. It had developed several years earlier: a sebaceous cyst, formed when a sweat duct clogged, causing trapped secretions from the sweat gland to compact into a hard, white, painless lump the size of a large pea. The doctor who had examined it back then said it would probably dry up and disappear one day. But in June of my fiftieth year, it quadrupled almost overnight, turning slightly mushy to the touch. It was infected and had to be lanced and then forcibly drained of bloody, putrid pus. For the next two weeks, I swabbed it three times daily with a Q-tip soaked in hydrogen peroxide, easing the whole head of the Q-tip into the minor excavation in my shoulder.

"Each time before you clean it," the doctor had told me, "apply heat for ten minutes and then apply pressure around the edges. You want to express as much debris as you possibly can." I resisted the temptation to tell him that I was no slouch when it came to expressing debris.

Three days later, I made an appointment with an ophthalmologist. For weeks I had noticed a slight puffiness under my left eye but thought nothing of it. One morning, curiosity got the best of me and I tugged my lower eyelid down to look inside. Instead of a healthy pink, it was a beautiful, flaming, sunset red. On the underside of the lid was a pale, opaque nodule. The doctor took one look and told me it was a chalazion, a sty on the inside surface of the eyelid. As he began explaining how ducts clogged, I told him I knew all about that, having recently had a cyst removed from my shoulder.

"That's exactly what we have to do with this critter," he replied.

He rubbed a cloth saturated with mild anesthetic on the outside of my lower eyelid. I couldn't believe how careless he was when I first realized he had managed to smear anesthetic all around in my eye. But the stinging made me blink, and the blinking spread it to the inside of the infected eyelid.

After the lid numbed, he held it down and pricked the inside half a dozen times with a long needle I tried hard—but utterly failed—not to notice. A few minutes after this local "took," he applied an ingenious little clamp that held my lower lid down so he could core the sty. I heard a sound like scissors cutting cloth and began to see red. For five to ten seconds, my whole existence focused on one goal: to suppress, if at all possible, the overwhelming urge to vomit. It rose from my stomach, worming its way up through my gullet. To ward it off, I opened my mouth and began panting rapidly, shallowly. The doctor frowned and posed what he hoped was a rhetorical question: "You're not going to faint, are you?"

"No, thanks. I think I'll just puke on the floor, instead."

The whole process, start to finish, took no more than fifteen minutes. Afterward, he put me on a thousand milligrams of tetracycline a day.

The eyelid healed rapidly, but two days later, I had an unexpected reaction to the tetracycline, one I thought only women got: a yeast infection. A few irregular patches of pink appeared on my foreskin, and the base of my glans was oversensitive to touch. Too smart for my own good, I decided to self-medicate, using an over-the-counter preparation: the "doctor-recommended" kind advertised on television. Three days later, purplish pink and in such discomfort that I walked with a slight yeasty limp, I paid a visit to my longtime urologist, who chuckled—why are these urologists such a jocular bunch? why can't they be as sober and somber as judges?—and prescribed Corque cream, a hydrocortisone ointment that cured me, limp and all, in less than a week. But he didn't chuckle or prescribe anything for that other problem I reminded him of: a phantom pain that continued to haunt me every time I even slightly overexerted myself.

About ten years earlier, to terminate an acute epididymitis otherwise unresponsive to treatment, he had performed an orchidectomy on me. So for a decade, I had been minus one testicle. But for some inexplicable reason, I now and then felt exactly as if the neighborhood bully of my childhood were squeezing my excised testicle, trying to make me cry uncle. If I thought it would ease the pain, I would gladly have shrieked, "Uncle! *Uncle!* UNCLE!" at the top of my lungs.

After prescribing Corque cream, the doctor shrugged, "Your phantom pain, again? Not much we can do about that. Take aspirin and cut back on physical activity." When I reminded him that the most physical thing I did was walking my dogs two miles every day, he deadpanned, "So? Stop walking. Sit a lot. Watch more TV. Read *War and Peace.*" I am probably the only person in the world whose urologist has prescribed Tolstoy as a remedy for phantom pain in a long-lost left testicle.

Passing the half-century milestone has brought me other unanticipated experiences. Like those damn trifocals I now have to wear. And the stool softener capsule I wash down every morning with a small glass of prune juice. And my appointment next month to have my colon scoped out—scoped, not scooped. Not yet, anyway . . . .

What do all these hypochondriacal confessions have to do with the wisdom of fifty?

A lot.

Really.

But it took me a while to realize this.

It has been said that the best place to hide something is in plain sight: the last place anyone would think to look for it. What I found at last, hidden in plain sight, is one of the secrets of life I always knew in the abstract but never really had to contend with here and now. But every day, here and now, I am reminded that my body is an intricate machine made out of meat. It has already started to decay, stumbling down that bumpy road of bodily decrepitude.

Sometimes I lie in bed at night, sleepless and afraid, sick with the thought of betrayal. How could my body do this to me? Other times, I look in the mirror and don't know whether to cry or to laugh at what I see: a hole-in-the-shouldered, puffy-eyelidded, one-nutted, prune-juice-guzzling, fifty-year-old manikin peering back at me, nodding his head up and down, trying to determine which of his three trifocal lenses to stare through. Should I tell him to just take them off? Should I tell him that sometimes blurred vision is a damn sight better than clear vision?

At times like this, I realize what a brutally funny sense of humor God has. The joke is on me, of course. Hell, the joke is me. I am growing older, smaller, weaker. My vices have all run off in search of a younger, more vigorous man. I am learning to live with certain inevitabilities I would rather not have to face. Grudgingly, I acknowledge them. And maybe this—which is hardly the Holy Grail that I years ago set off in search of—is the real wisdom of age. Acceptance. Acceptance of everything.

Lodged in slowly disintegrating bodies, we aging knights and our aging ladies fair—every man jack and woman jill—guide our battle-scarred steeds down that narrow path leading into the forest from which there is no return. We see the lengthening shadows leaning away from the soon-setting sun. We hear the rattle of dry leaves clinging to twisted limbs. A chill in the air snakes its way down our necks. Still, these last few hours of daylight fill us with joy and a strange sense of grace. We value what little we have, knowing it will soon be less, but convinced—against all reason, convinced—that we have been blessed.

Credo at Fifty-Five

Christina Lovin

I believe you reap what you sow
      but that sometimes you can steal
      your neighbor's watermelon
      and get away with it.
I believe that swallowing watermelon
      seeds will make a virgin pregnant
      in some states.
I believe in a state of grace, a state of confusion
      and the great state of Illinois.
I believe that once a Hoosier, always a Hoosier,
      that Missourians are exhibitionists to the core,
      and Rhode Island has a bigger heart than Texas.
I believe that the map of the world is drawn all wrong,
      that people are more important than borders.
I believe in no Borders, no Barnes & Noble,
      and no Amazon.com.
I believe the Amazon inside me
      when she says I can do anything
      and then I do.
I believe that anything we do is written in the Book of Life
      and that we will be judged by our words
      when the mother ship returns with them from Alpha Centauri
      where they are collected, sorted, cataloged, and preserved.
I believe in preserves: blackberry with seeds, orange with peel,
      and Preservation Hall with the doors and windows open
      so the cats down on Bourbon can hear the news.

I believe in good Bourbon and better Scotch:
>   Glenlivet, Glenmorangie, and Glenfiddich.
I believe in how things are in Glocca Morra and Bora Bora
>   and wild men from Borneo and wilder men from the West.
I believe I'm not in Kansas anymore
>   and that the people I see in Oz are doppelgangers
>   for those I knew in my real life before the twister.
I believe in Twister, Monopoly, Scrabble, and Pit.
I believe "The Pit and the Pendulum" was not fiction
>   and that anything published by the War Council is.
I believe in War, the rock group,
>   not the act or action or reaction of a nation.
I believe every action has an equal reaction,
>   but that an object at rest was probably just tired,
>   and that Newton makes one hell of a cookie.
I believe that all my exes don't live in Texas,
>   but that two states away is sufficient for a level of comfort.
I believe in dreams, but I trust nightmares
>   and that I am everyone in both
>   so I am both the black cat and the angel,
>   the chaser and the chaste.
I believe in Straight No Chaser, Take Five, Bitches Brew
>   and that Miles was Lucifer in the flesh,
>   full of light as he was here on earth.
I believe that angels fall from heaven
>   because they have such heavy hearts
>   and everyone I meet once sat in the back row
>   of the Ryman in Hillbilly Heaven
>   because we're all hicks at heart
>   and my granny was one for sure.
I believe all children should have a Grampy or Grammy
>   or at least an Emmy or an Oscar.
I believe in hot dogs. Hebrew National.
I believe we should know what we're eating.

A Birthday Toast for Peter

J. Kates

My oldest friend, if you know what I mean,
is younger than I am by twelve days.
And so I hear his voice on the telephone
begging for hoary wisdom, *Tell me*, he says,

what it's like to be sixty. I need to know.
There is an urgency. I have a week
to craft an answer, to stick an aging toe
into the water of time's latest tick

and take its temperature. Tepid, tepid—
I hardly feel a thing. No telltale sting
or numbness. No sign of creeping decrepit
acerbity. I still want to sing.

And know a lot more songs than when
we sat at a dying fire as boys will do.
The flames kick up. The lined faces of men
stare half in shadow.
                              Here's looking at you.

Inheritance

Glen Sorestad

My mother's family was plagued
by weak knees. Considering that ancestors
clambered down the tilted mountainsides
of Norway's Gudbrandsdal, then trekked
to the seacoast to emigrate to America,
it is reasonable to believe they may
have assumed a link between steep inclines
and their bad knees. Since I am an inheritor
of these genes, though several generations
removed from the ancestral slopes, I take it
as a given my wonky knees have
an in-built aversion to inclines past two degrees.

My knees prefer level paths, the flatter
and smoother the better. I'll happily walk
miles over pancake terrain, but give me inclines,
ladders, uneven ground, even rocks and my knees
whimper and whine like scolded pups.
It's the most elemental reason I can cite
for living here on the Canadian prairies.

Besides, I am past the age deemed safe
or even advisable for shinnying up trees,
scaling ladders, cavorting on stilts,
taking up extreme wall-climbing,
or joining any expedition up Everest.

But in deference to these knees
passed down to me from my forbears,
I admit they have served me well so far,
though not without loud and lengthy protests
of abuse, especially during my hockey days
when simply walking home from the rink
was a form of torture, some unseen hand
shoving a knife into each knee as I
hobbled along. The next day my knees
picketed me with unkind placards.

I think my knees increasingly want
to remind me at this stage of their service
they'd like to be treated with more respect,
with a little extra consideration, when I
blithely opt for a steeper path than I should,
or decide to clamber uneven rock-bound banks
to fish along the San Juan River.

> *I'm listening, knees, I'm listening.*
> *I really am.*

All I can ask is that you do your best.
We are—as you have so often
reminded me—in this together.

Los Feliz Uncle

E. Michael Desilets

In his seventh decade he'd
taken a liking to Italian
beer particularly
Moretti which his smug snob of a nephew
always futilely hid in the Sub-Zero
behind those old cold bold ignored cans of Moxie
but when he was flush with fuck-you cash
he'd also guzzle a few bottles
to complement bowls
of Rigatoni Bolognese
at Puran's on Hillhurst
then smoke half a pack of Benson & Hedges
at his sidewalk table and savor the satisfyingly
cluttered view of Albertson's parking lot.

Everybody
over there seemed to need
kitty litter and
Ring Dings.

Still on a bad night he might
revert to type and drink whatever:
shit lite at Ye Rustic Inn
crud suds at that place
across the street where his rolls of pennies
were always welcome and he could discuss
at great and grandiloquent length
the weltanschauung of ragged enraged
imperfectly aged assholes
with kindred spirits in hooded sweatshirts.

Eyeing the Alternatives

Diana Anhalt

No one agrees on what happened next, but apparently two armed men approached the van. One wore a baseball cap, the other a sombrero. As the first brandished his weapon at the driver, the second made his way around the vehicle and pointed his gun at the woman and two men in the backseat. Just then, a man leaped out of the front of the van, another emerged from the rear. Both carried rifles. I was seated in the back of our car between my children, aged nine and ten, when I heard someone scream and pushed both kids off the seat and onto the floor. Roberto placed the car in reverse and stealthily backed away from the holdup, while his aunt Rita reminded him that he'd been driving above the speed limit.

Although I was there, I'll never know for sure what really happened because I was groping around in the bottom of my straw bag for my glasses. By the time I'd found them, the assault victims had seized the two outlaws, thrust them face first into the side of the van and were roughing them up as they frisked them for additional weapons, oblivious to the getaway car, which had slid off the soft shoulder and disappeared around a curve abandoning the outlaws. I now believe, thanks to intuitive reasoning and an overactive imagination, that the people in the van were probably delivering a payroll to the Tenancingo bank, but, well prepared for any eventuality, had been able to counter the attack. I also realized that despite my front-row seat, my poor eyesight had deprived me—once again—of the opportunity to witness a singular event.

Up until then, I'd become reconciled to peering out at the world with eyes more decorative than functional. I assumed that as with fingerprints, naturally curly hair, and an allergy to strawberries, my borderline vision was something I'd carry to my grave. But the "payroll bandits" episode was an epiphany of sorts: To continue peering out at the world with the eyes I had was tantamount to living an existence strained through cheesecloth. I would have to find a solution. I did.

It was approximately twenty-five years in coming and, by that time, I was in far greater need of it than I had previously been. My solution arrived smack in the middle of what I now think of as the "Age of Impossibilities."

In much the same way history records a Golden Age, an Age of Reason, and the Age of Invention, we live in an era when much of what we had been taught to believe was contrary to the laws of nature no longer is. Today many former impossibilities have become realities: You can colonize outer space, communicate through cyberspace, alter and duplicate genetic structure, cross the Atlantic Ocean in four hours, bake a potato in six minutes and, as I was to learn, acquire a new set of eyes.

I first realized that my dream of recuperating my eyesight was no longer wishful thinking after reading about transplanting corneas in order to restore vision. That information inspired me. I wrote a poem:

> "After I die give my eyes away," I tell you
> and envision the surgeon screwing them,
> like two blue lightbulbs,
> into some child's blind sockets.

But having written the first stanza, I recognized I would never make a model donor, nor for that matter a recipient, and I wrote:

"Who'd want them?" you ask,
reminding me of progressive myopia,
chronic conjunctivitis,
childhood sties.

(I remember stumbling across a room,
head thrown back,
damp tea bags balanced on my lids,
two glorious peepers painted on my knees . . .)

"Do it anyway," I tell you.
Give my eyes, snapped shut like Venus flytraps,
around my memory of your outstretched hand
bearing an opaque sky afloat in a glass of milk.

No. I would never make a model donor, but at least I'd gotten a
poem out of it. However, the second alternative, that of becoming a
recipient, appealed to me, so for a short time I played around with
the idea that, along with a stranger's eyes, I could inherit his or her
understanding, experiences, and memories. In much the same way,
if I could be a donor, I could pass on my own store of erudition.
This fantasy did not last long. It was unsound, impracticable and, in
any case, I was not blind enough to become a candidate for corneal
transplants.

Soon afterward, I was puffing up the tree-flanked path skirting
Mexico City's Paseo de la Reforma, with the eighty-three-year-old
man I jog with most Sunday mornings. He told me that after sixty
years of myopia he'd thrown away his glasses. He also expounded
at great length on what, in those days, was a recently developed
procedure for restoring eyesight, laser surgery: After the surgeon
cuts a semicircular flap into the eye's outer layer he directs a beam
of light so intense toward the now exposed cornea it is capable of
slicing away a diminutive tissue fragment, thereby eliminating the

deformity responsible for faulty vision. His grisly description was enough to curb my enthusiasm—for a while, anyway.

Naturally, I still yearned to see everything. But I had mellowed considerably in the years following the highway robbery, having—or so I liked to believe—developed that wisdom and judgment which, we are told, compensates for the loss of other faculties. I was nearing sixty by then and, though I expected to live another three decades, I could also recognize that, along with its disadvantages, partial vision has its benefits as well. "Think of it this way," a friend wrote. "Perhaps nature arranged for couples to blur precisely in proportion to the onset of wrinkles, age spots, and thinning hair. That way, blinded by both love and fading vision, they can blissfully carry through life the image of their mate in younger days, bright of eye, springy of step, glossy of hair . . . ."

I am happily married, so my friend's observation could not be taken lightly. I recognized that giving up one pair of eyes for another was a trade and a risky one at that. How could I help feeling like Faust making a pact with the devil? Who knows? I might lose something essential in return—my perception of reality, for example. And for what? Twenty-twenty vision? In a literary turn of mind, I recalled the Nathaniel Hawthorne tale of a woman whose physical beauty was unsurpassed; her only flaw a tiny hand-shaped mole upon her cheek. Such was her husband's desire for absolute perfection that, in his attempt to remove the mole, he destroyed her soul.

In the end, I feared I might regret my choice. After all, the way we see things helps define who we are. An eye change, like a sex change, could permanently transform me, and not only might I regret my choice, I might end up hating the "me" I had become. Such a loss would be greater than the gain.

That's precisely what had happened to my mother. Following surgery to correct her partial deafness, she claimed the world was far noisier than she remembered. In time, the effects of her operation wore off. We pleaded with her to return for a second intervention, but turning a deaf ear—so to speak— she refused, preferring the drone of silence to the roar of reality. I wrote a poem about that too:

I shouted to be heard.
"Why do you whisper? Speak up, speak up," cried my mother.
"Don't you know nothing is lonelier than silence?"
But our exchanges blurred, tenuous as organza,
yesterday's promises,
smoke.

After her operation
my mother expected sounds she hadn't heard in years:
clatter of typewriter keys, kind words, heavy breathing—
to enter her ears politely,
like reception-line guests
or nuns on their way to mass.

She got barbarians instead,
operatic thunder, firing squads, climatic changes, revolutions.
"Stop shouting at me! Stop pounding on my door!"

Today, occasional stray truths slither through
or gnat-like, circle her head. "Give me back my silence please,"
she sobs.
"I need to think."

I sometimes wonder: Did she believe there just wasn't enough room in her head for all those sounds? (I could understand that.) When I remembered the scores of things I could no longer see without glasses—the casual gesture, the difference between grainy and smooth, raindrops cupped by leaves, spiders' webs, my own shadow, tears—I was afraid I too might end up with the visual equivalent, discovering I had far more to look at than two small eyes could conceivably take in. No wonder the metaphysical concept of the "third eye" is central to Hindu, Buddhist, and some Rosicrucian teachings. (Think of how much you could see if you could "grow" one.)

While myopia remained a convenient excuse for not being able to see, another possibility did occur to me: Maybe I didn't want to. I remembered a school counselor describing the response of a group of upper middle-class children who had spent the morning walking through an impoverished Mexican neighborhood. "When I asked them what they had seen," the counselor said, "they remembered very little. By the time they're six or seven they've learned to screen out ugliness and squalor." Quite possibly I had done the same decades ago: I had deafened my sight as my mother had blinded her ears. Maybe I unconsciously censored the things that offended me and preferred my amorphous images floating fishlike behind glass to a world as unforgivably incised as an Edward Munch etching. (Of course, if that were the case, laser surgery probably wouldn't make much difference.)

By now, I'd accumulated a lengthy litany of excuses for continuing to live out my dim-sighted existence in a perpetual squint. But, while well worth considering, my deliberations were not all that was holding me back. Terror was. Why submit two perfectly healthy eyes, the only ones I had, to a laser beam as capable of inducing eternal blindness as of restoring my eyesight?

In the end, following years of vacillation, I reached a decision. How much longer could I squander scores of visual experiences? The sun glistening off a seal's back as it leaped to seize a flung fish, a blimp floating outside the window of a friend's apartment, faces in the subway, Rudolph Nureyev bounding across the stage in *Swan Lake* the night I lost my glasses, and the bandits on the road to Tenancingo.

So when my daughter-in-law told me she was pregnant I decided I was not going to stand around and allow my first grandchild to crawl, ride a bicycle, or graduate from high school without being able to witness it properly. And, though I hesitate to admit it, unless I had that operation performed, my grandchild would never know what I looked like without glasses. (In the end vanity got the best of me.) "Provided man is not mad, he can be cured of every folly but vanity," Rousseau wrote. (He was right.)

Dress Code

William Borden

He's retired now. The ties, so carefully selected to harmonize with the button-down Oxford shirts and tweed jackets, hang forlorn as forgotten lovers in the dark corner of the closet, tiny gray ridges of dust atop each one where it curves over its own small hook. The ties chart the fashions for forty years, the narrow, the wide, the compromise; the silk, the knit, the paisley, the little golf clubs. All forsaken now.

Now he pulls on jeans with paint stains and a sweatshirt. He has sweatshirts with logos of the colleges where his children studied, sweatshirts advertising the companies they work for now, sweatshirts presented as gifts on various holidays and birthdays bearing clever and humorous slogans—*Life Is Short, Eat Dessert First, Einstein Couldn't Add Either*—others asserting political resolve emblazoned with wolves and manatees, bald eagles and pandas, whales and entire jungles of endangered species including a tree-burrowing ant. And of course he has the *World's Best Grandfather* and the *I'm Retired This Is As Dressed Up As I Get* sweatshirts.

He pulls on wool socks—it's winter—and slips his feet into the fleecy moccasins worn in the heels. He tunes up the home espresso machine, makes his cappuccino, eats his toast, watches indifferently the morning television show tell how to keep toddlers safe, how the government wasted a billion of his tax dollars building an airport in the desert, why the aerosol can he keeps in the garage has caused the hole in the ozone, global warming, and the imminent extinction of life as we know it. He perks up when the subject turns to health for the senior citizen but wanders away as the slim young woman in tights demonstrates a yoga position he could not have achieved thirty years ago.

Still, he reminds himself that he should get more exercise, walk at the mall maybe, except he resists joining all those old people lunging back and forth, arms swinging insanely, their two-hundred-dollar walking shoes with the air cushions squeaking on the tile as they stride past the closed dark stores. Too much like life, he thinks, that endless round of pacing, going nowhere, and leaving just when the stores open and things get interesting.

Dress Code

Barbara Diltz Chandler

A Vancouver store advertises "Menopausal Apparel."
I'm aware of hot flashes, night sweats, mood swings,
but hadn't realized there was a dress code, too.
Window mannequins pose polyester in assorted sizes,
in shades of matron and moribund.
Must *a woman of a certain age* hang these in her closet?
Does she need purse and pumps to match?
Must she nip this attitude, tuck that behavior?
Trade her frayed denim for refined, defined, dignified and disciplined?
Must gray ponytails be shorn pert and prim?
Must *provocative* morph into *appropriate*?
Must we, the menopausal, finally get serious and act our age?
I'm too old to slip into something less comfortable,
too young to exfoliate tight jeans,
too spunky for a polyester transplant.

Estrogen: A Letter

Ann Fox Chandonnet

> *Words are the voice of the heart.*
> —*Confucius*

Yo, girlfriend,
you bitch,
you backstabber, you ingrate.
(I won't say "slut"—
though I'm tempted.)
I thought we were pals, bosom buddies,
BFFs, so to speak.
Now I glimpse your slimy hidden agenda:
You set me up for a really big fall.
In the autumn of my life,
you skedaddled under cover of darkness,
pruning my vocabulary like an apple sucker.
Tongue-tied, stumbling,
I suspected as much,
but now medical research confirms it.

Oh, I could just spit!
Words were my shining weapons, my flow-blue tea set,
my wettest tears,
my arms able to embrace the world.
How dare you, churlish girl!
Silly giggler!
I've given you the best years of my life,
burnt offerings of cramps, ruby crystals

and scarlet candles for your altar,
all that good stuff.
Not to mention:
       stammering before midterms
       stained mattresses in several states
       one ectopic pregnancy
       one gall bladder set with hundreds of pink pearls
       one miscarriage

You always craved my gingersnaps,
my blonde brownies and rum-raisin cookies.
But don't expect any more care packages,
you ingrate.
This is my final communication.
You'll find my phone unlisted
and my address changed.

Pig!
Here I am balding,
quite chapfallen (those puppet folds).
I can hear you mutter, crone;
I can hear your annoying open-mouth breathing.
Go ahead, gloat.

Now I'm prosaic as a buzz cut.
Inability to retrieve the right words
frustrates me no end,
infantilizes me.
Maybe we needed a prenup.
But enough about you.

Girl,
you were my chemical muse,
racheting up my creativity during ovulation.
Now I'm a bass out of water,
high and dry.
Bitch.
Hang your ugly hair over here so I can yank it.

188

Her Eighth Gray Hair

Karen de Balbian Verster

When she renews her driver's license on her fifty-fourth birthday, the photo portrays her own hair for the first time in sixteen years, which, her hairdresser reluctantly admitted, wasn't as gray as she'd thought it would be. Oh, the hairdresser had put up a struggle when asked to cut off her client's dyed hair, suggesting she consider lowlights, and talking her out of that insane idea to hack it all off. So she went home and did it herself with a pair of nail scissors, which was pretty easy since the gray/brown dividing line showed her exactly where to cut. She missed a few spots, but having curly hair came in handy because it all kind of swirled around and camouflaged her errors.

She studies her new self in the mirror. She likes this unvarnished self, this truth-telling self. She remembers her eighth gray hair. She was still a brunette, so the wiry, pigmentless strand (like albino pubic hair, really) stood out. She was thirty-seven. She remembers it because, unlike the first seven gray hairs, when she plucked it from her head, it detached with no tug. This happened because she'd been receiving chemotherapy for a month. This happened because she had Stage II breast cancer. This happened in 1991 when thirty-seven was considered pretty darn young to be getting cancer.

And what was she thinking, anyway? That she could stem the tide of age by plucking out her gray hairs as they appeared? Not a winning strategy, but unfortunately a lot like those she applied to the rest of her life—that is, until she was diagnosed with cancer.

How important were eight gray hairs in the face of that? Maybe she would die before there were eight more.

Chemo made her bald, scary at first but liberating. She looked good bald, ageless without hair. People thought it a fashion statement. She felt sexy without hair. Which reminded her of how she felt sexy *with* hair in 1973 when she stopped shaving her legs as a feminist statement while wearing hot pants and dating a man who golfed.

Her curly hair had never been in style (except briefly when Jon Peters permed Barbra Streisand, who, though very talented, would never be a trendsetter), so for fun she got a wig with long, straight russet hair. This wig was perfect. It swung and swirled like a girl's in a shampoo ad. This wig was glossy even when it was humid. (Not a surprise since you were supposed to cleanse it with furniture polish.) This long, straight russet hair would've taken ten or more years to grow if it was real. Ten or more years she might not have.

After chemo her hair grew in even curlier if that was possible. And all those gray hairs that had gone unplucked had lain in wait for their chance to rise up and sing, to proclaim their allegiance to life, to a life lived not in black and white but now in shades of gray. She actually paid someone (oh, she was horribly cheap) to apply blonde highlights to camouflage these pesky gray hairs. After all, she was reborn. She had survived cancer. She kept getting more highlights until somehow she became a blonde. How great is that, she thought, now I can have more fun!

She ate organic vegan meals, did yoga, meditated. People thought she was in her early thirties. But at forty-three, she began to notice a few stray hairs on her chin. And a few varicose veins around her ankles. Her skin got a little drier. Her period got a little heavier. Then a lot heavier. A real gusher. Geez, she couldn't leave the house for fear of flooding the floor. She'd never been a slave to her period, never thought of it as the curse like her mother. Was this cervical cancer?

Then she got a migraine. The kind where black dots advanced

from the edge of her vision until they shrouded the scene before her like a sandstorm. She almost passed out and had to sit on the floor until the nausea passed. Where did that come from? She rarely got headaches. It happened again. Did she have a brain tumor?

When she was forty-seven her period receded like the ocean at low tide—just sucked back out to God knows where. It became erratic. (It had never been all that regular to begin with.) Sometimes it was just some drops of blood. Then months went by. Then a scant flow or more drops of blood. Was this cervical cancer?

She who once slept through the piercing shrieks of alarm clocks, who had to set two at a time to ensure wakefulness, now slept as lightly as a soldier on a battlefield. Her husband tried to be quiet on his trips to the bathroom but his ankle popped like gunshots. Then she would have to get up to go to the bathroom too. And when she tried to fall back asleep would be disturbed by his breathing. And then would wake easily to the melodic tones of her alarm but would be logy and grit-eyed all day.

She didn't get hot flashes. She got hot flushes. Her body would suddenly heat up like a microwaved sausage. No sweat but unbearable warmth. Her blood pressure pumped up like an overfilled bicycle tire. Her head was a big fat beefsteak tomato that someone had just shot with a BB gun. She walked around with this big-red-tomato-head feeling like a hissing Headless Horseman hot air balloon. She got so mad over insignificant slights she spit fireball retorts. She got so sad over tepid setbacks she wept rock-salt tears. She ranted and raved. People looked at her like she was crazy. She *was* crazy. She who had always prided herself on her sound, her logical, her acute, powers of REASON.

She got puffy and baggy and striated as stretched-out Lycra. And then, just in time for her fiftieth birthday, she lost thirty pounds. She, a sofa spud, suddenly got good at sports. In summer she played doubles tennis during the week with young mothers. She poured her craziness into every shot. Her serves were scathing. Her returns excruciating. In winter she skied weekdays with retired people. The fastest guys took her under their wing. She learned to ski the black diamonds like death was on her heels, spraying snow in his face with her rooster-spur turns. She was a babe again. Taut as concertina wire. Guys might actually want to sleep with her. But she didn't want to sleep with them. Besides she was happily married. Besides she only had one breast and she just couldn't see herself trying to assuage any man's disappointment ever again.

After watching several TV makeovers where women were transformed from blowsy blonde to cheery chestnut it occurred to her that blonde was no longer de rigueur when it came to self-improvement. She wondered if it clashed with her skin tone, if that's why her face looked so red. And while we're on the subject, she thought, doesn't everyone and their mother have blonde hair? Blondes, once so fine and rare, were now a dime a dozen. It seemed like every woman over the age of fifty was blonde. And the young ones were blonde too, although they were allowed to have roots. When she was in high school, only sluts dyed their hair blonde, but even so having roots was inconceivable.

When she turned fifty, she thought, Well, this is it, I'm middle-aged. But what's middle-aged nowadays? Like our economy, there's no longer a middle ground. You're either rich or poor. Young or old. Celebrities, even the feminist Gloria Steinem (who probably started this whole thing by posing on a magazine cover which proclaimed her the new fifty), dyed their hair, perpetuating their youth well past their fifties, hell, even into their seventies. (Think Mae West and Ginger Rogers with Goldie Hawn hot on their heels.) When do we get to be our age, she wondered. She looked around. It wasn't just celebrities dyeing their hair. It was everyone. And not just women, either.

She looked good as a brunette, but people no longer guessed she was in her thirties. They were guessing forties. She turned fifty-three. And had this wild idea that maybe she'd stop dyeing her hair. And then she'd look in the mirror and say, I'll stop when I'm sixty.

Her husband, the lucky duck, had stopped dyeing his pitifully sparse hair and now shaved his head. He looked younger and more vital. She worried that if she went gray she'd no longer look younger than he. But the idea wouldn't leave her. She started going longer between dye jobs, examining her gray roots, trying to envision how she would look.

She'd watched her friend Jane arduously grow out her gray like Rapunzel letting down her locks one inch at a time. And just when Jane grew it out and got it back to the early-Hillary style she normally wore, she changed her mind. And dyed it back. Maybe people told Jane how old she looked. Maybe Jane told herself how old she looked. *She* certainly thought Jane looked old. *She* certainly thought Jane looked better when she dyed it again. Certainly her own hairdresser, who cringed and pouted every time she said she was thinking of growing out her gray, would agree. She knew her eighty-year-old mother, who still dyed her hair, who said, If you stop dyeing your hair you'll make me look old, would agree.

Somewhere between fifty and fifty-three her period ceased. For good. For ever. She'd never minded her period. But she did mind the estrogen, since her cancer had been estrogen-receptor positive, which meant her cancer was exacerbated, maybe even caused by her own estrogen. And then she read that estrogen was nature's way of subduing pubescent girls. Of taking the guts out of their gusto. Of making them amenable to a male-centric world. Or at least amenable to a non-female-centric world. A woman's job was to pump out the eggs. Month after month. To ensure the continuation of the species. Year after year. But never, oh never, to create a female-centric world.

And now her estrogen had snuck out of her body like a slow leak from an air mattress. But instead of flattening her it expanded her. Made her happy, joyous, and free. Made her sizzle with possibility. She went back to work on her old passion. And then another passion bloomed. And then another. She felt ageless again.

Until she looked in the mirror. Unruly eyebrows. Dingy teeth. Receding gums (which gave new meaning to the term "long in the tooth," since her teeth protruded from her gums like adolescent legs outgrowing trousers). Sagging jawline. Puckered upper lip. And were those hairs on her upper lip really that black? Was she getting a moustache, she wondered as she peered into the 10x magnifying mirror. Best not to look there too often. Fortunately, her unaided eyesight, while still good, gently blurred the edges of things. (And presumably blurred her flaws when her husband wasn't wearing his drugstore reading glasses, which thankfully he did not wear during sex.)

She ran into Sally, whose long hair was gray on the top half and brown on the bottom and said, Oh, you're growing your gray out! Sally looked at her quizzically and said, No, I'm not. I just forgot to dye it. Good Lord, she thought, that woman could hide her own Easter eggs! Six months later she ran into Sally looking the same way and said, Oh, you're growing your gray out! Sally looked at her quizzically and said, No, I'm not. Why do you keep saying that? Probably thinking, Good Lord, that woman could hide her own Easter eggs!

Then she had her epiphany. Now she looked like a haggard forty. But if she had gray hair she'd look like a healthy fifty! Suddenly those big ropey veins in her right hand would not look so out of place. (The chemo had desiccated the veins in her left hand.) Ditto the crepey skin on her thighs and the dry skin on her heels. And when did her toenails get so gnarly? (Now she understood why every woman over fifty got pedicures.) At least tennis and walking with hand-weights had tautened her flabby biceps.

Finally, her hair grew out enough where she was in danger of looking like an inmate of a state mental institution if she continued to cut it with the nail scissors. Sadly, she hung them up for good, knowing this idyll of cutting her own hair was over, and somewhat fearfully returned to her hairdresser, who asked if she intended to persist in this lunatic pursuit—what she really said was, So how's that workin' for ya? as she sardonically looked her client over. Great! she said, realizing it was great. I am what I am, Popeye's delight, what you see is what you get.

She pities her eighty-one-year-old mother, who still rolls her hair every day on hard pink rollers, who still wears heels albeit short ones, who takes three hours to get ready even to go to the grocery store, who refuses to wear shorts on ninety-degree days because of her varicose veins, who has no life. Nothing. Nothing at all but the *National Enquirer* and "The View." (Thank God Rosie is gone and banality reigns once more.) Here is a woman who relied too heavily on her looks because she feared to rely on her brain. Here is a woman who squandered her A+ in Psych 101, the top grade in the class which set the curve, in order to marry a man who would keep her worried about her looks her entire life. Even after he dumped her. Her mother is a constant mirror that reveals what happens to a life half lived.

With her gray hair she feels on the threshold of a new world. A world where she is fully present and realized. A world where her voice is heralded and heard. A world where her artistry is applied to her work rather than her looks. And she is only fifty-four! Almost exactly middle-aged, since she plans to live to be one hundred and four. What magnificent things she will accomplish! What a legacy she will leave! Inspiring a generation of young women to place their humanity before their gender!

When I'm Old

Mara Hart

For Kitty

When I'm old and longtime widowed,
I'll wear hot pinks, blues, and turquoise.
I'll live with my sister Kitty
In a cottage by the sea.

We'll have our own bedrooms
And need our own baths,
A screened porch with wicker,
A ramp, just in case.

We'll have books. And paintings
By masters of light:
Vermeer, Bonnard, Van Gogh.
We'll have cats.

We'll grow
Irises for her,
Roses for me,
Violets in memory of Mother.

Mornings we'll walk or garden,
Singing old love songs.
Afternoons I'll write, Kitty will paint,
Or maybe we'll just nap.

I'll cook,
Kitty will do the dishes,
Both of us will read,
Neither of us will clean.

Evenings, giggling like schoolgirls,
In wingback chairs by the fire,
We'll cheat at Scrabble,
Gin rummy, or chess.

We'll reminisce about the bookshop,
The cat that fell six stories,
The flashlight down the toilet,
The crackers full of worms.

We'll smile
As we remember old loves
And laugh at the time we told Grandma
Penises grew up.

Saturday nights we'll entertain men friends:
Linen, sterling, china, crystal,
Oyster stew, Caesar salad,
Salmon, wild rice, asparagus,
Champagne, Drambuie,
Chocolate mousse.

Then we'll dance slow and close
To Vaughan, Sinatra, Clooney,
And with luck, one of us
Will need the guest room.

We'll drive our red Volvo
To concerts and plays,
To children and grandchildren,
And visit New York every fall.

I'll help Kitty hear,
She'll help me see,
We'll help each other walk.

Two women,
In our seventies
Eighties, or nineties,
Ending our lives
As we began them,
Together.

Aging

Karen Nelson

She curls her almost fifteen-year-old body
into my lap—then begins examining my skin:
checking age spots, places where she can stretch
skin with her fingertips, pulling up the excess while
saying, "How thin your skin is—not to mention that
flip-flop, jiggly stuff under your arms."
She counts as she flips the jiggles with her open palm.

She traces my face's age lines, comments
on new ones she hadn't noticed before.
She pauses, looks straight into my eyes with
her dark ones—"I think you're beautiful."
"You should have seen my high school pictures!"
I add softly. Even with my wrinkles and crinkles,
as she called them at eight years old, she repeats:
"You're beautiful!"

Seven Days in May

Marsha Dubrow

My parents died seven days and seven years apart in May. That changed the merriest month into a dreaded month.

Every year I think it will be easier. Some years it passes gently. But other years May slaps me hard across my face, like Mother did only once.

I try to reconvince myself that spring is, as Henry David Thoreau termed it, "an experience in immortality." But for me, it's closer to Ralph Waldo Emerson's comment, "What potent blood hath modest May." May's blooms remind me of death.

Another reminder is forgetting words. Not multisyllabic, Styronesque words, but everyday take-for-granted words like "hand" or "jar." My vocabulary splinters.

This once-a-year word loss began immediately after Dad died on May 3, 1983. I was back at work as press secretary of a U.S. Senate committee, and urgently needed a notepad for our hearing that was about to begin. An intern asked what I was looking for. I stammered, "A—a—uh, um . . ." But the word had vanished, so I replied, "Thanks anyway; I'll find it." I couldn't find a notepad or the word although I always carried a notepad to jot down everything about our legislation and our chairman.

What was I to say? "It's paper, with lines, for writing, bound, yellow or white—I forgot the word?" Instead, I pawed silently and frantically around our supply closet until I found one, and its word. "Notepad," I declared, grabbed it, and rushed to the hearing.

Odd, yes. Surprising, no. A writer, a communications person, losing words after losing her father. For seven days each May, my vocabulary is shattered. I still stutter over the simplest words, and use more synonyms and circumlocutions than I use during the rest of the year.

While ordinary words hide from me, unusual names repeat and repeat in my ear.

My father savored names, except for his middle name Hyman. The more exotic, the more hypnotic. He repeated incessantly "Ish Kabibble," a comedian, and "Thanom Kittikachorn," a Thai premier. After years of intoning "Sessue Hayakawa," a Japanese actor, Dad's fascination switched to "S.I. Hayakawa" when the educator S.I. became a U.S. senator from California.

Last May, triggered by a recent trip to Cambodia, "Pol Pot" kept resounding in my mind as did visions of skulls piled up at the late dictator's "killing fields."

Another May event, ever since contending with my late father's personal effects, is spring-purging rather than mere spring-cleaning.

After Dad died, I walked into his closet and gasped as I gaped at three decades' worth of bills and their cancelled checks. All were in their respective surgically slit envelope, arranged chronologically. I recalled that slitting envelopes with my fingers instead of a letter opener enraged him. I dared not ask why his temper flared at this, or at chewing ice, or leaving cabinet doors open—or at asking any question. His hazel eyes would turn spring green, and his cheeks would turn the shade of his cherished Pink Peace roses that burgeoned each May in our Houston garden.

I jammed these thousands of stuffed envelopes into seventeen body-bag-size Glad bags and hauled each down the exterior stairs of my parents' cramped apartment. I could understand saving the architect's bill for the house we had built on Heatherglen Drive, but all utility bills? All Southwestern Bell telephone bills? Every single cancelled check?

I wondered what deficit had made him hold onto all these throughout four moves to successively smaller dwellings. Was it proof that he had met all financial obligations despite having arrived impoverished in America as an eight-year-old Russian immigrant? He had always warned me, "Never owe anyone anything." His tone had been as cutting as slivers of dry ice, so frigid that it burned.

I found almost nothing personal among his personal effects until I opened the last drawer. There I saw every letter and postcard I had ever sent him. Only then did I cry.

Yearly since then, I gather my rubbish while I may and lug away bags of files I no longer need. Last May, I tossed three bags from Hotel Pribaltiyskaya filled with information from my trip and article on St. Petersburg. The prior May, I heaved two hotel laundry bags' worth of background info about Anguilla, one from each of my visits and stories on the British West Indies isle. LexisNexis and the Internet save info for me, dust-free.

Ridding myself of other excesses is also key to annual rituals commemorating my mother, Pearl, who died on May 10, 1990. Two rituals involve hair. First, I tweeze any errant eyebrow even more meticulously than usual.

I remember the day Mother told me I was old enough to pluck. Facial hair is a rite of passage for females as well as males, especially removing it. She put my head on her lap, poised her sharply pointed tweezers, and said, "Honey, beauty knows no pain." Then ka-pow, right between the eyes. I yelped, she smiled, and we both laughed.

Afterward, she held a mirror to reflect both our faces with matching mother-daughter eyebrows. "See how pretty you are now?" Hardly hirsute, I wondered why only "now"?

I stole those pincers, the only thing I ever stole—from her. She must have suspected me, because they disappeared the day I left home for college. I have used her (our) tweezers for decades. They are part of Mother's legacy, along with vanity and almost impeccable honesty.

When the time came to help care for my aged mother, she asked me to pluck her eyebrows and also her chin. I tried not to grimace. I hesitated for a few moments, but then said, "Honey, beauty knows no pain." Soon I felt less like a member of the primate family grooming her mother, and more a member of our very private family.

Weeding her almost-seventy-five-year-old face gave me a horrifying view of what I may look like over time. Now when I spot a rogue tendril, I ease my shuddering by tweezing and uttering, "This one's for you, Mom."

As a young mother, she had worn her hair in French braids atop her head like a crown. Her hair was so thick that bobby pins sprang from the braids. And her hair was so black that it shined blue in the Texas sunshine.

Each May, if my hair is long enough, I wear French braids. Mother had braided my waist-length hair until I was twelve years old. Then she declared that I was old enough to take care of it myself, and added that she was tired of cutting wads of bubble gum out of my strands. So I learned to braid my own hair and to keep my mouth shut, at least while chewing gum.

Also on those seven days in May, I wear pearls in honor of Pearl. I had never liked them until she died. I used to agree with Philip Roth's description in *The Counterlife*, "They're absolute death, pearls." But now I have pink and black pearls, two styles of each color, as well as white cultured pearls, a present from a college boyfriend for my nineteenth birthday.

I had rarely worn the white baroque pearls until Mother's burial. I doubled the opera-length strand to form a choker. Minutes after the burial in sweltering Houston, my necklace broke. Pearls scattered across a bathroom floor. I grasped my throat, feeling that death had broken Pearl's choke hold. It sent chills throughout my body. Recalling that moment still triggers chills up and down my neck.

I also play Elvis Presley music. Elv the Pelv, the quintessential symbol of the generation gap, actually united Mother and me.

The first day KYOK radio played Elvis's "That's All Right," Pearl drove 65 mph in our Olds 88 to buy his 45-rpm Sun record. She always beat the local censors' ban, and built a coveted contraband rock collection. My pride at having the sole cool Mama was tinged with embarrassment.

The minute I got home from Oral Roberts Elementary School, she said, "You've GOT to hear this." I wondered superciliously, her new word for me, what in the music world could have transformed my opera-loving, jazz-adoring mother into a schoolgirl. As soon as I heard the first plaintive wail of Elvis, I knew. We played it over and over and over.

Throughout the years, his music evoked a time when Mother knew best and loved me tender, long before her "Mean Woman Blues" made our home like a jailhouse, with only music to ease the heartbreak. The only way I could cut short our most entrenched arguments was by blurting, "Remember that day you discovered Elvis . . ."

The Elvis connection continues to ease any strand of daughter-parent bitterness. Elvis's music finishes and I whisper, "That's all right, Mama—and Papa. Thank you both for everything."

Maybe this May, or surely next May, I too may "rest" in peace.

Helga the Horrible

Judith Sornberger

I'd heard she was a harridan
before I drove the county roads
dotted with falling down repair shops,
deer processing shacks, and dark-
windowed Bible churches
to teach a night class at her library.

This wasn't her idea, and she's refused
to order the one book I asked for.
Erotic poetry won't fly, she warned the board,
in her library, this valley where the Baptist ladies
battled—and won—against Harry Potter.

(She'd seen the word "Erotic" in the title
and thought it must mean "dirty."
God knows where she got the "poetry.")

How dare she censor me? I'm fuming,
as I brace myself on the bumpy curve
into Main Street, recalling the board member
who tried to calm me down, asking
could I blame her for trying to hang on
to her minimum wages in this job-forsaken county?
Anyway, Helga'd had some trouble in town once
upon a time, having grown up Dutch,
and you know how things are in Amsterdam.

Now here she is, elbow to elbow at the table
with her patrons—a gray wren of a woman
who chooses the purple spiral notebook
from the stack the grant provided.

Write for five minutes, say I, the teacher
from the college with earrings to her shoulders
and toenails painted fuchsia, *about the name
you wish you had been given.*

A few creased foreheads, some chair-creaking,
a few giggles. Helga harrumphing
to her neighbor, *A name is just a name,
after all*, as she bends over her notebook.
Ten minutes later, she's still at it, faster now
as though she's racing to catch up with someone.

I don't want to stop her, but the others
are tapping their pens, starting to whisper.
She comes up from her writing, cheeks flushed
and eyes blinking, as though I've reeled her
from an element she hadn't known
that she could breathe in.

When her turn comes, her wary eyes circle the table.
Then she shrugs and reads to us about *Lolita*:
a woman wearing flame-red silk that kisses
her ankles as she dances the flamenco.
Heads tilt, faces leap backward, as though
some dun-colored bird they have been watching
has turned into a scarlet tanager winging skyward.

Even I am startled by how the word has wizarded
her for a moment beyond censure, to stanzas where
she clicks her gypsy heels to scarlet music
that follows her back into this drab room
where I find we are dancing on the same page.

Vocabulary Downsizing

Maureen Tolman Flannery

It must be getting
crowded lately
on the tip of my tongue
with all those languid words
laid off, lethargic,
lounging around
in their underwear
in despair of ever
being called up again.

Asking

Sharon L. Charde

this huge slumbering thing
boxed inside my body

like my son's bones
in his coffin

a prisoner of war?
a thornless rose?

now my old dog
burned to a crumble

ashes, chunks
of cancerous bone
in a cardboard carton

I clean my grief
like a wife
scrubbing her pots

When in Fear

Ilze Klavina Mueller

I offer food to the hungry ghosts—oatmeal, hot chocolate
radio programs about cars and their owners
a book of moderately easy sudoku
bones and gristle to delay the pursuing dogs

When in grief

yellow leaves to the river
sheets to the clothesline
candles to the Virgen de Pátzcuaro
life to the striped beetles on the cucumber leaves
water to my dead friend's geraniums
howls to the silent house

When at peace

I offer a handful of berries to a driver taking a break by the roadside
two just-picked lettuces to a tired mother of three
a smile to the neighbor whose ex swore he'd kill me for trimming his tree
temporary forgiveness to the squirrels who beheaded my tulips

When in hatred

an automatic message on the machine
a stone clenched in a fist
a locked gate
burning eyes

When in bliss

I offer
a song to the morning
a full tank of gas to the car
a dollar tip to the barista who poured me my decaf
a kiss to the ash tree in front of my house
a broom to the stairs

FIVE

A TIME TO LIVE

Bad Mothers' Club

Deborah Marshall

Minutes of February Meeting

Four mothers attended.
Tea was served.

Deborah reported
her mother-in-law
still is complaining
that grown grandchildren
don't send notes of thanks
for Christmas presents.

Nyia described
her frustrations
with planning a trip
for her grandkids.
Their divorced parents
do not return calls.

Paula revealed
her ambivalence
about fostering
her adult son's dog,
a birthday surprise
from his ex-girlfriend.

Nora displayed
color photographs
of her new grandchild
born unbeknownst
to her last year
in a foreign land.

Unanimously
Nora was chosen
Bad Mother of the Month.
She graciously
accepted the crown
and pink tissue box.

March meeting planned.
Green beer to be served.

Closings

Betty Buchsbaum

Since a daughter's last e-mail I'm keenly aware
of closings—

sincerely   yours truly   regards
best regards   best wishes   fondly
love   much love   oodles of love
hugs and kisses   ciao   peace—

aware of both subtle and seismic shifts
in how people end messages—
this daughter used to sign love, helen
but now it's a breathless run-on loveme.

I do I do!—what's going on
in her life that she sends this SOS
yet writes of nice sunny weather
in Denver and dinner with friends?

Worried about her daughter in Kenya
working with children in a Nairobi slum,
tribal conflict expected
in next month's election?

Her college freshman son half a continent away?
Chronic back pain?
Menopausal lows?
Or something she can't bear to say?

Or is she saying *loveme   loveme*
you never loved me enough!—those words
lodge like small stones in my chest—
a chiselled *never*, dun-colored *enough*.

And is her father in the next room faced
with the same coded message? Timidly,
I ask him; he laughs, says it's simply
her hurried shorthand for *love, me*.

How wise to marry this man—such a clean
commonsense take on that missing hook of a comma.
Still, last night I dreamt *loveme*
slept in my arms, it felt like her body.

Legend

David Mura

An only daughter is a needle in the heart
was how, in one legend, a poet put it.
Thus the legends of the father at the start of war
say I must stand on a rocky shore
and beg the gods for winds to cross the waters
and battle and destroy the city Troy.
And the gods shout back: Sacrifice your daughter.
Or else, in the tale of seven samurai swords,
I first hide you from brigands
and then from the warriors
who would save us for daily rations of rice.
And what these legends tell us is
the desires of fathers are foolish
with fear of their enemies and hatred in their hearts.
And fear too of how his daughter will part
her legs and never be seen again
for this is what happens
when men write the legends.
Of course there is no father in these tales
who descends down the corridors of hell
and crosses those foul and mysterious waters
to retrieve from the underworld his only daughter
and finds the courage to return her each year
before the leaves may bud and the earth flower.
Today I wandered with you
through the aisles of Abercrombie and Fitch

where all beaming models are ruddy and blonde
and no dark face mars their endless summer.
And I want to tell you they are there
to make themselves rich
and not because they are foolish and fond
and love the way your black
hair shimmers down your lanky brown back.
But I know you will not listen if I tell you.
I am the father, my words could destroy you.
Or bar you from the one blushing samurai
who gathers flowers on the hill
and though he desires to know what it is to kill,
what he desires most is beyond her father
as she opens for him on a slope of bright flowers
this summer afternoon with no thought of death
or how someone must descend in cold autumn showers
and answer to darkness and darker desires.

Wandering Off

Thomas Shane

The first time, she misunderstood him.

She'd been home three days and after marveling, again, at the simplicity of his physical needs—three squares, an aspirin, and a stool softener—had taken up the watchful work of piecing together, from the little things that happen, a current picture of his mental state, which had slipped in the four months since her last visit, but subtly—an old lawyer is an old bluffer. When she came to get him for the week, the nursing home director had told her it was a sign of his extraordinary intelligence that he seemed so normal, and she might've told the man that she'd never once outsmarted him in a lifetime of trying and doubted she could pull it off even now. But he seemed to be taking everything so gracefully, blithely even, that she had begun to think maybe it wasn't going to have to be that way after all.

She'd read up on the subject so it didn't surprise her that he confused her with Margaret. Confuse maybe was the wrong word since, except for the rare moment when, as if something loose inside his brain had with a lucky shake suddenly clicked back into place, he knew her as his daughter and would pretend to have some knowledge of her life ("Ah, the theater"), it wasn't something that could be cleared up by any amount of patient explaining or by any other means she could think of. Calling him Dad didn't do anything; Margaret was the kind to call her husband Dad. She tried things, of course, quizzing him—"Who am I?"—or reminding him of little things about Margaret that, if added up, would surely prove they had nothing in common, and he just went right along with her, saying, "Why, you're my Liz, of course," or "Oh yes, your mother was funny about that, wasn't she," or whatever it was, but it was a game to him and he wasn't about to be tripped up in any game. Afterward, though, he was back to calling her "Maggie" or "Margaret, dear" or, most off-putting, the teasing "sweets." For any number of reasons she could easily imagine—Margaret had not been dead a year so it was, for one thing, a convenient way around whatever grief he was capable of—it served his purposes to merge her with her stepmother in his mind, and once he had done it, that was it as far as he was concerned, all tricks aside. For some reason, though, she didn't think it through all the way.

They were staying at the old house (she'd made arrangements to rent it out, but the tenants wouldn't be moving in until the following week), and they'd spent the better part of the day on a visit to "the half-in-law," as he referred to Margaret's half-brother, Uncle Edwin, who lived in Tenley, the county seat. So he was more tired than usual, and instead of dozing off in his chair as they watched the TV together, he surprised her halfway through "Murder, She Wrote" by "rising to his full height," as he liked to say, and announcing he was going "up the golden stairs," which is how he used to phrase the bedtime command to her when she was a kid and there was an upstairs to ascend to.

He shuffled off, exaggerating his feebleness with a fake stumble or two, which he'd been doing for almost as long as she could remember, but now that he was past eighty, it made her catch her breath, audibly, in spite of herself. He looked back at her with the most pitiful expression on his face, and she laughed, and then he almost did trip on the short step between the den and the kitchen. Anything for a laugh.

After a while he called to her. "Margaret," he intoned in his prideful, ageless baritone, then coughed primly, and she could sense it coming, the Charley's Aunt bit, even before he switched to a tremulous falsetto, "Could you come here a minute, sweets?"

"Certainly, Thomas," she responded at once, imitating Margaret, who had created in him, harmlessly while she lived, a monster of dependency for all the little things, like food and clothing, we need to survive.

He was in the bathroom, in his nightshirt, his thin fringe of white hair sticking out at angles and his face red and still damp from washing. Bowed slightly forward with his fingertips pinched prissily together in front of his chest, he was pretending, eyebrows upraised, to be searching through her cosmetics, which admittedly took up more than their fair share of counter space, for something pertinent to his toilet. "What, my dear," he asked through pursed lips, "would you recommend?"

With him, incongruities were the heart of comedy—if you knew W. C. Fields, whose little gestures and flinches he'd been practicing for fifty years, you were on to him—so he fully expected, this 220-pound ghost of a man, that the image he struck in his reverent contemplation of these elegantly bottled potions—"so bravely feminine," he said, mimicking the master's rasping twang, "in their resistance to mortality"—might raise some titters from an audience if he could get one.

"Too late, Dad; too, too late," she answered, with a throaty chuckle, thinking, involuntarily, of the nearness of her fiftieth birthday. She still carted the stuff around with her, obviously, but she found herself using less and less of it. What was the use?

He looked at her with mock surprise, and then, pretending hurt, looked away and began to rummage through the little drawer by the sink where his things were kept. "All right, then," he said, stiffly, chin up, "I am sorry to have troubled you," and he took out his toothbrush and a tube of Ben-Gay.

In the big mirror over the sink, Liz could see that if she did have her father's nose—the hump on the ridge like a badly healed break—still the difference in scale saved her. The tip of his nose, which seemed to have accreted over the years like a stalactite, hung now to just above his upper lip, and his ears, with their bent sprouts of colorless hair, stood away from his huge pink skull like stunted wings. He had bad skin, which she had inherited, but while hers was mostly just dry, he had those hard, scaly patches of yellowish psoriasis, not to mention the stubborn old wen on his left ear and now (since when? she wondered) that gray mole stuck, like a gorged tick, on his cheek. I don't look half so bad, she thought, mocking herself, well aware of her own signs of entropy: hair almost all gray now and the creases around her eyes and lips that made her look old-maidishly pinched and severe even to herself. Your spitting image, people used to say to him of her. God help us.

Thomas was making a show—slow enough to give her time to react—of squeezing the Ben-Gay onto his toothbrush.

"Let me have that, you old fool," she said, snatching it away.

"Oh?" he said, pouting.

"Here," she said, handing him the toothpaste.

"Oh, all right," he said, still playing offended dignity, "if you insist."

She watched him brush his teeth. "Is it true your nose and ears never stop growing?" she asked.

He stopped abruptly and spit, staring straight ahead at his image in the mirror. Without his glasses his red-rimmed eyes looked small and puffy and sad. "I hadn't heard," he said and resumed brushing.

She laughed. "Well, let me know if you do hear; it's important."

When Thomas finished in the bathroom Liz was in the kitchen emptying the drainer, and the teakettle had just begun to hiss. His bare feet made a sucking noise as he padded across the linoleum, and she turned to look at him. It seemed incongruous to her that an eighty-year-old man should be so sturdy, though most of his bulk, to be sure, was in his upper body—his gut and arms and shoulders, his thick neck—and the real incongruity was how smooth and pale and delicate his calves and ankles were. How did they hold him up?

"Margaret, dear"—he was absentmindedly holding the tube of Ben-Gay in one hand and waving to her to take the other—"you must come now and ease an old man's pain." And though he said it like that, matter-of-factly, like this was expected of her now so come along, he had a quizzical, oddly sheepish look on his face she couldn't quite place, which told her, somehow, he was anticipating a rebuff.

"Are you okay, Dad?" She looked at him hard for a moment, and the kettle started to whistle.

"Oh, you're having tea." He had that hurt look in his eyes, like before when they'd been kidding over the makeup, and he might have been kidding now too. "That's nice."

"Can I fix you some?" She took the kettle off the burner and put two tea bags in a pot.

"No. Oh, no. None for me, thanks. No, I'll just go to bed." He gave her a little forced grin, which was a dismissive signal of his, and turned and gave a weak backhand wave and headed off to what used to be the guest room. "Nighty-night," he said, and she felt the sting of his sarcasm.

"Where does it hurt?" she called after him.

"Ha, ha," he said, "rub it in, rub it in."

She followed him. "Dad, really. Here, give me the Ben-Gay and show me where it hurts." She was being brisk with him now, much as Margaret might have been, and she reached to grab the tube out of his hand.

He stopped then, in the doorway of the bedroom, and looked at his hand. He'd tightened his grip on the Ben-Gay, instinctively, and now he looked at it as if he was seeing it for the first time. "What's this?" he asked. He looked genuinely puzzled now.

She took the Ben-Gay away from him, slowly. "Here, lie down, Dad." She guided him gently to the bed and tucked him in and turned out the light. "I'll finish putting the dishes away—it'll only take a minute—and then I'll be back to give you a rub."

"I know, Maggie. I know. God bless you, dear. I'm a little tired now."

"Rest. I'll be back," she said and kissed him on his forehead, which felt cool to her lips. When she came back, he was asleep.

It's not so hard, really, to see how she could have misunderstood. The next time, though, he was more, well, direct.

Liz made a big breakfast in the morning, fried eggs and bacon and toast and juice, like Margaret used to feed him before all the advice about cholesterol, and a late-rising Thomas, positively bright with rest, went at it with pleasure and praise. Helpless though he was in all such things, he was unfailingly grateful to those who had the knowledge and full of wonder that it was his good fortune to be the beneficiary of it. At least that was the way he played it, though it was clearly his understanding, probably from birth since his mother had doted on him like everyone else, that he was not meant to miss a meal, and he could be quite the prompter if, as the appointed hour approached, those responsible for the necessary preparations appeared lagging. "Have I eaten already?" he might ask, "And did I enjoy it? That's the important thing."

After three solid days of cooking for him, Liz proposed they "do the town," as she jokingly put it, topping off with a visit to Burger King, which had become a favorite of his when Margaret was in the hospital. His brightness on rising faded fast, so they waited till the afternoon, which gave her a chance while he napped to talk on the phone with the real estate agent who was handling the rental. (Renting, in fact, had been the agent's idea; wait for the market to improve and maybe by then . . . maybe by then it will be easier.)

There was a time some years back when there had been some talk about selling the old place—it had gotten terribly expensive to heat after the price of oil took off, and anyway the size of it was getting to be too much for Margaret, who was more frail than she looked at first—but Liz couldn't listen to it.

As a child she'd been called moody, which seemed to give her license to be a little short with people (except Margaret, who used it as an excuse to be even shorter with her), but all she remembered of that was the feeling she got when the air changed in the fall and she'd walk out back past the barn and into the stubble of the cornfield, which had been sold off before she was born. There was nothing but open land as far as you could see in those days, rising on an easy arc to the west, and she would stand and shield her eyes and imagine herself walking out across the cultivated fields, feeling the superficial boundaries on the land, the accidents of ownership, fall away, and with them the accidental boundaries of her life, and everything was suddenly boundless and possible: the earth springing underfoot and the flocks of blackbirds scavenging among the leavings of the harvest, and the fields stretching on and on, infinitely, on a curve toward the sun. Everything would be quiet except for the cluck of the birds and her breath, and she would imagine the future out there, that she could just go and walk to it and there it would be. When she'd head back in, the long light, shivering through the trees at the edge of the field, would make the white clapboard of the house shine, and the windows would look like they were on fire until she got closer and could see in. Margaret would be in the kitchen bent over the oven or stirring something on the stove, pausing maybe once to push her glasses up or brush her hair from her eyes, and she'd watch for a minute, feeling a little superior maybe and thinking she knew something, though she couldn't have said what.

Anyway, that first talk about selling might as well have been about death; it hadn't been that long ago—eight, ten years—but even at that late date it hit her hard that anyone could consider just letting go like that, and it made her feel alone, suddenly, before the fact, like an orphan, at a time when the future had begun to seem to have less life in it than the past.

But, of course, she needn't have worried. Whatever the place meant to her, it meant so much more to Thomas, who had lived his whole life there, practically from birth. So the solution had been to close off the upstairs, add some insulation, and get better windows, and although Margaret let it be known she would have preferred the change to a different place altogether—without that silent upper story looming darkly overhead—it all seemed to work out pretty well for them those last years, a natural contracting of the space around them, but still familiar, which turned out to be important in Thomas's case as his loss of memory began to tell.

Now, though, for Liz, everything had changed. Each visit home since they shrunk the house, the town seemed to have swallowed another farm, and except for the cornfield—rezoned "commercial" but still being farmed for now—the open spaces had filled in, and it was as if the family place had been lifted up out of the countryside and plopped down in the center of a thriving suburban village. It was not unpleasant, really, compared to what was happening in a lot of other places, but there was so much traffic they'd had to move the mailbox to the end of the driveway from across the road, and there was too much light at night, and with the contraction of space outside matching the contraction inside, well, it just wasn't the same anymore. When Margaret died, Liz knew it was time to sell, and she was ready. The problem had become getting Thomas to agree.

Not surprisingly, he had his own idea, and it was that she would come back to live with him. It was impossible, but that didn't keep her from turning it this way and that, at first, to see if maybe it wasn't the right thing for her to do after all. Part of this, she recognized, was sentimental: a yearning, after all the years, to make a circle of her life, to find her way home. And too, though she'd reached the point where she was glad for her solitude, had made of it, she thought, her one great strength, the single life in New York had long since lost the enchantment it had once held for her, and the gypsy existence of the journeyman actor—all those dreary days and nights spent on the road playing regional theaters—had begun to take a toll. She had nothing to show for herself. Her grand life in the theater, which had begun as a brave gesture of independence, wild with risk, had become, after thirty years, as routine and pre-dictable a way to make a living as Thomas's lawyering had been, maybe more, and it disturbed her to find herself, with increasing frequency, just going through the motions, getting by with tricks. And of course, in spite of, or because of, all the time they'd spent at odds with one another—all that wasted time—Margaret's death had shaken her. Thomas was alone now. Maybe she should come and be with him, for however much time there was left.

It was as much because she was thinking like this as it was because it was the only way to get him to do it that she had presented the nursing home stay as a temporary thing. He had to have some stim-ulation, however unsatisfying the institutional setting might seem. He could lead songs there and call the numbers for bingo and oth-erwise gratify his urge to entertain, and she knew from playing the Grange with him as a little girl ("What are you standing on there, sir?" "Why, madam, ceremony, of course") what a good audience the old-timers would be.

"All right," he'd said, "but just until you come back."

"And when I come back?"

"The house will be there."

So that's where they stood. She hadn't told him about the tenants.

"Doing the town" meant looping around to the sewer plant to pay their respects to what had been the singular achievement of Thomas's tenure as town attorney, when laying the groundwork for growth was the farsighted thing to be doing, then crawling along the network of alleys branching off Commercial Street, touring, as Liz said to needle him, the town's *id*. ("I'll *id* you" was his comeback.) Here were the decaying remnants of the old rural industries: rail-road warehouses, cold storage, canning factory, basket factory, feed store, lumber yard, and the place that had gone from selling farm equipment to lawn mowers to pool supplies, and now announced itself to be the "Hilton Health Club." Most of the places, like the last, were still in use—plastic signs stuck over peeling stucco walls or weathered siding declaring, in block letters, "Welding," "Glass-cutters," "Equipment Rental"—but not the basket factory, which was a burnt-out ruin now. And not the canning factory. Seeing it, even with the windows broken out and large flaps of plaster hanging down, brought back to Liz the gagging smell of boiling fruit from her first summer job. She had been convinced then, when summer ended and she'd returned, practically shaking with relief, to school, that she would smell it, and smell of it, for the rest of her life.

"Do you remember sending me to work there?"

"Oh yes, you were so proud."

"I was so mad, I think you mean."

"Turning the age for a work permit, now that was a proud thing."

"You should have had a son."

"Didn't I?"

"Ha!"

They'd reached the end of the street where it dead-ended in the railroad right-of-way at the point where the tracks curled away from the town and headed south.

"Oh my god, 'the Burning Bush,' it's still there. Can you believe it?" Liz leaned forward on the steering wheel, taking in the sight of the weathered, ramshackle house on the opposite side of the track. A faded metal Carling's sign and a half-full parking lot were the only clues to purpose and habitation.

Thomas was grinning. He liked seeing this last redoubt of the grittier days, even if he was as responsible as anyone for the suburbanization that had sterilized the town.

"What was it called originally?" she asked. A long time ago a Christmas tree had caught fire there, and the original name fell out of use. He'd told her, more than once, but she'd forgot.

Thomas pushed up his glasses and pressed his fingers to his eyes. It was a habit he had to indicate deep thought. He used to do it when he was advising clients, and it seemed to give an oracular weight to his words. She'd hated it when he did it to her; "I am not your client," she always wanted to say, but never did. Now, though, she knew, he was only pushing himself to remember, and she was immediately sorry she'd asked. "It doesn't matter," she said, and when she put her arm on the seat back to turn the car around she squeezed his shoulder.

"I don't know," he said, slowly, eyes still pressed shut. After a moment he shook his head and opened his eyes, staring straight ahead, unfocussed, as the car spun around. "No," he added and gave it up.

Their last stop before Burger King was his birthplace. Liz had always known he was born in town, but until Margaret got sick she wouldn't have been able to identify the place. On their way back from the hospital one night, he asked her to go by, and she had to say she didn't know where it was for sure. He did a take, staring hard at her profile. "Do you mean it?" he said. She looked over at him and shook her head dumbly. "Well then," he said, and after that he'd made it a point to have her drive by any time they were in town.

Liz pulled the car over to the curb and let it idle in park. It was a sturdy house, white with green trim, with a big front porch and a small hexagonal window, like a third eye, between the two front-facing windows on the second floor. It looked well-kept from the outside, like all the houses along Maple Street, where the branches of the old maples, arching across the street, formed, as Liz thought of it, a green tunnel to the past—or one man's past, anyway, whose nativity, a little more than eighty years ago, was as far back as it went. He told the same story every time, about how his mother gave birth to him on the hottest day of the year, while his father entertained the doctor out on the front porch.

"Oh, they had a grand time. They sat right there under Mother's window, smoking their cigars, discussing world affairs—"

"Didn't she say anything?" A restive show of disbelief was Liz's way of keeping the story fresh.

"Yes, she did. She said the smell of those cigars was enough to make her sick."

"But really, Dad. I mean, didn't she ever say anything to the doctor?"

"Doc Norton? Oh no. Mother would never have said anything to Doc Norton. No. But that was the last child of hers he would deliver. Now that makes a point."

"Dad, you were her only child, period."

"Exactly. Mother could be truly . . . what's the word?" He closed his eyes and thinned his lips and, magically, the word came to him. "Vindictive." He had a look of real satisfaction on his face. "Yes, she could. Mother was quite a woman, you know."

"And you're quite a guy." She leaned over and touched his cheek. He'd shaved unevenly with his electric razor and there was a rough spot, which she rubbed gently with her thumb.

"You mustn't say that, dear." Displays of affection had always embarrassed him, giving or receiving.

She took her hand away and put the car in gear. "Bacon double cheese?"

"I thought you'd never ask."

When they got back to the house the moon, which was just a day or two from full, had already floated well away from the horizon. The night air was unusually soft for April, and they stood out on the front lawn for a minute looking at the moon. Across the road, in a shallow slice of woods that served to shield a pair of baronial two-acre estates from each other, the peepers were singing. Liz used to listen for the peepers as a girl, anxious for that first sure sign of spring, though Margaret always cautioned her they would freeze up three times before winter was really done. It was all woods across the way then, and the sound would fill the air at night, and it was wonderful after the endless dead silence of winter. There could easily be another freeze or two this year, she supposed, but there hadn't been a long, cold, snowy winter for years. "Nothing's the same anymore," she said, wishing immediately she hadn't.

Thomas was back on his heels looking straight up at the first stars. "Sir?"

"Nothing. And don't call me 'sir.'"

"None of that now. I heard something."

Two cars sped by, noisily, in quick succession.

"All right: *Où sont les neiges d'antan?*"

"*Gesundheit!*" One of the flaps of Thomas's shirt collar was bent up over the collar of his sport coat, and with his head thrown back and his tie too tight as always he looked, as only a man habitually oblivious to comfort can, perfectly uncomfortable.

Liz couldn't remember the last time she'd stood and looked at the night sky. "That's some moon, though, I'll give you that." She imagined it, like the jolly sing-along moon of childhood matinees, to be grinning at them, madly.

"Oh yes, we have always had the nicest moon here in Hilton," he said, then turned and with a little gentlemanly bow gestured for her, the lady, to lead the way into the house.

The night routine was television, mostly, with Thomas simultaneously trying to read the paper and going over the same story again and again, or going straight through the whole paper and putting it down, then discovering it again near at hand and starting over without any memory of having just been through it. From time to time, he might launch into one of his half-dozen or so favorite vaudeville ditties or a number from his community theater days, which seemed to float in a circle on the surface of his mind like leaves in an eddy. Pretending they were for her entertainment, he would do them song-leader-style, pointing his finger like a pistol. Now and then he'd hit a blank spot and close his eyes and concentrate quietly; if nothing came he'd just take it from the top again, and again, as often as it took or until she intervened. After a few days of this, she began to sense there might be something desperate in it—as if he thought if he could just hold on to these old tunes he could hold back the darkness that was overtaking him.

The ones she hated hearing most were the Gilbert and Sullivan patter songs she'd helped him learn at the height of his amateur career, such as it was. He would be the "Lord Chancellor" or the "First Lord of the Admiralty" or the "Major-General," while she was expected to play the part of sycophantic chorus ("with many cheerful facts about the square of the hypotenuse"). It had always worked before—he with his deep baritone and his chin against his chest hitting just the right note of self-parody—but now that an obsessiveness had crept into it, it was his self-centeredness that came through, his need for attention, and it irritated her to have to indulge him. This time when he started in ("When I was a lad I served a term as office boy to an attorney's firm . . .") she found herself, without warning, in tears.

"What is it, Maggie?"

"I'm not Maggie!"

"Of course you're not. Here, use this."

He handed her his handkerchief, and she did use it, wiping her eyes, then blowing her nose loudly. When she went to hand it back, he insisted she keep it, but she said she had no place to put it, so he took it, making a face before putting it back in his pocket, and she laughed.

"Oh, Dad."

"Yes, dear."

"Oh, oh, oh. Just, oh."

"I should say."

"I'm going to have to turn in, I'm afraid."

"By all means."

"Well, this is where I sleep." She gestured at the daybed, where she was sitting, next to his chair.

"You don't mean it."

"Where else?"

"Where else indeed."

She went and washed up and put on her nightgown and returned. "Aren't you going to bed?" she asked him.

"Not just yet."

"Well, don't mind me," she said, a little sarcastic herself this time, though he didn't seem to catch it, and she lowered the volume on the TV and turned off the lights, except for the standing lamp by his chair. "Goodnight, bub," she said and went to kiss him, and he turned his head to her and gave her his ritualized kiss, squeaking like a balloon through exaggeratedly puckered lips. "How charming," she said as she pulled away.

"Oh, dear, didn't I do it good?" Brow creased, eyebrows twitching, he looked at her, then away, then back again.

"Spare me." There isn't a trick of his I haven't used, she thought and smiled. "There now," she said and patted him, "it's all right."

In the daybed she propped herself up on the pillows trying to watch with him for a little while, but she felt her tiredness like a pleasant weight on her body, and she gave in to its pull and sank.

Whenever she was sick as a child she used to sleep on the daybed so it would be easier for Margaret to care for her. Before going to work Thomas would come and lean over her and press his thick hand on her forehead, firmly, and she would feel the ache go out from behind her eyes into his hand, which seemed to absorb it like a pad, and she would put her hand over the back of his, feeling the veins and the hair and the thick knuckles, and close her eyes and think of nothing until he took his hand away.

In her dream, he was leaning over a woman, her eyes sunken and sightless, lying still as death in a hospital bed. He was gripping a rosary in one hand and gently stroking her hair with the other, which made her head look small like a child's. "It's all right now," he was saying just loud enough to be heard over the sound of a baby crying, "You can wake up now." The soul of the woman, her mother, whom she'd never known except in dreams, hovered silently over the scene, a guardian presence Liz had often imagined as a child, visible to her but no one else, not even Thomas. "It's over now," he repeated, "wake up now." His eyes were as calm as God's; but the baby's cries kept growing louder and louder, and then, without warning, in a chilling voice, he roared: "Maggie!" He hadn't changed his posture at all—he was still leaning over her mother, calm and gentle—and the voice didn't appear to be coming from him—his lips weren't even moving—but it was his voice and he was repeating, incongruously, "Maggie," over and over, first roaring, then wheedling, then pleading, then roaring again. "Maggie!"

Liz bolted up in bed. The television was still on, showing a static rush of colored snow to an empty chair. Thomas's voice had come from the other end of the house. There was silence. Then a door banged and a wall creaked against the weight of a man stumbling against it sideways. Again he bellowed, "Maggie!" Then a dining room chair went over and dishes crashed in the hutch, and before she could throw off the shock of it all he was coming in a determined rush toward her from the kitchen door, pulling his nightshirt up over his head as he came.

"Dad!" Her voice, with all the stage command she could muster packed into it, hit him like a clap and he froze in midstride, his nightshirt hanging from his hand. She sat there, rigid, and stared at him, her eyebrows straight across, and the image she had of herself was of a school mistress breaking up a midnight pillow fight, so sudden was the shift of mood.

Thomas stood before her, naked, struggling for comprehension. His legs were slim and fine, but his upper body seemed to be sinking into itself, shoulders to chest, chest to belly. Large patches of psoriasis floated on the map of his skin like continents. The hair at his groin, as sparse and white and matted as winter grass, looked like a plundered nest. Hanging there, abandoned, was the source of her, plucked and headless, as dark and distended as an old wine bag. He had a warm, animal smell, a little stale maybe but not repugnant. "The thing itself," she thought, and the expression on her face eased.

"It's you," he said quietly and held the nightshirt to his crotch.

The pose was familiar to her from the occasional childhood encounter at the bathroom door, though the sight of his sex, she realized with some surprise, was new. Uncircumcised—the old pirate. "''Tis a naughty night to swim in, Nuncle,'" she said, softly, a little smile in her eyes for him, for both of them.

"I was looking for your mother." He stood there, still, lost.

Liz got up from the bed, pulling the top blanket with her, and put it over his shoulders. "Were you asleep?" she asked him.

"I don't know," he said.

Holding him loosely at the shoulders she guided him back to his room. "I'll be back with some warm milk," she said.

When she came back he was sitting slumped on the edge of the bed with his nightshirt on. "I'm sorry, Maggie, but even old men get the itch sometimes."

"I'm Elizabeth, Dad, your daughter."

"Why won't you sleep with me anymore?" As desolate as he looked and sounded, there was something ritualized in the question. He had to ask it, but he didn't seem to expect an answer.

"Oh, Dad . . ."—she handed him the milk—"have this."

He took the milk and sipped at it, at first, then drank it down. It left a white line above his lip, and Liz took a tissue from the bedside table and wiped it away. "Try to sleep now, Dad," she said and held the bedclothes back for him. When he lay back she put her hand over his. This was the familiar, defining texture of him—strong and male and secure. She slipped her fingers under his and he gripped her softly. She didn't know old men could have hands like this. She

wanted him to hold her, to anchor her, to keep her safe. She wanted
it all back. She wanted him back. "Good night, my good man," she
whispered.

It was their last night at the house that he wandered off. Liz
could have blamed herself for not hearing him, though the fact was
she'd slept so heavily all week—being there with him, and sleeping
in the daybed besides, she was thick with dreams—that the only way
to have heard him would have been to keep from sleeping altogether.
It was the cold air that woke her. He had gone out the back way,
directly off the den, leaving the door ajar, and gradually the night
air, lapping against her on a light breeze, seeped in under her blankets, and when she woke she was holding her knees to her chest.

"You have your career, I believe, Elizabeth," Margaret had just
finished telling her by way of explaining why she could not go to
town with Thomas, who was backing out of the driveway in the old
DeSoto, the car of her childhood. She had been crying in the dream,
so it was, at first, a relief to be awake. Then it hit her. "Dad?"

Though the way her mind was racing she felt like she was going
in circles, she was able to dress quite quickly, and when she went out
in the night she was wearing his heavy overcoat, retrieved from the
hall closet, like a cape. Altocumulus clouds, silver in the moonlight,
made the sky's surface seem like the cornfield's, which was freshly
disked. Walking felt like wading in the thick soil, like the sluggish
progress of dreams. How far could he have gone? she wondered and
held the bulky coat, which dragged against the clumped clods of
earth, tight against her throat.

Thomas had never been much of a hiker, so walking the width
of the cornfield represented a major exertion; having got that far, it
made sense to him to lie down. The broken ground, lumpy though
it was, conformed to him in general, a pleasing sensation, though
not having thought to orient himself with his head uphill, he began,

238

shortly, to feel a little full-headed and strangely like he was falling backwards, though the ground held him firm. He could see the clouds were moving, and then he thought he felt the earth moving too, rolling under him, and he with it, backwards, head first. He thought the damp cold was part of him and accepted it as such; he did not associate it with being outdoors in his nightshirt. The breeze felt like someone tickling him with a scarf, cool and silken, and it made his hair stand up. He lay quietly, and time passed. A memory came to him: his mother calling him, "Thomas!" and he lying in the corn with the guilty pleasure of invisibility, shaking with silent mirth.

Eventually, he started to sing, "They strolled the lane together, the sky was studded with stars . . . a . . . She turned her soft eyes to him . . . but there's nothing between them now. For he was only the hired hand, and, a, sheeeee was a Jeerseeeey cow." He couldn't sing very well in the position he was in so he leaned to one side and struggled up into a sitting position, and who should he see lurching toward him as fast as she could come, lifting her knees high against the suck of the earth—"Maggie!"

Liz fell on his neck, struggling against the anger she felt welling up now without warning. She held him too tight, wanting to squeeze the madness out of him. Straddling him, she pulled his coat from off her shoulders and threw it around him while he shook against her, giddily. "Maggie, Maggie, Maggie." His teeth were chattering but he didn't seem to be aware of it. He spoke like a drunk man, mumbling disjointedly. "Sing" she made out and "stars" and, improbably, "cow," but the rest was lost to her except, of course—he was talking past her now, as if she wasn't there—"Maggie," always "Maggie."

As she held him, his shivering began to come in hard waves against her, as if he meant to break them apart from within. Her anger left her as quickly as it came, replaced by fear of the danger they were in. How fast can it go? There would be no use even trying to move him. Even if she could get him up, which was doubtful, she would never be able to get him across the cornfield. She buttoned the two top buttons of his coat, which had the effect of binding his arms together in front of him almost like a straitjacket, and wrapped the open flaps as best she could around his legs. He had his shoes on, the same old business oxfords he always wore, but no socks, and his pale ankles reflected the moonlight. "Don't go anywhere," she told him.

"Dongwinnywear," he parroted her. His eyes were blank.

The distance to the house was not great, but the soft earth fought her every step of the way. The fat-faced moon, bouncing behind the rippled clouds as she ran, was laughing. "Honeymoon"—stop it!—"keeps a-shinin' in June." She began to feel dizzy, nauseous, and the clamminess crept over her, but she kept on, willing it down. Here and there in the distance, superfluous mercury vapor lamps, mimicking the moon, gathered small clusters of houses and tin-sided outbuildings into inconsequential circles of false light. Ahead of her, the old house, gray-browed, yellow-eyed, might have been a giant buried to the neck. Her shadow leading the way—longer legged, more elegant than she, but with the same resolute, forward-tilting trot—she passed the moon-washed barn, which was shining like a drive-in movie screen. "Faster!" she called out, "Faster!" But she was going as fast as she could.

On the way back to him, stumbling, she fell forward twice on her elbows, her face buried in the blankets she was carrying. "I'll remember this," she muttered the second time, to nobody in particular.

When she reached him he was rigid in the position she'd left him in. "Oh, Christ, Thomas, why, why, why?" She opened two of the blankets and laid them on the ground next to him and leaned against him until, like a drugged bear, he fell over on them and lay there, jackknifed, on his side. She pulled on his legs, managing to move him a little more, then took off her shoes, sat down behind him, and holding the edge of the blankets, pushed him into the center with her feet. Then she put the other blankets—they were four good, heavy army blankets—over him. "Everything's under control now, Thomas. Not to worry."

She was talking to herself, really, so it surprised her when, though she couldn't make it out, he did mumble something in reply. She leaned over him close and stroked his light hair. On the side of his skull, where his hair was thickest, was a long scar, a dent, from a childhood accident with an axe. She couldn't have been more than four or five when, finding her at play in the toolshed, he'd taken her hand and gently combed the tips of her fingers through his hair to feel the hidden crack. At the touch of it, she'd recoiled, as if from an open wound, and he'd laughed. "It's just something to keep in mind," he'd told her with a wink. Now she traced the contour of the scar with her finger. "Father," she said, self-consciously setting the word against the stillness, like a prayer.

She smoothed the blankets on him, making sure he was covered everywhere, then crawled around him on her knees and slid in beside him, face to face, scissoring her legs along his flank and rubbing him up and down. His eyes were unfocussed but his breathing was all right, and she knew she could warm him. She opened the buttons on his coat, freeing his arms, and pressed close against him, slipping her arm under the coat to embrace him. "You smell like a bear," she said. She thought, under the circumstances, she could say anything she wanted.

Shortly, she began to feel her own heat returning to her from the blankets. "Come on, come on." She pushed him on his back and lay on top of him, her legs flat on top of his, and rubbed her hands along his sides, avoiding the rough patches as best she could. Then she took off the sweatshirt she was wearing, careful to slide it up and off without letting in too much cold air, and wrapped it around his head. Her bare skin was against the thin fabric of his nightshirt, and she felt her body heat transfer to him. "God, your breath is awful," she said. "Really."

As the cold's grip on him loosened, Thomas shuddered. He

felt the woman on him, her animal warmth, and absorbed the heat she was giving him. In a little while he became conscious of a silver night sky and then her eyes, close to his, watching him, as familiar as a guardian angel's. Wherever I am, he thought, this is wonderful.

When she knew he was aware of her, Liz became self-conscious. Now what? she thought. She felt him move under her, like a man, and saw in his eyes, looking out from his makeshift bonnet, round as moons, the imbecilic hopefulness that went with it. "I called for an ambulance, Dad. They should be here any minute." She began to pull away.

Thomas looked at her. Who are you? he almost asked but didn't. Instead he raised his arms and pulled her back and held her to him, firmly, feeling her naked skin under his hands. "Thank you," he said, smiling like a schoolboy, "whoever you might be."

Naked Encounter

Ruth Harriet Jacobs

At age 83 I see
in the pool changing room
a painfully thin adolescent's back
completely covered with tattoos

I say to her "You are brave"
"Brave" she repeats
"It is an interesting word
My mother calls me stupid"

Hearing deep hurt in her
I reply "Your body is yours
to do with what you want"
but feel deeply for the mother

I wonder if she is anorexic
and whether the hopefully sterile
tattooing is better than self-cutting
and why life is so hard for our young

After the tattooed girl leaves
another old woman in the room
says "You were kind to her"
and both of us shed tears

The Daughter-in-Law

Cherise Wyneken

Ma pushed her round eyeglasses up on her nose and stared across her son's bed at Millicent, his wife. *Look at her. Mrs. Prim and Proper. She'll more'n likely worry him to death with her ever-lasting fussing. Why'd he have to go and marry her anyways? I knew it'd come to no good. Her being out of our faith and all. None of our people ever done that—married outside our religion. He should've known better—him being such a good churchman and all. Oh, I know he said it was his good friend from church what introduced them. But I know too—it was at one of them square dances down in San Ramon. Her with her fancy finger waves and fine clothes. And them peasant blouses what she wore to finagle him. He should've took one of them home girls back in Dakota—before we moved to here. Look what it got him. And him so good. Never missed a time to visit or to trim my toenails.* She *never come along.*

I can see it to this day. Him running in from play—soon as he smelled the fresh baked bread. He'd set there'n watch me take out the old bread-board and slice off a thick slab. Still so warm the butter melted into it and turned it yellow. Just like them dandylions blooming in the pasture. I can still see him wiggle his nose and say "Mmmmm," when I topped it all with chokecherry jam. Then he'd kick his heels against the kitchen stool and say, "I'm never going to leave you, Ma." It was a nice house there what Pa made us when we moved to town and I was proud as I could be the way I kept my hardwood floors. Just as good as hers. He always helped me shine the wax. Such a good boy.

Millicent looked across at Ma. "You look tired, Ma. Why

don't you take a break and go down to the coffee shop for some refreshments?"

There she goes—trying to get rid of me again.

"Ma, did you hear me?"

Just then a young candy striper came into the room with a pitcher of fresh water.

"Would you like a glass of cold water, dear?" Millicent asked her husband.

He gave a weak smile and nodded.

Look at her. So prim and proper. Blue suit—blue hat—blue purse—blue shoes. Not a thing don't match. Musta cost a pretty penny. Has to take off her gloves yet—just so's she can pour a little glass of water. He'll likely die of thirst—before the cancer gets him.

Millicent raised her husband's head from the pillow and offered him a sip. He took a couple of swallows, winked at her and said, "Thanks, honey." Then he gave a little cough, lay back down and closed his eyes.

"Would you like a little more, dear?" Millicent asked.

But there was no reply.

Ma looked around the room. *She should've kept him to home and nursed him herself. He'll never get well in this funeral parlor. Cold steel beds. Cold white walls. Cold white sheets. Even his face looks cold and white. Like when Pa used to butcher and the pig's blood was all drained out. Them were good days—grinding up the meat for sausage and squeezing in the sage. Oh how good it smelled. She'd never like to do that. Even though she was raised on a ranch. Ranch! California talk for farm. She—with all them brothers coddling and protecting her. She don't know what hard times is.*

"Walter. Walter," Millicent called, gently patting his shoulder. "Are you all right?"

Still no reply.

"Oh, Ma. I think he's gone."

"Gone? But he just took a drink of water. I seen him do it

myself."

Millicent headed toward the door. "I'd better call the nurse."

Ma stood up and stared at her son. *Who ever thought he'd go before me?* "Walter. Walter. Answer me."

The doctor arrived with his stethoscope and checked for any heartbeat.

"I'm sorry," he said. "He's passed away."

"No! No!" Ma screamed. "He's too young—I need him."

Millicent moved across the room and folded Ma into her arms.

Ma wept as she hugged her back. "Thank the good Lord—I got you."

Decision

Barbara Wade

Toes anchor at cliff's edge.
Berry black clouds loom above,
winter wind needles my neck and head.

My father's words tunnel through thick, moist air,
gather like gnats round my ears and eyes:
"Do something, do something, even if it's wrong."

Below, gray waves crash against jagged rocks.
I lick my lips, inhale, step off,
feel wings unfurl.

Living in the Past

John Lavelle

Carl, my neighbor, makes his way up the street clutching a plastic grocery bag in each hand, absorbed in this spring Sunday just past noon. Even though neither of us believes in a higher power, vague phantoms of our parents' generation haunt us. We're both old enough to have lingering remnants of beliefs in the sacredness of Sunday mornings, especially gorgeous sunny mornings after a hard winter. I know it's afternoon because I'm sitting in the cool shadows of the upstairs porch clutching a longneck beer watching him, and I never drink before noon. I say it's the difference between a drinker and a drunk. Call it a belief system. That's what Carl's always calling it, something to keep me getting out of bed every morning and dragging my ass into the shop and doing the same old thing day after day.

The season is spring. I know this because I'm in Buffalo. You don't sit outside without a coat unless it's really spring. And the cherry trees that crowd the sidewalks of this little dead-end street are in bloom like giant pink geraniums lined up on each side of the street between the sidewalk and curb. Lydia Slovecek, our landlady, planted a perennial garden in a little ellipse of earth right smack in the middle of the turnaround where everyone keeps running over it in winter. That doesn't stop her, though, from repairing it every spring.

Carl is walking slowly under the new-leaf-green trees. He's all smiles and hellos to the neighbors. Upstairs people in the row of apartment houses that line both sides of the street are setting out plastic window boxes on their porch rails full of new flowers. Thirty years ago the street was probably booming when Bethlehem Steel in Lackawanna was still fired up and putting out endless rows of sheet metal for all the stamping plants on River Road, lighting up the sky as if the sun could never quite set. But that was even before my time, and now the houses whisper of neglect, porches starting to tilt, old windows sloppy in their frames, time running out. One girl is scrubbing a small gas grill. She's new on the street and I haven't met her and probably won't. Last winter, after a heavy snow and no plows, a few of us men got together and shoveled the street out from turnaround to outlet and then we went back to our homes, but with a sense we could do it again if it needed it.

The miniscule front yards are greening and the pollen from the maple trees makes my eyes itch. I'm slouched in my lawn chair; my feet propped up on the rail. Today, I'm thinking about my life, the kid, the divorce. I kick little pieces of winter-loosened paint down onto the shrubs that are still waiting for their first trimming. The landlady has hinted that it'd be nice if I did the yard work, what there is of it, and I actually like doing it, but Carl gets pissed off when I don't ask her to pay me.

The street beyond is still silver-gray from the scour of the salt and sand heaped on the packed-snow ice by the city just a month or so ago. We get packed ice on the street because the city plows can't seem to find the street after one of the lake-effect snowstorms hits and all the neighbors have to run the snow down with their cars. We get two or three of the storms a year. The city comes along a week later and throws sand and salt all over it. It's also why older cars around Buffalo are rust buckets.

A younger man is washing a new car on the street. I don't remember if he was one of the snow-shoveling group. We were pretty well hidden under all the winter protection we wore. Despite the fact that it's barely seventy degrees out, he's got his shirt off. His chest is raw-chicken-skin white. His car is a bright red one with those disappearing headlights that won't survive one winter before

249

the ice jams one of them open or closed in a perpetual wink, burning out the motor or solenoid or whatever gets the lights up. He'll get it fixed a few times before he figures it's best just to leave them up. His open beer sits on the curb next to a bucket of sudsy water. He's dragged a hose out from somewhere around back. None of us have driveways or much of a lawn, front or back, so we live pretty close to the street.

I know I've got better things to do than sit here, but I drink my beer and watch cherry blossom petals fall to the almost-ready-to-mow grass because I'm pissed off at my kid again. He didn't pay his car insurance and it's lapsed, again, and the state has suspended his license—again. I know this because he got a letter that I opened. And the kid's still sleeping in the back bedroom after God knows what time he got home last night, and I'm trying to calmly decide how we're going to approach this, again.

Carl saunters by the man and peers down at his reflection in the polished fender. He makes a face behind the guy's back. I know he's thinking the guy suffers from some sort of bourgeois egotistical ownership mania spurred on by a lack of self-esteem due to a small penis. He says that a lot. I think the kid just likes cars and girls who like cars.

In one of Carl's bags is the square bulge of a quart of milk. There's the soft round bulge of a loaf of bread and what looks like a box of pasta. A stalk of celery peeks out through one of the hand holes. At the bottom of the other bag is the rectangular shape of a six-pack of beer.

Carl is shorter and stockier than I am, and younger, but with his full white beard and white hair, he looks at least five years older. He walks with the gait of a dockworker, not the way you'd think a drug and alcohol counselor would walk at all. He goes into the house next door, which doesn't have porches even though everything else about it and my place is the same, exact opposites of each other. All the houses on the street are the same, so any one of us could instantly find the bathroom in any other apartment in any one of the houses, if we needed to find a bathroom in a hurry.

Carl comes out a few minutes later with his own beer, a cheaper brand than mine. The cheap beer always strikes me as a little strange seeing how he drinks expensive scotch and good rum. "Hey," he says, staring up at me as I lean forward to peer at him through the porch rails, a big Cheshire-cat smile on his face. "What's up?"

"Nothing," I say, while tilting the bottle up toward my mouth. The way he's looking, I know he's got something cooking in that head of his. His smile is too wide and there's no I've-just-seen-some-thing-else-wrong-with-the-world look. Carl is a crusader. He's out to change the world for the better. I keep trying to tell him it doesn't want to be changed for anything.

Carl goes in through the side door, up the stairs, and walks through the apartment to come out on the porch. "I think your kid's up." Carl grabs the other lawn chair. He sort of wiggles into it like a nervous kid.

I don't say anything, but I get his drift. I'm just hoping the smell coming from the kid's room is from a cigarette. Carl tries to set his feet on the rail, but his legs are too short. I smirk at his attempts. I cross my legs slowly just to be mean.

We sit for a minute not saying anything. We're just taking in the day. I'm trying not to think of things that have happened or things going to happen, but I got this way where my brain is always run-ning in high gear and trying to figure out all the scenarios. I glance at Carl and he seems to be feeling the same way I am. We both know something's got to happen because, hell, it's spring in Buffalo, New York, and that only happens once a year.

I blow out a long breath. "Maybe we need to go for a ride." I nod toward my little Japanese sports car with the dual overhead cam engine and the five-speed that I bought new last fall before the snow had clogged the streets, a kind of present to myself.

Carl follows my gaze. "The Pink'd be good. I'm kind of in the mood for a steak sandwich."

I was actually thinking of doing what our parents did in spring-time, go for a ride in the country and, as my mother used to say, blow the stink off of us. And I know Carl's not thinking of The Pink, although they've got good steak sandwiches. We'll go for a couple of drinks and maybe the sandwich, but I can see he's itching to get to Clancy's. I think about it for a minute, pulling a pack of cigarillos out of my back pocket and lighting one up. There's something about getting a slow mellow buzz on a Sunday afternoon in a corner bar with the doors open and the fresh air seeping into the dark and quiet after all the cold and snow. I hold the tin out toward him. He waves it off. We both stare out at the new tenants of the upstairs apartment across the circle. Carl says, "I heard they're exotic dancers."

I study the girls for a minute. I don't see it. They're young, okay, but tiny. Neither one looks like she'd weigh more than a hundred pounds and both have the curves of twelve-year-olds. I light up my cigar dragging hard. It's not smoking worth a shit. It happens once in a while. And one of the girls is Asian. Who ever heard of an Asian stripper?

I scout the porch floor for a twig or a sliver of wood to poke up the end of the cigar. I can't find anything, so I lay it on the rail where I know it'll go out in a couple of seconds. If it's still there when I get home, I'll work on it. "I'll drive," I say, even though I know this will curtail my drinking, but I need the release, as Carl calls it.

Carl seems to think about it for a minute, still staring at the small Asian girl, who is sitting and stroking a mixed-breed cat. I'm wondering if he's thinking the same thing I am, that maybe we should go over and introduce ourselves. After all, if she is a stripper there could be a chance the age difference wouldn't matter and things could happen. But she's gazing down at the shirtless guy who is now waxing his car. So I think that Carl's wrong again and we're pretty much invisible to her, like we are to most young women.

I know Carl is weighing all the possibilities of taking my car. He likes when I drive and he can get blitzed, but he also knows I have a tendency to drive a bit aggressively when I'm pissed and he knows I'm pissed at the kid by the fact I got the beer in my hand early on a Sunday afternoon.

"What the hell," he says. He gulps his beer down and leaves the bottle standing high on the porch rail. I don't finish mine, but put it next to his, trapping the cigar between the two. Even cheap cigars don't come cheap.

Carl and I pile into the car and I head for downtown, catching upper Delaware so I can drive through the Park. Forest Lawn is on the left, the lake on the right as I weave in and out of light traffic while wondering if Olmstead ever figured his pretty little winding roads would be used to blow off steam. Carl's holding onto the oh-my-god strap above his head.

Now, there's a real nice thing about Buffalo on a Sunday afternoon in springtime—the streets are pretty much deserted. I figure people are salvaging what little is left of their lawns and such. I run the tach up to six thousand before I shift, then press down hard on the gas pedal so the little car jumps forward like a cat springing on a mouse. I get the green into Gates Circle, cross several lanes, shift down and punch the accelerator, shooting back out onto Delaware again.

Finally, when I weave in and out of three cars and jump a yellow, Carl says, "Whoa, he's really got you pissed off, big time."

I catch a red. I exhale in one long breath. "Naw, I'm just pissed that he had to grow up in such a fucked-up home."

Carl shakes his head. He knows how I feel about the boy growing up where the ex and I spent most of our time screaming at each other. Just like when I was a kid.

The light turns green and we slowly drive past pink-skinned people walking alone. They're wearing shorts and tank tops even though it still isn't that warm, but with such a short summer everybody has got to work on their tan as soon as possible.

The Pink is quiet and peacefully dark. It sits along Allen Street, crowded in with other buildings, none of which are more than four stories tall, some stone and brick, some wood painted in bright colors. It's as close to a bohemian lifestyle as a neighborhood is going to get in Buffalo—a lot closer than most cities. Small trees hold territory in square islands of dirt in the sea of concrete sidewalks. The smell of the thawing lake hangs in the air with the odor of the sun baking the dry rot out of the old buildings.

Carl and I sit where we can see Allentown, the name the artsy types have given their ten or so blocks. We watch the characters work the sunshine, sometimes looking up and blinking as if they forgot what the hell it was like. Some are walking by in heavy trench coats, staring down at their feet as if they haven't even figured out that winter's over, or maybe they don't pay attention to that anymore.

The ceiling is low. The walls and floor are dark, but not the nice patina of dark mahogany. They're just painted that way. The coolers are brushed stainless and the grill, down the other end, is hissing dark smoke from the steak for the sandwiches Carl and I ordered. The air smells of cooked onions.

A couple of grizzled-faced men smile and watch Patty the bartender work on the sandwiches. A young woman with brown shoulder-length hair walks down the bar from the dark interior. She watches me stare at her. I know she thinks I got the hots for her, but it's her short fluffy skirt that sticks out like something Shirley Temple would be wearing if she were still five years old. And it's the real long dark-blue socks or short stockings clinging to her skinny legs to mid-thigh, making her mottled skin look even paler. I know she's making some sort of statement like my kid, whatever that might be, but it's like she wasn't quite sure who she was when she got up.

Carl and I get our sandwiches and beer and play a game of pool with two fourteen balls, one pretending to be a three. The small room smells dusty. The pool table has a few stains of old spilt beer and the chalk is almost all used up. Carl's beating me, like most times, but like most times he drops the eight before it's time and I win.

He lays his cue stick along a rail and says, "What now?"

I say, "I don't know." And I don't know, but I'm thinking I should be doing something for, with, or to the kid. I can't seem to get into the mood of blowing off the day drinking and playing pool. "What do you want?" I'd just as soon play another game to give me some more time to think, but the strange girl is looking this way. I'm really not in the mood to feign stupidity while she weasels a couple drinks out of us. She's not even close to being either one of our types and I know we aren't hers. I suppose just coming out and asking us to buy her a drink would be too much?

Carl looks down at the table for a second, then says, "How about Clancy's?"

The kid's probably up rousting around in the cupboards looking for cereal or maybe he's just in the mood for a pop and a cigarette. More than likely he's got plans anyway and they don't include me. "What the hell," I say. "Life's been going like shit anyway." I lay my cue stick on the table.

Carl's a bit upset by my talk but he follows me out. He thinks I'm a bigot because I don't like going someplace I don't belong, but sometimes I get the feeling he's actually one in some way.

The drive to Clancy's on Main takes me about three minutes. I come up south of the building and park opposite it, facing north. Across the sidewalk from us is a tall chain-link fence guarding an empty lot. Actually the lot is the size of two football fields, mostly weeds surrounding remnants of what once was a building, large slabs of ragged concrete with rebar hanging off it like broken insect legs. There are a couple of low buildings around it and down further an empty warehouse striped with fire escapes. Someday a developer will stumble onto them and attempt to make trendy lofts or what-ever out of the space. I figure as long as the city is so bad at clearing snow-clogged streets and the busses quit running at nine at night, the neighborhood isn't in too much danger of losing its culture.

Clancy's is an old bar from the days when the area was still Irish, just a beer-bottle throw north of the theatre district, where all the well-to-do suburbanites come to reinforce their belief that they've got taste. If they're lucky, they never look a block or two away where most of the buildings are boarded up and empty. Those that are occupied have steel bars across their windows and doors that'd make Attica proud.

Clancy's shares the first floor of an old redbrick building with a laundromat. There's a large picture window with Irish-green letters painted on it. Several black men in baseball caps sit with their backs to the street.

I follow Carl in. The few men and women drinking at the bar this time of day shift in their seats. It's like there's no color at all in the bar until we show up and then there's all that history and this is one little place that's theirs where they can just be people. And we walk in. Except to my surprise an old white guy sits at the far end of the bar. He's wearing an old black cowboy hat. His white hair sticks out from under it and over the frayed collar of a long black coat. The bottom of the coat is stained with the white residue of a long winter. His face is the dull gray color of a man who spends most of his time hunched over a drink.

The walls are plain, almost unadorned, painted a bright green. Still, it's cool and quiet. Business seems light. Doris, the afternoon bartender, is there. She's a middle-aged woman with short hair and hips that have borne children. Carl and I belly up to the bar in front of her. She's got Carl's beer sitting in front of him before he's settled in on his stool, but she doesn't acknowledge him with a hello. She asks me what I'll have.

I say, "A draft." I stand quietly behind Carl surveying the area, making sure nobody wants to get two hundred years of slavery straightened out.

Black children dressed for church walk by the big window, the little girls with ribbons in their hair, the boys dressed in sweaters with tee shirts poking out of the neck openings. They're all smiles and taunts and swift dancing movements on the wide sidewalk.

Carl stares back at Doris with a shit-eating grin on his face and I know it's going to get to be a bad time. He orders a Bacardi on ice to drink with his beer. I look at mine, knowing that I'll be spacing them out and I'll be dragging Carl out of there in about seven hours when he gets shit-faced and cut off.

"Chantal been in lately?" Carl asks when Doris comes back with the fifth of rum.

I hadn't heard that name before. I glance first at Carl, then at Doris, and then back to Carl, trying to size up this new situation, knowing I don't need any more trouble than I've already got and this looks like more. That's Carl for you. He'll give you details on everybody's life except his own, but pieces are starting to come together as if a film was running backwards in my head, remembering things he'd said and his comings and goings, which didn't mean anything at the time.

Doris doesn't speak while pouring his drink. She glances up at him with her big dark eyes in what looks like a reproach. Doris sets the bottle on the back bar. "She's one pissed-off bitch," she says to Carl when she turns back to him. Doris walks away, not looking too happy. Carl takes a drink of his rum, then a swig of beer.

I get the missing piece that's going to connect everything else. Carl's been playing with fire here and it'd be real easy for both of us to get burned. I want to jump all over him like I want to jump all over my kid, but I scratch the back of my head and say to him, "So that's what you've been up to."

Carl opens his mouth to say something but nothing comes out. Something's on his mind. I can almost see the words percolating behind his eyes, so I go back to my drink waiting for him to come clean. Our reflections stare back at us from the long mirror behind the bar. Mine looks like a man who's got kid problems.

Carl is staring back, too. He looks as though he knows he's adding to my troubles and that somehow he's compromised his position as the world's savior. He nudges me and points down the bar at a lone figure hunched over a draft gone warm and flat.

Carl says, "That guy was at Los Alamos."

"What?" I ask. "What the hell was he doing there, besides falling down drunk, I mean?" I take a drink of my beer, but I've already lost the taste for the stuff today.

Carl grabs his drinks from the bar and stands. He does this in a short, quick movement. He has a habit of doing things like this in bars, so I'm not surprised. "He's a physicist. He worked on the A-bomb," he says.

"Was a physicist, you mean." I pick up my beer out of habit, knowing we're going to be trying to converse with the old drunk, which I think isn't a bad idea as a way to take my mind off things.

We slide onto stools on each side of the old man. He doesn't flinch, but then Carl looks like a red-faced Santa and I'm just some guy not aging well and fearing I'm getting shorter every day.

Carl says, "I told my friend here you helped build the atom bomb." I know Carl's insinuating the man's a drunk out of guilt for helping usher in the atomic age. What I don't know is whether Carl knows the old man knows Carl thinks he's a drunk from guilt.

But Carl's a real left liberal, maybe as a way of defining himself. He says most people are always trying to redefine themselves. Rewriting their identity is what he actually says. I figure Carl is carrying around guilt for being upper middle-class and white in the sixties and he thinks everyone's doing the same thing.

The old man's voice is whiskey-rough when he finally speaks. "We live in the past," he says to neither of us, probably having learned to avoid eye contact with would-be troublemakers a long time ago. Except Carl and I couldn't make trouble if we had a manual.

I can't believe he spoke at all, and now I'm thinking maybe Carl's right. I brace my head against my hand and slide my elbow along the bar trying to get a better look at the old man's face.

Carl says, "Yeah, we all carry around baggage." Carl's bouncing around on the stool nervously, a bit too enthusiastically. He's trying to get me to forget that he's gotten himself into some kind of a fix.

The old man smirks, and then mutters the words again. "We exist in the past."

I lean over and stare at the side of the man's leathered face. "You speaking scientifically?"

The old man nods. I know he's a drunk and anything he says is probably going to be pure bullshit, but I like translating for Carl. Deep down inside I get the feeling Carl's always talking down to me, so playing a little game with him and the drunk might be a way to even the score. Make Carl feel even more left out. I sip at my beer trying to figure out what my next move ought to be. I could use a little entertainment, but between my kid and what Carl will be doing in the next few hours, I figure I'll get more than my share.

The two men by the window are laughing about something. Doris is a few feet away doing her job but staying in the conversation. The conversation is just quiet enough not to be heard and I wonder if Carl and I weren't there, if the laughing would be louder and what might get said.

Carl motions to Doris when she glances his way. She strolls halfway over to him before she remembers she's pissed off. Doris stares at both of us like she could crack a bottle of beer over our heads.

I'm not so sure anyone would care if she did it either, and I could get a little pissed off myself for Carl having put me in this situation just so he could look up some one-night stand. I roll my eyes and Doris smiles. I'm thinking about the kid doing the same thing, dragging me into shit I don't want to get involved in and I'm getting disgusted with people in general and I decide I really need to bust somebody's chops, Carl's or the old drunk's. It doesn't matter now. I point down at the top of the black hat and say to Doris, "Bring this man a beer."

The old man mumbles, "Whiskey."

I nod to Doris. I say, "Okay, you got it, fella." When the shot arrives, I say, "Tell me this scientific theory of yours."

Carl walks off down the bar with Doris, who's scowling at him. He asks, "She doesn't come in anymore?"

Doris says, "Knows your sorry ass might show up."

Carl sits four stools down from the two black gentlemen who seem not to notice him at all, but become quieter. Doris leans in closer to Carl. The muscles in her face are tight as she talks under her breath at him. Carl's face is reddening under the white beard and he's shaking his head.

The old man sips the whiskey. "It's the big bang," he says, coughing the words out.

"I know all about that," I say. "I watch educational TV. Trying to get my kid interested in learning something."

"Maybe a leak," he says.

"A leak?" I ask, and then laugh. "We sprung a leak?" I really don't know that much about science. I'm just a tool and die maker, like my father, but he had a union job. Been that way since I was my kid's age, but I know a crackpot idea when I hear one.

Down the bar Doris is talking to Carl through clenched teeth. She's stabbing the bar with her finger. I twist up to get a look at Carl and Doris, hoping I can read their lips, although now they're starting to get loud. I see the irony of this. The ex and I were always trying to break into his upper-crust world and Carl's spent most of his life trying to break into this one. It's like the space between is where all the shouting gets done.

The old man's gazing down into the whiskey. "A string of energy forced into a nondimensional universe."

The vision of what he said brings my attention back to him. "A universe with no dimensions?" I start to laugh, but I'm trying to imagine it and realize it's pretty weird or complex. I think of lighting up a cigarillo. I even rub the back pocket of my jeans where the tin case is stuffed, but I know how they smell and how impolite that would be. One time no one cared anything about a man lighting up a stogie in a bar.

"Energy crushed into matter." He picks up the shot and sips it like it was Chivas Regal. "The explosion creates a shockwave. That's the universe," he says between sips. The old man runs his tongue around his dry pink lips. For just a second he glances at his reflection in the mirror. "Before the edge of the wave is nothing."

"You mean empty space?" I'm really tired of my beer, so I slide it away from me.

He shakes his head like I'm some know-nothing. "No space, no time, no existence."

It hits me kind of like a shockwave itself, the concept of nothing. "So?"

"Space is time," he says. "Or time is space." The old man makes a small circular gesture with his right hand, the most I've seen him move other than to pick up the shot glass. "There's no future."

"For some of us." I think about my kid, who is probably still in bed while Carl's half in the bag already, getting his ass chewed good.

One of the two men at the window seats calls for another round. The anger on Doris's face softens to a large grin. Carl watches her intently like a small child as she pours the men their drinks. Doris is avoiding his gaze. Finally Carl gestures plaintively with his hands. He says something to her.

"I know you little fuckers," Doris says, loud enough for the bar to hear. She glances quickly around the room.

I turn my attention to the old man, but before I do, I see the two black men stare down at their drinks. The one on the left pulls his baseball cap down lower over his eyes.

"No, no," the old man mumbles.

"What?" I say loudly. Carl and Doris stop their conversation and stare at me for a second. Carl's eyes are red and wet. I know it's not Chantal he's crying over. The eyes are from being outside looking in. I've been there before with the ex, with being on welfare as a kid, being the poorest family in town. With the kid, not being able to get inside his head and make him understand he needs to get his shit together before it's too late.

The old man's glass is empty. I point down at his head again and Doris brings over the bottle. "Okay," I say once she pours the drink. I don't know if he knows what he's talking about or his brain is just pickled, but what he's saying doesn't jive with what I learned in school.

Doris smiles when she takes my money, but I see the exasperated look on her face as if she doesn't understand why I bring Carl here or why I don't drag him out right now and make her life a whole lot easier. She glances at me quickly and for a moment our stares meet and I see disappointment in her eyes. I think she had as much hope for Chantal and Carl as Chantal did. Not so much for the love, but for the possibilities.

The old man slowly sits up and glances around the bar as if surprised to find himself there. He pats his shirt pocket looking for a pack of cigarettes. They're on the bar. I slide them over to him and pull my lighter out of my pocket, a Christmas present from the kid, and hold the flame in front of him.

The old man is sitting up straight on the stool. He takes a couple of hard drags, then cracks a smile. "The edge of the wave is the present," he says. He thinks he's figured it all out.

I think about it for a moment. "Where are we now?" I ask.

He holds the cigarette and glass in the same hand, waving them in small circles as he speaks. He reminds me of a professor. "The wave is time rushing out, pushing against the nothingness. It's compressed. We—" he says, holding his other palm up. I know he means everyone in the universe "—are far enough behind it where time is fairly stable. In the past."

Carl's gazing into his drink. His thoughts are someplace at the bottom of it. Doris is speaking to a black couple who have just come in from the laundromat.

"So there's a future. That makes you wrong," I say. I can feel my hand quiver, little quick vibrations. "Someplace between us and that edge you think is out there." I stare at my glass of beer, remembering I don't want it.

"Just less past." He starts to slouch again.

I want to press my hand on his back to straighten him up, and I want some answers. "Sort of like you can never get ahead, just caught up?" I ask.

The old man doesn't answer. He stares down at his drink. He seems to be gone back to the place he was before Carl and I disturbed him. He isn't what I thought he was. Maybe a lot of us, like Carl and me got it all wrong and have been giving out all the wrong information? Maybe the guy's just an old drunk with a line of bull that gets him drinks?

I think about what he said, how time—or space—how it's moving so fast and everybody is trying to catch up and nobody can because nobody can travel that quickly. I look out beyond Carl, beyond Doris and the black couple, out to where my car is waiting in the sunshine, thinking how I always needed to drive fast to catch something, something I'm never going to be able to catch. I want to tell the kid how I'm really not pissed at him for sleeping late, how I really don't want him to have to end up like me or Carl, living just to catch up and never quite doing it. I reach into my pocket and finger the car keys on the old key ring my kid made me for Father's Day when he was in the fourth grade. But then I never knew how to tell him I love him so much.

O World Unknowable

Bruce Barton

Sometimes John worried that maybe he had done something to cause Buddy's . . . predisposition. Or lifestyle. Or whatever the hell the right term was. Of course, the closest he'd ever come to admitting this even to Beth was during one of her recitations on genderification or the spectrum of sexuality or some such that she'd read about. She was making herself into an expert on the topic and over dinner often felt the need to share any new knowledge with John, who generally just grunted and kept eating. But something she'd said caught at him that evening, and he'd asked, "So it's probably not really the parents' fault then?"

"Fault? Fault?" she had blazed. "See, that's the kind of attitude that contributes to hate crimes."

"Okay, sorry, sorry," he had said. Lately Beth could get huffy over anything.

Like when she told him that Buddy was bringing a friend home on this year's summer visit. John had said, "A friend or a *friend?*"— which had seemed a reasonable enough question.

But Beth right off got snappish: "The man he's been living with the past five years. Don't worry, they'll be staying at the Comfort Inn."

The bedroom in the northwest corner of the house had been Buddy's. Beth had long since laid claim to the dresser drawers and closet for her wardrobe overflow, and had cluttered the walls with oversized prints of those blurry French paintings, but the single bed was Buddy's, and on the wall above the headboard was the shelf Buddy had built, still crowded with the trophies, plaques, medals, and ribbons he had won in high school sports. If he hadn't been so smart, Buddy could have gotten a scholarship in track, swimming, or football. He might even have made it in the pros as cornerback. When he visited, the room was his again. Each year before his arrival, John had to remind Beth to clear a drawer and some closet space for him.

"Five years?" John had said. "How come he didn't tell us before?"

"He told me," Beth had shot back. "His friend isn't well. His heart. So you behave."

"Since when do I say anything?"

For the past fifteen years Buddy had come home eight to ten days each June. He might miss Christmas, but they could count on him in June. Ten years ago he had sat John and Beth down in the living room and explained about his "sexuality." He loved them too much, he'd said, to hide any part of his life from them any longer. And they needn't worry: He was responsible, didn't do gay bars or the leather scene. He'd hoped they would understand.

"Oh, honey, of course we understand," Beth had said, sounding suspiciously unsurprised. "We'll always love you and always want to know everything about your life."

"Well, sure," John had managed after Beth's sudden elbow. He'd been trying to imagine what a "leather scene" might be. During the uncomfortable hugfest that followed, he didn't mention that there were actually plenty of things he could live without knowing.

To John's relief, after the revelation Buddy didn't start wearing jewelry, or dressing and talking funny in front of them. In fact, his and Buddy's relationship didn't much change. During Buddy's phone calls, John would put in his five minutes, commenting on the weather here and in Buddy's region—John was a weather channel devotee—and maybe talking sports a bit, and then turn the receiver back over to Beth. On Buddy's June visits, Beth and Buddy would do their things on the weekends: shopping, the art museum, fancy coffee at Barnes & Noble, and lunches at those Oriental-type restaurants whose food was too slimy for John to stomach. On weekdays, if it wasn't raining too hard, he and Buddy would drive to the golf course John managed. He wasn't sure how he'd ended up as manager, intending that first summer after retirement to just drive the big fairway mowers a few days a week for something to do between fishing trips. He'd never even liked golfing all that much. But after the elderly previous manager dropped dead of a stroke, John had been talked into taking the job, temporarily at first, until they could find someone qualified who was willing to work for minimum wage, then not so temporarily, and now no one could imagine anyone but him in charge. He was actually pretty good at it, had even read up on course management and taken a correspondence course one winter to get officially certified in chemicals and environmental stewardship.

When they'd get to the course, he'd send Buddy off alone on a cart for nine holes while he took care of whatever crisis had occurred because he hadn't been there. Then he'd join Buddy for the second nine, taking over the driving so that he could point out the changes he'd masterminded: the blue bird houses he'd put in as 150-yard markers, the refurbished drainage ditches on three and five fairways, the new bridge over the creek between seven green and eight tee that he'd designed and mostly built himself.

Maybe it wasn't some hoity-toity country club—nine holes twenty miles outside town, whose players wore sneakers and jeans, and spent as much time in the woods searching for their balls as on the fairways playing them—but it was pretty and natural, its short, slender fairways bending through sixty acres of woods. No car horns out here. Just bird calls and wind. And you might see a doe leading her pair of fawns to the creek, or a hawk making off with a rabbit. One entire afternoon a young bull moose had commandeered nine fairway and all but demolished the cart John had used to try to chase it away.

Beth liked bragging about how Buddy was a professor at that university he was at out East, but what John liked was that Buddy wasn't at all like most of those professor-types. He didn't put on airs. By the second or third day home, some of his home region's up and down lilt and drawn-out vowels would return to his speech, and he'd refind the working-class phrasing he'd grown up with, start kidding with Pete C and Pete K, the retired farmers who worked the grounds and treated Buddy like a visiting hero, bragging all year to the hacking regulars about how Buddy could drive the green on the two-hundred-ninety-yard ninth—and they'd seen it. Buddy flirted with fat old Dorthea Klatt, who ran the till and worked the computer for John. She dressed in her best frumpy summer dresses when Buddy was around and giggled like a schoolgirl at his attention. Everyone liked Buddy. Always had. John saw no point in letting anyone know about his predisposition.

In the evenings, after dinner out at Red Lobster or barbecuing burgers or steaks while downing a few beers, John and Buddy would plant themselves in front of the Twins game, John in his recliner, Buddy on the couch, John's commentary eventually expanding from the new kid who'd been called up to replace their All-Star shortstop the Yankees had stolen to the woes of major league ball in general since the inception of the designated hitter.

By the third or fourth inning, Buddy would make them a Manhattan, the drinking restrictions John had pledged to Beth after his second DUI—no bars and no drinking of any kind past six—blissfully lifted during Buddy's visits, at least when it came to the exotic cocktail Buddy had introduced him to. After all, what was the harm in a father and son having a drink together, especially one that included a cherry?

Then Buddy would return to his other life, and John and Beth to theirs, and for a week or so John would be a little crabby. "Oh," Beth would say, "You're just missing your Buddy."

Buddy's friend—Arthur, not Art—turned out to be at least John and Beth's age. Short and delicately built, with silky silver hair moussed into place and talking like one of those guys who narrated historical documentaries for PBS, Arthur needed a whole five minutes to charm Beth into gaga land. He'd lived in London and Paris, had traveled all over the world, told stories whose characters' English, French, or God knows what all accents he could mimic ever so cutely.

"Bu—John sent me your book," Beth said. All evening she'd been trying to call Buddy by his given name.

"Which one?" Arthur asked.

At Beth's perplexed expression, Buddy said, "The Tennyson, Victorian gloom, yadda yadda."

"Why would you do that to your mother?" Arthur said.

"She asked," Buddy said. "Cheaper than tranquilizers, I figured."

Arthur smiled and shook his head, telling Beth, "These rough-hewn Americanists give us no respect"—as if Beth were part of his "us" crowd.

"Isn't he funny? So . . . urbane," Beth gushed to John in the kitchen. They had evidently finished with the skinny crackers and slab of duck liver—which basically had tasted like braunschweiger to John, though he bet it was twice as expensive—and now he was helping her, as instructed, carry out bowls of cold greenish soup. She had almost popped an eyeball when he suggested he might microwave his a bit.

"It's supposed to be chilled," she hissy-whispered.

"Guess I'm not urbane enough," John muttered.

That afternoon Beth had transformed their kitchen into a "Twilight Zone" cooking show. She had spent most of her time on a sticky rice concoction with clams, chunks of squishy-looking meat, and vegetables they never ate—well, except for the tomatoes and peas; its top was spoked by what looked to John like giant insect larvae, but turned out to be prawns. All and all, it looked pretty scary.

"*Paella mixta*," Beth called it.

"Taken from the wide, shallow frying pan the Spanish originally used in its preparation," Arthur tossed in. "Actually, it's sometimes called *arroz a la paella*. Beth, it is simply wonderful."

Beth beamed. "That's real angler fish, but I'm afraid I could only get it frozen."

"And calamari," Arthur noted approvingly. "It tastes like you made the broth from scratch."

Beth nodded, just tickled pink. "I even used the spine of the angler and the shells and heads of the prawns."

None of this was doing much for John's appetite. "What's calamari?" he asked.

"That would be squid, Dad," Buddy said, giving John a bemused smile.

"Simply wonderful," Arthur reiterated.

He and Beth fell into a discussion about women mystery writers; Beth was part of a book group who called themselves the Women of Mystery—just a bunch of housewives as far as John could tell. Arthur preferred "cozies"—big surprise—but Beth didn't mind a bit more edge. They agreed that anything by P. D. James was simply wonderful, and Arthur was determined Beth get to know Sayers's Lord Peter.

Meanwhile, John was trying to figure out how to crack open the clam shells the rest of the way with a knife and fork, as Arthur had done, and when he finally succeeded, with a bit of covert aid from his fingers, the glob of snot inside hardly seemed worth the effort. He avoided the squid as best he could.

Over coffee and dessert, a soufflé thing with a sweet amber sauce that could have used a dollop of Cool Whip, though John was wise enough to forgo such an observation, Arthur said, "Okay, I can hold back no longer. John refuses to gratify my curiosity about his nickname. 'Junior' I could understand, but from where did 'Buddy' arise?"

Beth beamed yet again. She loved telling this story.

"John, big John," Beth began, "was getting ready one Saturday to visit a friend in the hospital. Little John was tagging after him. Couldn't have been more than four."

"'Where you going, Daddy?' he said. He went through a stage when he was anxious whenever John was gone.

"'Going to visit my best fishing buddy. He had an operation,' John told him.

"You should have seen that little face try to hold in the heart-break, until finally he burst out with, 'Ain't I your best fishing buddy, Daddy?'"

"Oh, how dear," Arthur said, smiling, his eyes actually getting a little misty, for God's sake, and his hand snaking over to curl around Buddy's forearm.

Buddy rolled his eyes, then said, "Actually, Dad's quite a fisher-man. He and his partner won a walleye tournament last year. You each won, what, a thousand bucks?"

"Thousand fifty," John said.

"Arthur was a junior state champ in tennis," Buddy said.

Arthur finally removed his hand from Buddy in order to dismiss his remark with a flutter of fingers.

"I can see Buddy inherited his build from you," Arthur said to John. "You must have been quite an athlete in your day as well."

"Never had time," John grunted. "Started working in the mill after school and weekends by the time I was fifteen. Put in forty-five years." He felt uncomfortable with the thought of Arthur imagining his body in any of its shapes.

John helped Beth clear the table and offered to rinse and load the dishes into the washer so she could join Buddy and Arthur on the back patio.

Beth stared at him.

"What?" he said.

"Nothing," she said. "Just thought I sensed hell getting a little chilly."

"You being urbane now?" he said.

He could hear them through the screen door as he worked, mostly Beth and Arthur, the new best chums for life. For some reason Beth arrived at an explanation about why Buddy was an only child. There were the miscarriages, her pelvic inflammatory disease, the adhesions so bad they positively gummed her fallopian tubes together in places—Jesus Christ, Beth, John thought—"and John probably had a low sperm count, though of course he wouldn't have it checked out"—JESUS CHRIST!

Buddy surprised them in their thirties, a miracle baby, really. Beth had had to spend the last two months of her pregnancy in bed, her mother moving in to care for her. John remembered how fun that had been.

When John finished, it was 8:30. He poked his head out the door. "Almost time for the Twins. Late game with Seattle."

"Actually, Dad," Buddy said sheepishly, "we need to get back to the room. Arthur has his medication to take and really should get to bed at a decent hour."

"For heaven's sake," Arthur protested. "We can stay for your baseball game."

"No, we can't," Buddy said. "I know what the doctor said as well as you do." And that was that.

When they were gone, John surreptitiously poured the watery remains from the Manhattan pitcher into a glass, added some bourbon, and carried the drink into Buddy's room. Since his retirement, he often watched TV in there at night, sprawled on top of the covers, lights off, doors closed, sometimes falling asleep and spending the whole night there, Beth more than happy, he was sure, to have a few walls between her and his snoring.

They had reached a kind of truce in their marriage, the boundaries and junctions well in place, a companionable enough distance solidified between them. John had learned the value of keeping his mouth shut. But this Arthur situation bothered him. Beneath that expensive haircut and clothes and no-doubt fake tan, something was wrong with him, something bad. His heart? Maybe. But John had read the newspaper articles, had seen parts of that Tom Hanks movie on HBO—an epidemic, they called it, your own body turning against you, wasting away.

When he wanted, John could still see Buddy on that center block beside the pool, the highest one, for the winner, second and third on either side. The other boys might shiver and hunch, but never Buddy. Back straight, shoulders solid in the hazy, sparkling air, he'd bow to receive the medal around his neck, then straighten again, and give the world that grin of his. Maybe John hadn't been able to make it to many of the swim meets, but he'd made it to some, and that image of Buddy was still fresh to him. If something happened to Buddy, John would do something, no matter what Beth said. He'd take matters into his own hands, and there'd be nothing urbane about it.

Arthur came along golfing, though he didn't want to play.

"I'd only be a nuisance," he said. "I'm just coming for the walk. And I want to see this golf course I've heard so much about."

"I can get another cart. For you and Buddy, if you want," John said. "No problem."

"No, I need the exercise," Arthur insisted. "You two ride together."

"It'll be fine, Dad," Buddy said, though John could see he was concerned.

No one at the course really knew what to make of Arthur. In his creased white shorts, Panama hat, and silky shirt decorated in exotic-looking yellow and pink flowers, he might as well have been a Martian. Dorthea out-and-out gaped at him. Pete C asked, "So, what part of England you from?"

By the seventh hole, John had had just about enough Arthur for one day. It was bad enough that he was traipsing along after them in his getup, but he also seemed to think that John was to be his personal golf tutor: What must one do when the ball flew off into the woods? How did one curve the ball so drastically to the right in midair? Why was it called a sand *trap*?

Of course, he was also a gardening expert. Yes, thank you, John knew the rhododendrons would do well in shade when he planted them. And that aubretia bordered nicely in sunny spots—okay, so he had no idea what aubretia were—but he'd decided to go with marigolds to have something for the fall. Nobody planted flowers on this course without his explicit permission, though a few ladies on the board had tried.

"That's something you two have in common, Dad," Buddy said. "You should see Arthur's rose garden at home."

Arthur did his finger flutter dismissal. "Not anything like this," he said and swept his hand across the course.

John had a surprise waiting for Buddy at the eighth tee, which sat on a shelf of earth extending over the creek. They rounded a stand of birch, and there it was.

"Wow," Buddy said.

The back half of the tee box was rimmed with three-foot-high shrubs filled with large, golden buttercups.

"Sunshine shrubs," John said. "I planted them three springs ago. Eighteen separate plantings."

"I'd just thought they were a dwarf hedge of some sort," Buddy said.

John nodded. "They've been blooming late, in mid-July, and pretty scraggly. The board wanted me to put in peonies, but I told them, 'Just wait and see,' and now this." He spread his hands before him.

The yellow blossoms shimmered against the blue background of sky, the creek gurgling below, bees buzzing in a kind of halo. This is how he'd wanted Buddy to see it. He'd worried that the weather would be bad.

Arthur said, "Simply stunning," and then suddenly intoned, "O world intangible, we touch thee, O world unknowable, we know thee."

Buddy tore his consideration from the blossoms. "What's that from?"

"I guess these young men don't know everything quite yet," Arthur said to John. He seated himself on the back fender of the cart, which was flattened and rubber-coated. "Should I try you with something easier: 'but every hour is saved from that eternal silence, something more, a bringer of new—'"

"Cute," Buddy said, grinning.

Urbane, John thought. "Anyway," he said, "Let's tee off. Your honors, Buddy."

Buddy's drive was straight and long, the rustiness worked out of his swing by now. John topped the ball and it ping-ponged to the ladies' tee. John waited for another of Arthur's annoying questions, but none came.

"I know what I'm doing," John said. "I'm looking up. I just have to play more."

Arthur remained perched on his fender seat. "Do you mind if I hitch a ride on this hole?" he said.

Buddy walked to him. "You okay?"

"Just a little winded. Really."

"You sit in my seat. I'll walk," Buddy said.

"No, don't be silly."

"You can't ride there," Buddy said. "That's only for when the cart's at rest. It's against the rules."

"It's okay," John said, slipping behind the wheel. "Nobody will say anything to me."

Buddy took his passenger seat, glancing dubiously back and telling Arthur, "Raise your feet and hold on." To John he said, "Take it easy, Dad."

John nodded and didn't quite punch the accelerator pedal all the way to the floor, leaning out to the left as he drove, inspecting the grass.

"This is ridiculous," he said. "A fairway should be no more than an inch and a half this time of year. I'm going to have to have a word with those Petes."

The cart suddenly hit a bump that sent it airborne for a moment. "I meant to do that," John said, but his and Buddy's laugh was curtailed by an "Oh!" from behind them.

John stomped the brake pedal, and they both turned to find Arthur sitting on the grass behind them, shaking his head. John slammed the cart into reverse, and, with the "be-be-be" warning sounding, barreled an efficient path back to Arthur. And just as efficiently ran over his right leg with a back wheel. An accident. An honest-to-God accident. It could have happened to anyone.

"Oh!" Arthur said again.

"Jesus Christ, Dad!" Buddy bellowed, leaping from the cart.

John switched the gear to forward, silencing the "be-be," then locked the brakes and leaped from the cart as well, suggesting, "Don't move him."

But Buddy had already slid Arthur away from the cart and, with one arm behind his back and the other sliding beneath his knees, was about to lift him.

"I don't think you should move him," John tried again.

Arthur was trying to push Buddy away. "John, no," he scolded. "For heaven's sake, I'm fine. I really think I'm fine."

Buddy desisted begrudgingly. Arthur's leg displayed a brush-stroke of whitened skin below the knee. Nothing more. Buddy insisted on examining the leg, his large hands squeezing along the shinbone gingerly.

"Does this hurt at all?" he said.

"No," Arthur said. "You do know that you're not this sort of doctor?"

"Not funny," Buddy said, and began his squeezing exam anew.

John felt clueless about what he should be doing, so he merely watched Buddy's ministrations and couldn't help but notice how much his son's hairline had receded. And the twin furrows between his brows did not completely disappear when his expression eased as he lifted his face to Arthur. John tried to remember the last time he had studied his son so closely.

"I don't think it's broken," Buddy said.

"Of course not," Arthur said, and began to rise to his feet, slapping away Buddy's attempted aid. He took a few experimental steps, then a few more, and then broke into a kind of jig, a goofy smile on his face.

"Are you crazy?" Buddy said, stepping forward.

"Don't be such a ninny," Arthur replied. "I believe my leg was in a hollow of sorts and the cart just cushioned it into the grass. I'm not made of glass, you know."

Buddy looked unconvinced. "I'll walk. You sit in the passenger seat now." He cut off Arthur's protest and to John said, "Take it easy, Dad."

They played the remainder of the hole in relative silence, John topping and skidding his ball to the green, finally getting down in ten, Buddy with a tight smile, Arthur trying out a few questions, then giving in. John had a knot in his throat. Maybe he could tell Beth what had happened and she could explain to Buddy how it was an accident, how he'd been overanxious to help or something. Beth knew how to talk to Buddy about such things.

At the ninth tee Buddy said, "Nobody behind us. I believe I can't wait until we get to the club house to see a man about a horse." John knew the horse thing was for him, not something Buddy would say anymore in his real life, a kind of offering, and he felt a bit better, though all he could say was "Ya, okay."

John and Arthur sat together on the cart, watching Buddy disappear, and then waiting in slow silence, John feeling every second inch by. Finally he said, eyes still on the woods, "Listen, we can stop at the hospital on the way home. I know a guy in X-ray at the clinic. Don't worry about the cost."

"John, I'm quite all right. Truly."

More seconds. Minutes. John said, "Well, I don't know if a bear got him or what."

"Don't those woods slope down to where the creek spills into a side pool?" Arthur said.

"Don't think so," John said, though he didn't really know. That part of the creek was past the course, so the area had never much concerned him.

"A pair of beavers dam it each year," Arthur continued, "or repair their old dam. There's a miniature meadow of sorts there in a largish opening of trees where John likes to spend some time each summer 'checking in on the beavers,' as he puts it. Probably he's making a quick hike there."

John was looking at Arthur now. How did he know this?

"John told me," Arthur said to John's unspoken question.

"Don't know why he's taking a break when we still have a hole to play," John said.

Seconds. Minutes. Arthur broke the silence this time: "Probably he's trying to collect his self-decorum. He's frustrated with himself for becoming irritated with you and overprotective with me. You know how John is, always trying to keep everyone happy. He's a fine man, though maybe a bit neurotic. But then aren't we all? He loves you, you know."

John flicked his attention back to the tree line, not certain if he felt irritated or embarrassed. What was the matter with this guy? "I'm the one who did the fool thing," he croaked. "Listen, you want me to go get him?"

"Let's not intrude," Arthur said. "Besides, I've been wanting to ask you if you had ever fished Maple Leaf Lake."

"What?" John said.

"Maple Leaf Lake. Have you ever fished there?"

"Around here?"

"In Canada. North of Lake of the Woods."

"Never fish much up there," John said.

"I caught a twenty-three-pound, ten-ounce muskellunge there."

"You caught a twenty-three-pound muskie?" John said, barely attempting to hide his skepticism.

"And ten-ounce," Arthur said.

"That's something," John said, still skeptical, but grateful for the familiarity of this sort of conversation.

"Yes." Arthur smiled. "I was only six or seven years old—I know, that makes the event seem even less likely. It was in that odd purgatorial time during the war. You remember how it was. One summer my father, who had always had a fragile heart—a genetic predisposition—and certainly had never been accused of being outdoorsy, announced that he and I were going on a fishing expedition. I have no idea where he came up with the plan. He certainly knew little more about fishing than I did. A born and bred, upper-crust Boston boy. Always in a coat and tie. Very proper and aloof—shy, actually, I later realized. Perhaps he sensed that he would be dead in a few years and wanted to take his son on an outlandish adventure."

John thought this fish story was taking its sweet time getting to the fish, but he found himself paying attention, stealing glances at Arthur's face.

"We spent a small fortune on gear and clothing, flew to Minneapolis, drove a rental to the border, and then hopped a single-prop to the lake. I don't know its condition now, but then it was isolated, one single-room cabin on the entire lake. A Franklin stove. No electricity or indoor plumbing. Father and I were quite helpless and our pilot-guide simply babysat us. Cooked, kept us dry and warm, doctored the hives Father had contracted either from his unlaundered flannel shirt or some local flora, managed to keep us from shredding each other's eyes with our errant hooks. His name was Freddy Duval. For two days we caught nothing, which should have been no big surprise. I don't know who was more anguished at our lack of success, Freddy or Father. 'De goddam fish, day ain't 'ungry. Sons-a-bitches,' Freddy would say. Father suffered in silence, half his body encased in calamine lotion. The world at war. Millions of people slaughtering one another, entire cities burning, the Bomb being built in the Southwestern desert, and there we were, fishing. My God, the nights were so big and lonely. I have never since seen so many stars."

John for some reason was remembering another night, a certain Saturday night before Easter a long time ago. It was a recurrent recollection, coming back to him after decades and then persisting. He had put in a full day of overtime and stopped by Duffy's for a beer with some of the guys, as he sometimes did, and lost track of time, as he also sometimes did. It was just so nice to loosen up—a whole day off ahead of you, feeling unencumbered, articulate, even rather witty—not qualities that would generally characterize him, he knew. On occasion, a few women had even found him charming, or so they had said.

Since Buddy's birth, Beth had abandoned her practice of waiting up to provide him a scolding on these nights. But this Saturday—Sunday, actually—she was sitting at the kitchen table when he stumbled in, a basket of brightly dyed eggs before her.

"It's almost two in the morning," she said.

"Happy Easter," he said, a fuzzy contentment still surrounding him.

"Aren't you cute," she said.

"I stopped for a few beers, big deal. I'm off tomorrow."

"How nice for you," Beth said. "Did it just slip your mind that we were supposed to color Easter eggs tonight? Buddy and me finally colored them ourselves at ten, though he wanted to wait longer for you. I had to tell him you'd probably have to work all night. That you'd be here in the morning when he got up."

"Oh, geez, sorry," John said. "I'll be up early to help hide his chocolates."

"No, you won't," Beth shot back. "You'll sleep in. And when you do get up, we'll all tiptoe around like nothing has happened."

The house was whirling around him a bit, closing in. "I said I'd get up, so I'll get up, okay? Stop being such a nag." Beth's eyes fired lasers at him. He hated when she did that. "You selfish bastard," she said, and suddenly picked up an egg from the basket and chucked it at him.

It bounced off John's chest and for some reason he felt he should catch it, fumbled for it with his hands and ended up falling over a chair.

"Go ahead, wreck the house now," Beth snarled.

John had no idea what got into him then. He wasn't a violent man. Beth could never say he'd ever raised a hand to her. But he regained his feet, kicked the overturned chair into the refrigerator, and snarled back, "Wreck the house? Wreck the house? *I* pay for this house! *I* painted it! *I* shingled it!" It was his turn to pick up an egg. He flung it at a wall, bellowing, "*I* sheetrocked that wall." And then he was inexplicably beelining eggs at walls—pink, yellow, red eggs, eggs initialed by a wax crayon, eggs stickered with bunnies and ducklings smashed into the walls around him. He thought he heard Beth give a little scream. Then Buddy was there, in that room, just staring at him, not far into grade school then. At the time, and for years after if John was honest with himself, John had always assumed that once Buddy was in his room, he was dead to the world, that he was not a part of what occurred in the rest of the house.

John didn't remember what happened then. Somehow Buddy was back in his bed, Beth in theirs, and he in front of the TV in the living room. Then he was in the car again, still a little drunk, but with a plan. He would buy more eggs—two, even three dozen—and more dye. He would decorate the eggs himself, two basketsful, and would have them waiting for Buddy and Beth when they awoke. The only trouble was, no supermarkets were open at that hour, years before the twenty-four-hour superstores came to town. The only trouble was the mist, so thick he became lost on these streets he had known all his life. And it just kept thickening, the mist . . . no, no mist. There was no mist in his story.

"It covered the entire lake, rising four or five feet, as if a gray cloud had settled in a clearing to nest," Arthur was saying. "You couldn't see the water at all, just hear the lapping on the shore. So quiet. I don't know why I was up so early, even before Freddy, though he had probably realized that we were definitely not morning people and had decided to sleep in himself.

"I was aware that I probably shouldn't, but I took my rod and shoved off into the grayness anyway, and just drifted. No shore. No trees. It was quite exhilarating. Freeing, really.

"I cast once, with this red and white striped thing Freddy had put on the line, and before I heard a kerplunk, my rod almost tore me from the boat. I was frantic at first, but I hung on. I don't know how long I was out there, reeling in, sometimes just letting the line spin out because that was all I could do. Freddy must have put on harpoon line. Or the fishing muse was smiling on me. I don't know. I just hung on, and the mist burned off slowly around me. And there I was in this wooden boat on this impossibly clear lake surrounded by conifers with a monstrous log of a demon fish lolling to the surface beside me. I brought it into the boat with my bare hands, lifting it somehow—luck most likely, its slipping and leaping at the right moment, its entire body snapping in the air above me, then landing at my feet, in the boat. I literally fought it there, that huge, daggered mouth, those razor fins, like wrestling a sword. At the time I swear I thought I might die, be eaten, I don't know. 'Goddamn me,' is all Freddy could say later. 'Goddamn me to goddamn 'ell.'"

A figure had come out of the woods. John felt a bit confused and bleary, wiped his eyes with his forearm. Buddy. Why was he standing with his back to them, staring into the woods?

"Then it became still." Arthur's story refused to let John go.

"Out of the water too long, I guess. I was pressing it against the side of the boat with both feet, my back braced on the other side. Its skin was torn away in patches where I'd stomped and gouged. I looked squarely into that flat, unhuman eye, and a thought struck me—I remember this clearly: To it, we were the monsters."

Silence. Silence. Buddy approached, slowly, first pointing toward the woods, then putting a forefinger to his lips in a shushing gesture.

"I know it's silly, but I still feel badly about that fish." Arthur was whispering now. "Father, however, rather than being angry, was ecstatic, had a taxidermist prepare and mount the poor thing so he could hang it on his den wall, mainly because Mother wouldn't allow it anywhere else in the house. Whenever a friend or associate stopped by, for however briefly, Father would insist I recount my epic struggle to them. And, despite my regrets, I would tell my tale with embellishments and wild gesticulations because it pleased him so. Ah, the small and foolish ways we show our love for one another. Well, here's our boy."

Buddy stood before them and John tried to get him into focus. He whispered, "There's a red-breasted grosbeak over there."

"Where?" Arthur whispered.

"Don't have any of those here," John whispered, his voice seeming to come to his ears from a long ways off.

"Now you do," Buddy said, and circled behind them to put a hand on John's and Arthur's backs. "On that low branch to the left of the little oak. Beside the two big maples."

"I believe I see it," Arthur said.

John asked, "What does it look like?"

"Red on its breast, like it's been shot through the heart," Buddy said.

John looked hard, into the darkened confusion of brush and weeds and hanging branches, feeling a bit foolish, but searching nonetheless. Then, on a low branch, a small movement.

Un Titled

A. D. Winans

Old man hobbling on cane
Young man feeling no pain
Old man singing the blues
Young man in spanking white shoes
Old man with no teeth
Young man balling under the sheets
Old man in Palm Beach
Young man out of reach
Old man with young dreams
Young man unraveling at the seams

A Time to Live

Carmen Anthony Fiore

"Pop's only sixty-seven, still got a lot of good years left." I had been telling myself this ever since my sister's phone call.

"Rushed Pop to Saint Francis Hospital this morning." Mary's voice crackled electronically. It was the sixties then, before the Internet, cell phones, and BlackBerry gadgets took over our lives.

"Lousy connection." I could hear a distant loudspeaker paging a doctor. "What's wrong with him?" I struggled to get the words out of my dry mouth.

"Everything!" She stifled a sob. "He's got a swollen aorta. Had a stroke, too—and his blood pressure's sky-high."

I dug an eraser end into my desk. "Be right down, bye."

The trip to the hospital took twenty unbearable minutes through Trenton's early afternoon traffic on what seemed like the hottest day of June. I hurried through three amber lights, catching the first glint of red each time.

I found driving the narrow urban streets of the Chambersburg section annoying after living so many years in the wide-open expanses of the suburbs. The familiar brick row houses in "the Burg" were packed together like cereal boxes on a supermarket shelf; prosciutto hams and links of salami and pepperoni hung in store windows; the sidewalks were filled with the vowels and the culture that southern Italians had brought with them at the turn of the twentieth century. I tried to recall the last time I had had a tomato pie, the Burg's version of pizza.

Pop had always advised me, "You get an education first. Then you get a job where you wear a suit. No be a barber, like me."

I had done what he told me to do. I had moved on up to the middle class, with my college degree and a professional position with New Jersey's Department of Transportation, and I was wearing a suit.

At my first step, my first sniff inside the hospital, my nose twitched at the sickening blend of disinfectant, alcohol, and ether. I hated hospitals, from the starched nurse uniforms and antiseptic odors to the world-weary doctors and their medical argot. The people in the halls were just blurs between me and my destination— Pop's room on the fourth floor.

Mom and Mary were already there, and their sad, tear-washed faces would have told me he was in big trouble, even if I hadn't seen the thin old man lying under the white sheet. The left side of his mouth angled downward. His eyes remained closed. His chest heaved. His gray hair lay in damp scraggly clumps over his forehead and spread out on the white pillow; nothing like when he worked in his barbershop. He always combed it straight back with no part, and he liked to keep it slick with fragrant hair tonic.

My mother had begun sobbing into her hands as soon as she saw me. My sister placed an arm around her shoulders and led her toward the door. I followed them out to the screened lounge and waited until my mother was seated before I motioned my sister to step into the hallway.

Mary's small face was pale. "Dr. Ferris says Pop needs an operation."

"For what?"

"His aorta."

"He's no young kid. Could he take one?"

"Dr. Ferris thinks so."

Her bleary brown eyes were framed with tiny lines, and her thin-lipped mouth drooped at the edges. I could see the sadness mixed with hope.

"What's Mom think?"

Mary wiped her eyes with the corner of her damp hanky. "She's for it."

"Anybody ask Pop yet?"

"No."

"He's got to give his consent."

"He won't. I know he won't." Mary grabbed my right lapel. "When he comes to, talk to him. He always listened to you."

Mary was still holding onto my suit while I stared past her down the hallway. Crazy thoughts flashed inside my head, like pictures on a television screen. I saw my father dying on an operating table because I had talked him into it, then dying in a hospital bed because I hadn't. Five minutes must have slipped by before I said, "He's a stubborn mule, but I'll talk to him."

Mary smiled. "Good, I feel better now."

"I want to talk to Dr. Ferris first. Is he around?"

"Let's go ask the nurse." Mary turned as if to lead the way, then she stopped and said, "No, you go—I better stay with Mom."

I was lucky. Dr. Ferris was on duty and I cornered him in a basement corridor.

"I'm concerned about my father's age. Could he live through the operation?"

"His chances of pulling through are good. He has a strong heart. A surprisingly strong heart."

"When would you do it?"

"Soon as possible. Can't chance any more swelling. Might burst anytime."

"Would he die, if it did?"

"Yes, from the internal bleeding. He needs to have the aneurysm removed right away. Get him to consent. Otherwise, he probably won't last more than a month, maybe less."

That was all I had to hear: Pop had only a month—or less—to

live. I went back to Mom, Mary, and my sleeping father, but I didn't tell them. It was my personal burden—my penance for being a son. So I stood like a mute in that warm hospital room with my guts slowly twisting into knots.

The following night I went back to the hospital to see if Pop was able to talk. I was on edge, knowing he needed to get the operation in a hurry, while facing the difficult task of persuading him to submit to it without scaring him.

My father is old-country *contadini* rural stock, and they don't believe in operations. Yet, knowing what I was up against—a "hard-headed" man, a real *capotosto*—I wouldn't have had him any other way. I loved that old guy.

At least Pop was still an "Italian." I couldn't say the same for myself.

After I walked into the hospital room, one silent step at a time, I gave my sister the high sign with my eyes and a quick nod of my head, then waited until she talked my mother into going out to the lounge for a breath of fresh air.

My father and I exchanged glances; then I asked him, "How are you feeling?"

"No good." He spoke in a whisper, nothing forceful like the strong baritone I remembered as a kid that had me shaking when he caught me breaking a branch on his favorite fig tree.

If my suburban neighbors saw me fussing with a fig tree in my backyard like my father used to, tying the branches together and wrapping them with blankets and tar paper to help it survive the winter, they would think I was getting a little whacky. Lawns, decks, and barbecues were *de rigueur* out there.

"You want to feel better?" I asked.

His laugh was weak. "Sure."

"I talked to the doctor. Said you have a good heart, but you need an operation."

Pop shook his head. "No cut me like a pig," he said, his speech slurred from the stroke.

"Dr. Ferris says you've got to have the operation right away. Can't chance any more swelling."

"So I die. I'm old, sick, my time to die."

"Look, Pop, operating on the aorta is a simple operation today. You have a strong heart. Dr. Ferris says you'll pull through it with flying colors. He knows what he's talking about." I paused. "Don't you want to live?"

"How much more I live?" He shook his head again. "No cut me like a pig."

"Now you're being ridiculous!" I waited a few seconds before I said, "You don't want to see your first grandson?"

My father's dark eyes widened.

"We just found out, Pop. Catherine's going to have a baby. You're going to be a grandfather. I didn't even tell Mom or Mary yet."

My father smiled weakly on the good side of his face, barely lifting his upper lip.

I hesitated a moment, then asked, "You want to die and miss seeing your first grandson, just because you don't care anymore, just because you're old and sick?"

He didn't answer.

"Look, Pop, you've got to have the operation. This old-country notion is ridiculous. So they cut you a little bit. So what! As long as you live—to see your first grandson christened with your name." I leaned forward and rested my sweaty hands on the bed. "We decided that if it's a boy, we'll name him after you. And Catherine has orders. She better have a boy, or she gets a good old-fashioned Italian *schiaffo*." I waved my right palm.

Again Pop's smile was faint, his mouth still slanting downward on the one side.

We grew quiet. I sat and stared at that old man I wanted to see live forever, while he gazed upward, with his head on the pillow, at some spot on the white ceiling. His face had that inward expression it always got when he was worried or thoughtful. I could tell by the way he blinked his eyes and the long time he kept his dark pupils fixed on that spot up on the ceiling.

He finally aimed those eyes at me. "The doctor say I live?"

"Sure, you'll live. You've got a heart like a bull."

He didn't reply, but went back to that spot on the ceiling. I kept quiet, rubbing my slippery palms together. When he turned toward me again, a slight crooked smile brightened his ashen face. "Okay, you tell the doctor I do it." He went back to that spot again. "I live . . . to see my grandson."

I could have hugged my father and kissed him right there, but instead I remained seated and wrung my hands dry, nodding my approval. I couldn't remember the last time I had shown him any real affection.

A minute or two later, I stood in the doorway and said, "Don't go away. Wait right here."

Pop grinned at my feeble attempt at humor.

"I'm going to tell Mom and Mary."

They jumped up when they saw me. "He agreed to have the operation," I said.

"How'd you do it, Lou?" Mary asked.

"Told him he's going to be a grandfather, and that he better live to see his grandson."

"You didn't tell us," Mary said.

"We just found out yesterday for sure."

My mother grabbed my hand and tears poured down her wrinkled cheeks, while my sister kept wiping her own eyes.

"I'm so happy for you," Mary said, "and I'm so relieved you got Pop to agree."

"When we go back to his room," I said, "let's act calm, like everything's normal. Nothing to get excited about, or to worry ourselves sick over, right?"

They nodded and I herded them back to Pop's room, where we

put on a "good front" for the rest of the visiting time.

Two days later he was under the knife. I was proud of him, knowing how he felt about it. He was doing something against his nature for his family, especially that important little guy who was forming inside my wife. But I admit I did a lot of sweating and worrying and by the morning of that second day, I could hardly sit still in the hospital lounge chair. I kept flipping magazine pages as if I were interested in the moving blur of print and pictures.

Every now and then I'd glance at my mother and watch her finger black rosary beads, her lips moving steadily. My sister stared straight ahead, but I suspected she was praying, too. As for me, well, I couldn't pray. I gave that up long ago. All I could do was fidget and sweat. My armpits were a soggy swamp and my shirt felt damp, as if glued to my back.

Watching my mother and sister brought back my days as an altar boy. I couldn't remember the last time I had said the rosary, and forget going to confession to make my Easter Duty, like a good practicing Roman Catholic should do each year.

The doctor had said it would be over by noon. I kept urging the time forward by sneaking glances at my wristwatch. There wasn't any need for words. It was a time for silent hope. I sat and turned pages until the tiny hands on my watch pointed upward. Then I hurried down the hallway to wait by the elevator for Doctor Ferris. It would be better for me to act as the shock absorber in case of bad news. I would deliver it with more sympathy than could be expected from a doctor. But it was nerve-wracking. I paced back and forth, wiping sweat off my hands with a smudged handkerchief.

After four false alarms, Dr. Ferris, still dressed in a surgical tunic, stepped off the elevator. He walked slowly over to my side of the corridor where my feet seemed frozen to the floor. My face must have given away my feelings.

Dr. Ferris smiled at me. "Your father's in the recovery room." He placed his hand on my shoulder. "Came through the operation like a trooper. He'll make it. Tell your mother and sister that everything's fine, just fine."

I breathed an audible sigh. "Thank God . . . thank God for that!" I forced my weak, trembling legs to move until I made it out to the lounge.

"Dr. Ferris says he'll make it. He's in the recovery room." My voice sounded hoarse, as if I had a mouthful of gravel. Even my breathing sounded labored. If I hadn't known better, I would have sworn I was hyperventilating.

"Our prayers have been answered," Mary said. "And yours . . . ?"

"Yes . . . yes," Mom mumbled into her handkerchief. But I wasn't worried about her tears of relief.

Mary put an arm around my mother's stooped shoulders, and whispered something in Italian to her that I didn't quite understand. My foreign language skills were getting rusty, and I don't know for sure when I stopped being an Italian-American and became "unhyphenated." I wondered why. Was it to "fit in" better with the people who didn't have a vowel at the end of their last names?

"Let's go down to the snack bar and get a glass of iced tea," I said. "Pop'll be in the recovery room a long time."

My mother mumbled something in Italian to my sister, who looked back at me. "Mom wants to go to the chapel and pray first. Will you come with us?" Mary stared at me, her eyelids unblinking.

I couldn't remember the last time I had ventured into a church or a chapel, not since I had joined that vast army of nonpracticing Catholics in America. But I do remember my mother asking me, "Why you no go to church anymore?"

"I don't know for sure, Mom," I had said. "Maybe someday, when Catherine and I have kids, I'll have to go back. Can't let the little rascals grow up heathens like me, huh?"

My mother had patted my hand. "You was so cute when you was an altar boy, helping the priest say Mass."

Mary was still staring at me. I shrugged and said, "I'll come, too.

The iced tea can wait. It's time to replant my roots."

I put my arm around my mother's frail shoulders and led her out of the lounge. My smiling sister followed us. And when we entered the quiet serenity of the chapel and knelt together in the pew, I got the funny feeling that I was home again.

Uncle Sterry

Michael Shorb

This old house, set off the road
to Valley Falls, aged to
birch white and peeling
like shingled skin, this mapled
driveway
   lost in autumnal hues
clay-stained leaves
running wild in antlered sun.

A strong man, neighbors called him.
Good as any ever wore
a pair of shoes.
   But now, with his wife
living in town
   nursing a broken ankle,
TV glows and drones,
blue parody of the burning bush, as we
approach the door.

The homogenized babble of talking heads
looms incongruous here
in Rockwell country:

   any voice to fill
the twilight now,
   any mode of sleep.

We talk of the madness of California weather.

"All the same, son, day after day.
No seasons. Like a neon tube.
Must confuse animals. With animals
you need seasons.
        Rain, snow.
The exact gold of October.
There's a time to rest the mare and a time
to foal.
        The same with sheep, and cows."

The only thing he regrets, says Uncle Sterry,
is giving up his car
        because of cataracts.
That, and letting his delicate wife
Blanche sleep alone by the dining
room heater the night
she rose from troubled
sleep and stepped
        through a closed glass door toward the warmth
of relatives in town.

As evening wears on
Uncle Sterry reveals
ghosts and skeletons
of apple butter country.
The Irishman
        crazed by debts and whiskey
who bludgeoned his wife and two boys
burying them beneath flat rocks
in a field of stubbled corn.

"Or you take the Millers now.
Stu and Aurelia? She had
that slight hunch back, don't you know.
Hadn't oughtta had no children, them two.
Six kids born.
Three was normal. Three was dwarfs.
Hadn't oughtta
          had no children."

The time to depart grows like a shadow.

We say goodbye to
Uncle Sterry
          shaking those burled hands
that once milked and sowed and
baled hay in the course of morning.

I don't even know what I felt
driving back
          light beams cutting
the air like molten snow.

A loss.
Not sorrow exactly.
But cheated,
          and a fear.

Fist, Palm, Hand

Dane Cervine

> *Your hand opens and closes and opens and closes.*
> *If it were always a fist or always stretched open,*
> *you would be paralyzed.*
>
> —*Rumi*

During my mother's stroke, her left arm swung
suddenly at her side like a stranger. She called out,
was rushed to the hospital by ambulance.

Now, recovering, her hand won't unfold—fingers curled,
supple, but unable to fist or extend. I think of this,
standing alone outside St. Agnes Hospital in Fresno at night
by the stone statue of Jesus, at the end of a spiral stone path,
my palms extended in prayer or defense under the thousand blind eyes
of heaven, sparkling. I make a fist, then open each palm,
then fist each hand again and again, remembering.

The next morning, I wake in the Red Roof Inn's pale room
next to the Korean Mart and the Jack-in-the-Box—the incessant
air conditioner already battling the incessant heat. I stare at a photo
of my father, dead four years now, but still speaking to me.
His hand on his tool belt, his heart full of fists, of waving palms,
the valves opening and closing, opening and closing, finally
closing. If he were always open, rather than mysterious, even dark,
I would never have questioned, never pushed into the depths,
would have been paralyzed by light.

Holding my mother's arm as we walk now to the car, we pause
by a fountain, a statue of two young girls running to touch
six birds escaping into flight, hear the sound of falling water
on blue tile. The stone girls will never reach even one bird,
but my mother, already, begins to flex the fingers
of her stricken hand open, then closed, then open.

The Stones We Bring with Us, the Stones We Take Away

Carlos Reyes

The small ones in my shoe
The pebbles stuck in the sole

Of my old shoe—maracas
Your mother says when I walk.

The flat stones like the ones
I skip six times across Lost Lake

Before they sink
Into the icy water beneath Mt. Hood.

The stones we take from the path
To ease our passing,

The stones we bring with us
To this cemetery,

Brought from places
You have been or not

Or places we would have liked
Or could have gone with you,

Now rest atop a tombstone
With a Jewish star.

We bring them in remembrance
And in some small attempt

At keeping in touch.
The stones, postcards

Though you are gone
Beyond our reach.

Signs

Brent Robison

When Arnie Beers woke one morning to find a sign planted on his front lawn, he was amused. He chuckled as he pulled the sign's flimsy posts out of the ground and held it up for his wife to see from the picture window. They both smiled and shrugged. In simple block letters painted in red on a two-foot by three-foot piece of white cardboard, the sign simply said: ARNIE & MAUDE BEERS.

Arnie was a small-town judge, recently retired after a satisfying thirty-five-year career. He took the sign as some sort of reverse vandalism, even a pat on the back. An anonymous citizen saying, "Take a bow—go ahead, you deserve it!" He felt proud, in a modest way. But he didn't really want a sign on his front lawn; benign though the gesture was, it was a little out of bounds.

Best to nip this in the bud, he thought. He put the sign in his garage.

The next morning another sign was on the lawn. It was virtually identical to the first. The mosquito of alarm that buzzed a split second in his ear was not loud enough to get his serious attention. Into the garage went the second sign.

Arnie didn't get annoyed until the third day. "OK, that's enough," he said aloud into the summer morning, looking around him at the empty yard, the quiet country road.

Nobody heard. There was a sign in place again on the fourth morning. Maude said, "Why not just leave it there this time? Maybe that's all they want. What does it hurt?"

So Arnie begrudgingly left it alone: one day, two days, three days. Nothing was quite right. He met his friends for their usual golf game, but he found himself unable to relax. His swing was off. His friends laughed when he told them what was bothering him. "Just some harmless wacko," Vern Denning said. "He'll get bored soon; just wait 'im out."

Skip Schultz said, "Or wait up all night with a shotgun. Give 'im a helluva surprise."

A week passed with the fourth sign on the lawn. It seemed that maybe Maude was right. Her way had always been to presume that benevolence reigned in the world, a trait that served her well during all those years as a fourth-grade teacher. Despite causing the occasional spat, her optimism was one of the things Arnie loved most about her. And, after all, nothing had happened; the thing just stood there, as if the signmaker were satisfied. Arnie, however, was fuming; he wasn't about to just hand over control of his little plot of land, of any fraction of his life, to some unseen stranger.

A whole week was damn well enough. Arnie ripped the sign from the lawn and tossed it into the garage. But he still wasn't ready to violate his sleep pattern.

The next morning, when he saw the new sign, he phoned his friend Joe Vitalo, the town chief of police.

"There's really nothing I can do, Arnie," Joe said. "No crime, no perp . . . . You know I need the manpower for other stuff."

Arnie grumbled, "You gotta ride herd on the wackos, Joe."

"Tell you what—" Joe said. "I'll have whoever's got the shift cruise past your place a couple times in the wee hours. We'll keep our eyes open."

On each of the next three mornings, Arnie found a new sign planted on the lawn. Joe Vitalo said, "Look Arnie, give 'em a chance to go away on their own. This is the best I can do."

The newest sign went clattering onto the jumbled pile in the garage. The time had come to catch the vandal himself. He decided to sit up all night in an easy chair facing the picture window, watching. He didn't have a shotgun, had never owned a gun of any kind, so he armed himself with a big bright flashlight. He imagined surprising the bastard in the act, a deer in the headlights. Maude protested, "Arnie, really, you're just going to make yourself ill. It's not worth it." But he couldn't be budged. She made him a cup of herbal tea, wrapped her robe tighter around her breasts, and disappeared alone into their bedroom.

Arnie sat in the darkness as minutes, then hours, crept past at a glacial pace that seemed almost spiteful. The indistinct shadows of trees cast by a waning moon drifted in imperceptible inches across the dim lawn. An old ache began its slow bloom in his lower back. This was a bad idea, he knew it.

Arnie never would have taken it this far if not for the fact that something felt deeply awry. Three months earlier he had attended the funeral of an old college friend, who had finally lost his two-year battle with lung cancer—a man who had never smoked and was fit in every other way. Since then, long before the first sign appeared, Arnie had become aware of something—a trace of disquiet, a vague imbalance—growing like a tumor. Not in his body, but in a secret, walled-up chamber in his body's general vicinity.

Now he wondered if the sign marked him as a target. Was there a hit man on the way to their door, a black car cruising the country roads, looking for bloodred letters on a white board? Did someone hate him so much? He ranged back through thirty-five years of courtroom memories, calling up every sullen backward glance of a jail-bound miscreant, every dark scowl of a victim's family member whose bloodlust he, the arbiter of justice, had not satisfied. There hadn't been many; after all, this was a peaceful little town. But . . . it only takes one. And a worse idea: what if there were someone he could not recollect, had no awareness of, someone whose life he had damaged unknowingly, wrapped up as he was, always had been, in his blind, petty, self-absorption . . . someone who'd been simmering in hatred for years, and was finally taking revenge? Maybe he deserved it, maybe justice was about to be served, a hand from on high poised to slap him down from his arrogant perch, to knock him tumbling from his bench, from that pathetic, deluded inner throne that he had trundled about on his back all his adult life. It was becoming appallingly clear: not only did he lack the wisdom of Solomon, he couldn't explain even the simplest events in his life. And, if that were true at his age, then obviously his days on this earth had been an utter waste, nothing learned, nothing accomplished, zero value, absolutely zilch.

Arnie's eyes popped open at 5:12 a.m. A hint of rose from the east lit the hazy scene before him. Shaggy trees across the way, wet black street, sweep of muted green lawn, and there it was: the sign had returned. A curse leapt to his lips, but before it could erupt, it sank under a rising swell of discouragement. He was old and tired and ineffectual. He wanted all this to just go away and leave him in peace. Creaking up from the chair's clutches in stiff stops and starts, he shuffled his slippered feet to the window and yanked the drapes closed.

Late that afternoon, Arnie and Maude ignored the sign on the lawn as they backed out of the driveway, and they didn't mention it during the thirty-minute drive over the ridge at Highmount and along the country roads lined in day lilies, into the village of Woodstock. The plan was to meet their daughter Donna for an early dinner, then go to the Center for Photography, for the opening of a show called "A Portrait of Protest: Fifty Years of the Anti-War Movement in Images." Donna was an activist, and while Arnie agreed in general with her politics, he found her too often shrill, sometimes seriously annoying. Fingernails on a blackboard, setting his teeth on edge. Although, truly, Arnie was immensely proud of her, he had never found it easy to say so.

The day had been hot, oppressive under a gray sky, and when

Maude and Donna, giddy at their rare mother-daughter reunion, entertained the idea of dining alfresco, Arnie put a grumpy stop to it. He took their elbows and guided them firmly into the air-conditioned depths of a chic Woodstock eatery.

The two women giggled and chatted and touched each other like best girlfriends, and while Arnie felt a glimmer of gladness to see Maude enjoying herself, he couldn't seem to escape the bubble of irritable gloom that surrounded him. With altogether too much fluttery hand motion, Donna jabbered nonstop: she was so excited about being able to arrange for the photography exhibit, which they would visit after dinner, to come to a gallery near her home in New Jersey. She had even met one of the photographers. Arnie had to restrain himself from interjecting, "So are you going to give your mom or dad a chance to say a word?" even though there was nothing he wanted to say.

Finally, as they finished up their entrees, Donna surprised him. She interrupted her incessant chatter, touched his arm with a look of genuine concern and asked, "Dad, what's wrong? Are you feeling okay?"

His out-of-practice voice had a croak in it. "I'm fine. Just didn't sleep well last night." He knew Maude was avoiding eye contact with him, and he felt grateful he could trust her to stay silent about the signs on their lawn. He changed the subject: "What's up with Al? Why isn't he here with you?"

It was Donna's turn to avoid his eyes as she picked at her broccoli rabe polenta. "You know, working at the hospital all the time. And complaining about it. I'm pretty fed up, actually."

Arnie didn't show the stab of worry he felt at hearing that. "Hmph. Tell him I expect him here next time. Gotta have another man in this crew."

"Yeah, Dad. Well, we'll see. You guys want dessert? Or should we get over to the show?"

At the Center for Photography at Woodstock, in a building

locally famous because Bob Dylan had once lived upstairs when it was a café in the sixties, huge photos hung on stark white walls and people milled about holding plastic cups of white wine. The walls held images in black and white from Korean and Vietnam War times, people costumed in period clothes and hairstyles, marching, shouting, holding placards. The pictures seemed to Arnie, even as ancient as he felt, somehow separated from the real world, as if all that passionate protest had been just a movie, an old Hollywood drama meaning nothing more now than absurd nostalgia. And then there was the more recent work, in color—often splashy, garish, violent color—of other people, a newer, somehow more real sort of people, so much the same but so subtly different in their modern style, still marching, still shouting, still holding placards, protesting Desert Storm, Afghanistan, Iraq. Everywhere were hands brandishing signs, signs, those blank rectangular shapes with their four, always four, sharp corners like shards of glass, and on which carefully etched or sloppily dashed words screamed out vital, meaningful, incomprehensible, dangerous messages, and it was all too much for Arnie to take.

An open door led from one side of the main gallery into a small triangular room containing a photo exhibit called, according to a plaque on the wall, "Odalisque Amerikai." Arnie found himself grateful to be alone in the claustrophobic little space and began taking a close look at the images. Crafted by a photographer whose name contained, in Arnie's estimation, entirely too many consonants implausibly jumbled, the prints were cleanly arrayed in a single row around the room. Each was sixteen by twenty inches in a simple black matte frame. The photos were nude studies rendered in an infinite variety of subtle but glowing shades of black, white, and silvery gray. In every one, a woman reclined outdoors in an unlikely setting: an industrial railyard, an automobile scrap heap, a ramshackle barn, an empty desert highway. The first thing Arnie found interesting about the images was not the setting, however. It was that they did not depict impossibly svelte and beautiful young models as one might expect, but real women, women like your next-door neighbor, your sister, your wife. There were wide hips, heavy thighs, pendulous breasts. There were cellulite and stretch marks. Some eyes were downcast, others gazed out at Arnie with a direct calm that held both kindness and sorrow. These were mothers, women at the age-less pinnacle of lush femaleness, bathed in an otherworldly light and transfigured into sensuous angels of mercy, miraculously captured in exquisite detail on the flat surfaces of platinum prints.

Arnie moved from one to the next, at first nearly breathless, surprised by his own response. He was not an art lover; had often joked about not having an aesthetic bone in his body. Then he realized the source of the emotion rising up in him. These images flung him back to a time long gone, summer after glorious summer, when he would take Maude and baby Donna camping: the Adirondacks, the Rockies, a willowy bank of the Colorado, a remote beach on the Yucatán. The three of them would laze about, totally naked, laughing, playing, free of all care. He and Maude were in their early thirties then, working hard together to build his law practice; he had often felt these nature-communing vacations were their key to sanity and a lasting marriage. It was like living a miracle: a few days of primitive pleasures erased months of complicated stress. But as Donna got older and responsibilities changed, nude camping faded into the past. He hadn't thought of it in years, and now, standing in the gallery with memories reeling out like movies before his inner eyes, he felt a groundswell of gratitude begin rising up to replace the self-pity he'd been lost in.

During the time Arnie, Maude, and Donna had been inside the gallery, the sky had turned dark as slate and nasty gusts were kicking up. It was clearly time to head home and, after quick good-byes to Donna, Arnie and Maude scurried for their car. But they hadn't gone a block when Arnie suddenly said, "Wait." He grabbed Maude's elbow, turned her around and guided her with rapid steps back to where Donna still stood under the gallery's awning. He gathered them both into a hug, his big arms strong around their shoulders, pulling them in until their foreheads touched his cheeks. For a moment, he held them like that, still as stone, and then he said, "I love you. I love you both." As he kissed their heads, big rain-drops began to splatter the sidewalk.

His wife and daughter were too surprised to react; they barely had time to look at each other wide-eyed before he pulled Maude away and, his arm around her shoulders, took her dashing through the rain toward their car.

The trip home became more and more tense as they drove. Wind lashed the trees and sent debris flying. The car shuddered, slammed by gusts. Rain blasted their windshield as if shot from a fire hose. Arnie hunched forward, gripping the wheel in two fists, peering into the deluge, slowing to a crawl at the worst spots. The journey began to seem endless.

By the time they turned onto the county two-lane that led to their house, the rain had thinned considerably, revealing an eerie, slanting light that bathed a wet world strewn with the broken branches of trees. Occasional mean little squalls still buffeted the car, but Arnie and Maude knew they were on the home stretch. Then, less than a mile from their driveway, as they rounded a right-hand curve, a tall pine caught by an errant gust came toppling its full length, out of the vertical forest, falling toward horizontal as if in slow motion. Every possible combination of steering and braking seemed in Arnie's mind to simultaneously appear for consideration, as his feet and hands did something all on their own—something, probably even the best thing, but not enough. His vision was sud-denly engulfed in wet green pine boughs and his ears deafened by the terrible heavy crunch of wood on steel, drowning Maude's scream.

For the second time that day, Arnie's eyes popped open after an interminable blank. He knew immediately that he was alive and, remarkably, not in pain. He looked at Maude, who looked back at him with moon-wide eyes before her face crumpled into a sob. He understood what the sob was for, because he felt it too. Even more than shock, it was gratitude that they were both alive and uninjured. The two-foot-thick trunk of the tree had slammed to the pavement ten feet in front of their bumper, and a big limb lay angled across the ruined hood amidst an impenetrable tangle of smaller limbs and tufts of needles. The windshield was cracked but not shattered. Steam hissed from the engine. The car was a mess, but everything was glorious, because Arnie and his beloved were whole.

As he leaned and hugged Maude, her tears subsiding, he was startled by a knock at the window. A bearded man had appeared as if from nowhere and was speaking loudly, "Everybody okay? Sir? Ma'am? If nobody's hurt, please get out of the car as fast as you can."

With the man's help, Arnie was able to wrench his door open and Maude was able to crawl out his side. Calm and in command, the stranger guided them to sit in his own pickup truck as, all at the same time, he called the local police on his cell phone and signaled an oncoming car to slow and stop. Arnie was dazed and compliant; Maude was silent. For an unknown length of time, they sat in the cramped truck, his arm around her, her head on his shoulder. Later, these minutes seemed blurred, gone, lost behind the single thought that loomed foremost in Arnie's mind. He could have died. Had they been moving a half-second faster, they would have been in perfect position to be crushed.

What did this mean? Was it a warning? A message from somewhere unseen? He was not a believer in any mainstream God; he had in fact, until so recently, found his strength in his own imperfect self, without the need for a supernatural parent. He didn't feel likely now to venture far from that, but he was suddenly mystified, engulfed with wonder. What forces were at work, out of sight, filling the air all around him like radio waves, ready to kill or bless at an instant's whim? Sending cancer, war, a daughter's failing marriage . . . but also split-second protection, helpful neighbors, warm memories of sunshine on bare skin? He had no answers, but he knew one thing: he was glad that he had told his wife and child that he loved them.

Both rain and wind had faded to a strange, dripping stillness, and dusk was approaching. At the bearded stranger's summons, a police cruiser had arrived and the officer was directing traffic, a county road crew had appeared and set up cones and detour signs, an orange-vested man was standing by with an extinguisher in case the engine caught fire, other men prepared to attack the fallen tree with chain saws, a tow truck was waiting to free their car, and Police Chief Joe Vitalo himself had come to give Arnie and Maude a ride home.

"That guy who . . . I didn't get a chance to thank . . ." Arnie mumbled from the back seat, where he and Maude sat in the chief's cruiser. They were just finishing the long looping route that took them around a mountain, to approach their house from the opposite direction.

"Yeah . . . Tony. Ex-cop from the city. Good man. I'll tell him you said thanks," Joe spoke as he turned into the Beers' driveway.

"Arnie, look." Maude whispered.

The sign, ARNIE & MAUDE BEERS, still stood in their front yard. Impossibly, it had survived the storm, looking only a bit twisted on its two thin stakes planted deep in the lawn. Joe brought the car to a stop, put it in park, and turned to Arnie, acknowledging with a silent nod and a raised eyebrow that, indeed, the sign was still there, and he was still ready to help if he could.

Arnie glanced at Joe, then took a long look at Maude's sweet, tired face, lit by the last blue remnants of daylight. Inside his weary heart was a muddle of inarticulate protests and ancient fears. Answers, control, the laws of an orderly world—these had always been his anchors. But now, someone was out there, watching. For good or ill, entirely unpredictable.

All he could do was follow his body's impulse. He let out a heavy sigh as he turned to look through the glass at his yard, his house, his world.

In the summer twilight, the sign's crimson letters on their snowy field had turned to purple on gray; still, the names were clear: those words, those strings of symbols that identified himself and his life's love. But in that moment, just before he opened the car door and entered his home as if for the first time, the words seemed instead to describe something ineffable, something eternal that he would never understand.

Arnie was surprised to discover that this sensation gave him, not pain, but a fine, subtle pleasure that lingered like faint perfume, long into the evening and beyond.

Some Somes

Louise Jaffe

Some rumpled morning
an amnesiac sun
forgot it was supposed
to rise,
faceless computer addicts
forgot to stop trading inane e-mails,
cliché-bloated hope
forgot to mock despair,
and heedless seasons
forgot how to change
as the weary world we've grown
to know and dread
finally remembered
to end.

Some flustered dusk
a senescent sun
forgot it was expected
to set,
waves of scheduled-for-shedding light
forgot not to ripple
through incredulous skies,
and distrusting gapers
forgot the taste of hate
and stretch-ego schemes
in politically correct gyms

as inch by inch
a verdant world finally remembered
this might be the time
for it to begin
again.

SIX

FLIGHT

Chant for Folding Clothes

Sarah Getty

Fold the fresh-laundered clothes,
the dryer's heat still fading. Fold all
these gifts, earth-grown and woven—
cotton, linen, seersucker, chambray, lawn—

all that lay light on the body, moved
through your days, May to October.
Now, on All Saints' Day, grasp at last
that the last warm day came, stayed,

and, while you weren't looking, passed.
Fold the old khakis that gathered
the red dust of Bryce and Zion.
Fold the gauze shirt, Roman-striped,

you wiped your face and neck with,
dripping sweat in Santa Maria
in Trastevere. Fold the tee shirt
from Pompeii, the tank top that toured

Herculaneum. Fold the cropped pants,
madras plaid, that roamed Brookline's
streets behind your grandson's stroller.
Fold the terry swim robe, the shirts

long-sleeved and tick-proof for walking
the path to the pond beneath the cool,
breathing leaves. Fold them with devotion,
lay them gently away, like prayers.

Fold in thanks and praise. Fold in petition—
for summer, passed, to return. For strength
to weather winter, wrapped in wool—to last
until the last cold day, unnoticed, passes.

The Curse of Ambrosia

Tracy Robert

Prologue

I sit on the scalding leather of our Lincoln Continental, rocking from one half of my butt to the other till each adjusts to the heat. My mother trots out a punchbowl of fruit salad for me to hold on our trip to church. I feel important in this duty, first of all because I love the stuff—marshmallows, oranges, pineapple chunks, sour cream, and coconut, folded up in a dessert she makes only when she wants to impress the church women—and secondly because my friend Phoebe is joining us, but she won't be the one holding the bowl.

Her mother the model has put her in a navy blue dress with a huge white collar, big as a toilet seat cover folded in half, and a red straw headband with netting. Phoebe has tiny dots of sweat on her nose and upper lip; I think she looks both pretty and ridiculous in her getup. I wear my usual white pleated skirt with the chocolate stain at the hem, and the only blouse I could find that was ironed. As part of my summer tradition, I've successfully hidden most of my dress clothes under my bed and at the bottom of my doll chest. Of course, on my head I have the obligatory lace mantilla my mother thinks is part of the Catholic uniform. She converted in order to marry Daddy Otto. I'm supposed to call him Daddy, but in my mind he's Daddy Otto.

With the ambrosia and a promise that I could bring a friend, my mother bribed me into going to this church social. Daddy Otto is the only true Catholic in the picture, but he never attends church or anything to do with it.

"It's hotter than hell's hot dog stand," I say to Phoebe as we wait. My butt has finally adjusted and I'm thankful, for once, for the added protection of underwear. Usually it just seems pointless. I flick a mosquito bite on her leg.

She says, "Hotter than athlete's foot in Africa."

We giggle and snort and roll our eyes, until my mother arrives at the car, putting a towel across my skirt and the bowl in my lap.

"Hang on to it for dear life, Dessa, my darling," she says. "The ladies of Saint Mel's are depending on you." The tinfoil is loose, so I crimp it tighter, and we're off to the Summer Faith Spectacular. Try saying that with a mouthful of milky fruit.

I see the lunatic suitor before my mother or Phoebe. Actually, I see him in my mind before I see him with my sight. What my mind shows me is not really him, but a warning of him, somehow: a slow motion film of the Rose Parade, which I am forced to watch with Daddy Otto every year on January first, while eating what he calls his "famous flapjacks." There is nothing famous about them; they're just regular pancakes made from Bisquick and water.

I've experienced warnings like this before, but they usually happen in dreams. Once I dreamed an entire night of tornadoes, and when I picked up the newspaper in the morning, opening it before Daddy Otto just to see how much it would annoy him, the front page photos were ruined Midwestern towns and funnel-shaped monsters like those in my nightmare. And we live in California. Tornadoes are as rare here as Indian-head nickels or icebergs.

"Mom!" I say, as she steers the car around a corner, and there he is, only you can't really tell he's a man. He looks like a bouquet of four dozen red roses scurrying on two skinny pant legs, and he's no more than a couple of car lengths in front of us. "Mom, stop!"

She stomps the brake pedal as if it were vermin, the tires shriek, and everything tumbles forward: me, my friend, our hats, the bowl, and even one of Phoebe's patent leather flats ends up in the grit and carpet fuzz mixed with the ambrosia. Phoebe has a stray glob of it on her platter collar, and I look like I've used it as a skin treatment. We're stunned, and unroll like pill bugs from beneath the dashboard.

"God damn-o-rama city," my mother says. When she uses foul language she makes embarrassing attempts to disguise it. "Are you girls okay? Let's see your little faces, front and center," and she checks us for blood and breakage. "Hands and fingers?" she says, swiping at me with the towel, but I know we're okay. I know because Phoebe is doing her best not to burst into hysterical laughter, which fuels itself like atoms in the hydrogen bomb we've heard so much about.

To avoid my own urge to laugh, I peer out the window at the man behind the flowers, the cause of this mishap, who's now made it to the sidewalk but is still not showing himself. I think he might be able to see us between the leaves and stems, though he remains faceless to me. I cock my head at him.

"Gotta go," he says, backing toward an apartment complex. "I'm gonna propose, if it's all right with you." And just like that, he reaches sideways for a familiar latch, and disappears behind a wooden gate.

My mother gazes after him, her mouth hanging open like something mechanical that's stuck. Finally, she murmurs, "May your children be in diapers till they're dating." She leans back in the driver's seat and exhales a colossal sigh, massaging her abdomen. Her linen sheath stretches so tight over it I can see the stitched outline of her girdle's control panel.

"Fudge sticks," she says, with a kind of tremor in her voice. "To top it all off, I've got the Curse."

Phoebe and I are old enough to know what the Curse is, yet, ever since that day, I've taken my mother's meaning as this: Whenever a bowl is chock-full of something delicious, something you love, it is also doomed to be dumped and lost before it can be savored.

I write this for Theo, so he knows.

Chapter 1
Eggs in Viable Shells

It began with the first pelican dead from algae bloom, washing up on the Balboa Peninsula.

It began with sewage systems.

It began when a guy named Benz got the brilliant idea to power a carriage with an internal combustion engine.

It began with gunpowder, or maybe hairspray.

It began with life forms we didn't recognize but helped create.

It began with hurricanes, quakes, blizzards, droughts, floods, tsunamis, and more so-called natural disasters than we could keep up with.

It began as a strange odor, like burning sugar and shoe rubber, we noticed at first then got used to.

It began as dogs and prophets howled mournfully, and we laughed at them.

It began as smoke that stung the eyes but made for beautiful sunsets.

It began when someone paired intelligence with permission to destroy.

Somewhere in all this, it began, the end did. And one afternoon, right around the time I realized I would live to see the end, my friend Phoebe Dunn, after sixty years of absence, came back into my life, and we started the doctrine of Might As Well.

Of course, I didn't recognize her at first. We'd been in a strangled knot of people, had ducked and wiggled our way to the start of it, and were wearing Enviromasks. Phoebe's was a caramel color that blended with her face, mine a bright violet. I figured if we had to wear these contraptions to survive, they might as well be obvious. No matter what color they were, though, the masks almost completely obscured faces. All but the eyes.

Phoebe and I reached for the same two cartons of eggs at the same time, the last two. Some rancher close by had managed to shelter his chickens enough to keep them laying eggs with actual shells instead of fragile, mushy membranes. Most eggs were sold in cartons, like milk, or in fake plastic shells similar to those filled with jellybeans and hidden at Easter egg hunts. The real thing, eggs in viable shells, was cause for near riot at the supermarket, and Phoebe and I, by virtue of the invisibility of advanced age, had managed to finagle our way to the forefront of the mob.

These are the first words I said to my old friend: "Let go of the eggs, ancient bitch, or I'll rip your wig off." I was hoping intimidation would work and I could slink out of the crowd as invisibly as I slunk in, twenty-four eggs richer.

But Phoebe was Phoebe, and if she didn't recognize me, she recognized my style. "How about we share them, like sweet old-fashioned grannies, and leave these people in shock?"

Which is exactly what we did, toddling away with our arms around each other's waists, out through the scanner that read our Magnabags, into the boiling haze of day.

When we began to laugh, halfway down the street, she had trouble stopping, and that, combined with her peering dark eyes, was how I knew it was Phoebe Dunn.

She invited me to her floor for an omelet. "I have some dried avocado just for the occasion," she said. Avocados were a junk food invented in heaven: bright yellow-green and smooth inside a bumpy exterior, so buttery and rich it was hard to believe they were good for you. No matter how firm they were when picked, they wouldn't keep longer than a day anymore, so were immediately sliced, freeze-dried, and sold far cheaper than the fresh specimens.

Lettuce or any crisp vegetable was a wilted thing of the past.

It had been a while since I shared a home-cooked meal at a friend's place, and we had decades of blanks to fill in about each other. So, despite her nabbing a carton of gourmet eggs I might have made off with myself at the Superplex, I joined her.

I kept Phoebe talking.

I didn't want to tell her about my two divorces yet, or why I lived in a room with a shared bath, rather than having an entire floor to myself, as she did. That what I settled on from my ex-husbands was mostly dependent on Social Security, and, well, pamphlets and pundits try to explain how that fairy tale ended. I stashed away enough to survive on, as long as I didn't live past ninety. That was one good thing about the end—it lightened my financial worries.

I didn't want to speak of my gift, either, though whether I mentioned it or not, it always affected my relationships. I tried to ignore it when I was a teenager, forcibly forgetting my dreams and acting oblivious with friends, but, like most things we ignore, it came back stronger and with a vengeance.

Since Phoebe had been a teacher, a social anthropologist, and paid into a state retirement system, since Phoebe had never married, she had more to live on than I, who'd married two millionaires. I was the reason they'd made their money, investors and my gift, you see, but my gift could not be classified a profession on any tax form. And men are excellent at forgetting during divorces all the help that women were to them, and men are also talented at burying money, the way dogs bury bones.

Phoebe had made a living studying happiness. "A barren area in anthropology," she said. "Happiness mystified me. I thought if I studied it, I could bring it closer."

I didn't tell her the day her younger brother tried to hang himself all those decades ago, I'd known it would happen. Or that the reason I threw up was not because I'd seen Pierce dangling by a dog leash, but because I'd noticed the leash the day before in the Dunns' garage and imagined blood on it. He'd always been a strange kid, yet no one could've seen that coming without, well, without outside help.

"Do you have any children?" I asked her.

"Never married," she said, and set the omelet, steaming, on the table. She began to slice it, carefully like a holiday roast.

"That never stopped a gal from having children."

"Didn't actually stop me either. The drug my mother took when she was pregnant with me did, however. Another egg problem."

I didn't tell her about the child I gave birth to, prematurely, probably because of the abortions I had in the seventies combined with the drugs I took. The child I held in my arms till he died, and named, and buried in a tiny white casket. Whose death depressed me so much my second husband divorced me, saying, "Jesus, Dessa, snap out of it. I married you because you knew how to play."

I forgot how.

"What have you learned about happiness?" I asked her.

I listened as she explained how we North Americans had it all wrong, that being an individual, establishing yourself as *someone*, was not the key, as we'd seen time and again with the divorce and suicide rates of celebrities. Balinese culture, for example, discouraged individuality. In fact, children were given the same names, regardless of gender, according to their birth order: Wayan, Made, Nyoman, etc. The people of Bali had little money, and hence no personal worries. Few had any delusions of getting ahead. They ate simple and mostly fresh foods, and created beauty wherever they could with offerings of fruit and flowers and incense at Hindu altars, so numerous you had to step around them on sidewalks. Happiness was theirs until the waves that leveled most of the islands of Indonesia. That was when Phoebe retired from academia.

"Still close to your family?" I asked, before she could ask me anything.

"Pierce. Every so often. His wife keeps him on a tether, and needs to. He drinks, often quite a lot. My parents are gone, of course. Slugged it out in court till he had a heart attack and she inoperable cancer of the pancreas." Phoebe took a few more bites, chewing slowly, and stared out the window. "The poor pathetic dears loved each other that much." She studied another bite of reconstituted avocado she was about to take. "And your folks?"

Oh, she was clever. Start with my parents, then sashay on to the topic of me.

"Dead, both of them. Lung and heart disease, and one within a year of the other."

"Yes," she said, nodding. "If smoking didn't get them, the environment did. The world went from boundless to spent in their lifetime, or thereabouts. We're the ragged end of it. I marvel every day that I'm still here."

The omelet was so delicious, spongy and rich, that I chewed for a period of time without speaking. My eyes were open, but pictures started forming in my mind, nonsensical at first, roads and trees and stones, dirt and traffic signs and blankets blowing by me like a storm, then the images settled into steadiness. I saw a long line of men in dark suits, among them one who was naked, a splotch of pink in all the sameness.

"Ever fall in love?" I asked her.

Phoebe dabbed at her mouth with a dishcloth. "Truly, deeply, and inappropriately. He was married. I lied to myself and to him when I said I could bear it."

"Bear what?" I said. "The competition?"

"No. I didn't want all his time and attention. It was my own yearning I couldn't put up with."

I must have looked confused or interested, because she continued. "Crept over me like sickness. When I was with him, I was so relieved and so depleted by the yearning, I had no energy for him, the object of it all. I mean, essentially I curled up next to him like a cat who wanted to be stroked. Not like anything human."

"Dramatic ending?" I asked. I slid another hunk of omelet onto my plate.

"Hardly," she said. "An airport. A goodbye I didn't realize was the last. A cliché."

"Rain or fog involved?"

"No, thankfully."

When I married, both times, it was simple: I assumed he would take care of me and I would take care of him. It worked out that way for a while, then we parted. Not much yearning involved, except at the very beginning, and it disappeared like smoke, showing us the truth of our common arrangement. I'd wondered what it was like to be madly in love, even as a girl. My relationships always seemed like something expected rather than something that took me by surprise.

"Dess?"

"Uh huh?" I thought she'd bombard me now with all the questions I hoped to sidestep.

"Listen," she said, and busied herself with a bottle of wine she was attempting to uncork. "I hope this isn't vinegar. I never drink alone, and consequently, hardly ever drink."

Avocado and wine, I thought. Life is good tonight.

We clinked glasses. "To old friends," she said. "Very old. Incidentally, this isn't a wig. I've managed to retain my hair, not to mention a few of my teeth."

"Cheers," I said. "Sorry. My mistake." Her hair was arranged in such a thick white puff of a pageboy, it really did look fake. I was still tempted to try to pull it off her, but restrained myself. What little hair I have I keep cut in short wisps under a baseball cap.

"Dess?"

Okay. Here came the questions. I slugged back my entire glass of zinfandel, in case I had to leave quickly. I could always say I didn't feel well from the food. Usually, I ate from packages and cans.

"How shall I say this? I worked hard as a public servant, but I know what happened in the private sector. You see what I have here." Her age-mottled hand swept the air to the left and right of her.

"You want a round of applause?" Why was she lording it over me? It wasn't like Phoebe Dunn to brag. Was this some reckoning for the tricks I played on her as a child? All the challenges I won? Was she giving me a sunset nanny-nanny-nanner? I looked around, and the place wasn't so fabulous: two bedrooms and a bath down the hall, worn bamboo floors, large living and dining area and respectable kitchen, all painted a soothing beige, so soothing it irritated me. A butter-colored leather couch with at least a decade of use. Dingy window blinds. "Let's give a big cheer for public service," I said.

"Shit," Phoebe said. Her face drooped like old ladies' socks. Like our socks. "I didn't mean for it to sound so self-congratulatory. What I meant to do was ask if you want to stay here. Indefinitely. Move all your belongings in if you'd like. I'll give you the room I once used as a study. There's nothing really to study anymore, short of how the planet's dying, and I'm as bored with that topic as everyone else."

If her face had drooped, mine must have stood at attention. "What?" I said. Kindness and generosity were not in abundance these days as people struggled to survive, as if we weren't all going to perish by the same sunspot licking into the atmosphere, or wall of water, or viral plague, or explosion meant to teach a lesson we already knew too well. As if one of us might somehow outrun what was coming for us. My mother, before she died, said the struggle was because of hope, and I said it was because of stupidity. They might be two sides of the same attitude.

Phoebe remained silent. This was worse than if she'd at that moment asked me about marriage and children.

"Are you serious?" I continued, and she looked at me like a subject in one of her happiness studies. "I'm not homeless, you know. I have a place in the Apartments Formerly Called the Promenade.

There are lofts. It's a swanky joint." It was swanky if you were lucky enough to have a loft, only I had a studio with a shared bathroom from which I often had to scrub a stranger's filth, or else sit on it.

"Dessa, I know you're not homeless. You're nothing like homeless. I was asking for selfish reasons. We could keep each other company, play cards, share cooking, wait for the inevitable together. Maybe get into some trouble like we did as girls. Why not? There's not even a future to leave as a legacy." Her voice was quavery with contained emotion, maybe even embarrassment. I knew she was serious.

"How long do I have to think about it?" I said.

"Long as you want. Take your time." She poured more wine in my empty glass and took a seat again.

"What kind of trouble were you thinking about?"

"Anything our impaired brain cells can come up with," Phoebe said. My friend looked up from her lap, and grinned.

I Dot-messaged her two days later, after a vision I tried my best not to have.

I'd watched movies on the wall monitor, old mindless movies about adventure and plunder that winked at what such pursuits really led to. Then, when my Per Diem Energy Cache expired, I sat in the suddenly quiet room, looking out the glass block window that distorted everything I might have been able to witness outside, and it was just as well. The blur of a passing HoverBug, or the metallic bundle of a midair collision (and what was left of the people in it) sinking to the ground under a forlorn rag of white emergency chute. Smoke in an array of grays, yellows, and beiges. Angry exclamations muffled by masks, or listless eyes with nothing left to say.

I thought of the loneliness I felt, now that I had been offered an alternative. Before, I hadn't realized I was lonely; I had just spent my days as if they were in endless supply.

My message to Phoebe read: *Hw mch r u askn fr rnt?*

She Dotted back immediately, which told me she'd been waiting:

Nt mch. A thsnd inclds evrthng.

That was less than half of what I paid for a cramped hovel whose corners had so many layers of grunge it was part of the building's structural integrity. Still, I didn't want to seem too desperate. *Mght as wll*, I Dotted.

My vision was something clearer than what showed through my window, though not completely formed. In it, an orange glow illuminated skin and sand and water. A palm tree burned, but the flames were shaped like the fronds, almost as if the fire grew slowly on its subjects rather than attacking them. Around me were many, many people, some I sensed I knew and some I didn't. The only one I recognized was by the puff of her white hair taking on the orange.

Ys. Mght as wll, she Dotted back.

Chapter 2
Live Ones

What had I gotten myself into?

Moving from solitude to built-in companionship overnight was a lot like waking from a state of sleep and finding myself in the middle of a convention without belonging to any political party, and not too keen on picking one. I was sometimes cross with Phoebe when I had no legitimate cause to be—when she'd laugh at a passage in one of her beloved books she was memorizing for the umpteenth time, for example, or when she asked me if I wanted rye toast, as if it were a delicacy whose appeal was born again each morning. Or when she stared, slack-jawed, at the news we watched on the monitor wall, and her head bobbed down and up in a prelude to sleep. We had blocked out times to use our Per Diem Energy Cache for the floor we occupied, times when the monitor was hers, times when it was mine, and times when we watched together. Our PDEC was far more than the allotment I'd had in my single room. Still I begrudged her the time she had control of it. I had to pause and remind myself, *Dessa, you agreed to this*, yet often I was overcome with resentment to the point I'd banish myself to my room. There I sat with my Hawaiian-style furniture, too tropical to blend with her Danish Modern pieces throughout the rest of our living space, and stared out the window my eyes could actually see through. I confess I even resented not being blind anymore to the outside world, and turned away from the haze that seldom cleared and the people who were far less lucky than I was in their living arrangements. Some of them slept on the damp concrete of public bathrooms. There was a recent court case involving a man who sued LA County, claiming to have been misled by official signs that directed him to *restrooms*. Shortly thereafter, new signs were stamped out pointing the way to public *lavatories*.

I planned to move again as soon as I found a studio with a private bath. In dreaming of this escape from companionship, I calmed down enough to accept it. Maybe that's how we learn to live with anything—by plotting a way out, and day after day deciding to stay put.

Besides, the move was not without benefit.

I loved leaving the decades of congealed grime, and sorting through the garbage of my life. I left a note for my unseen bathroom mate: "Hey Big Guy, Please learn to clean up after yourself so the next person doesn't gag on your messes. Who toilet trained you—a wooly mammoth?" I disposed of divorce papers governing agencies cared nothing about, having more pressing concerns on their dockets, and time working against them; I threw out photographs no one would be left to care about, keeping only a few I might want to pore over to remind myself of wedding days, birthday parties, vacations at lost and lovely places. Maui. Bimini. Apollonia on the island of Sifnos. Venice. I tossed cards and letters from people I had forgotten or wanted to forget, but kept those that reminded me I'd lived a life. I sensed every now and then I'd need to assure myself of that.

I saved the receiving blanket I'd wrapped my son in, Theodore Hauser Daly, small and slim as an evening purse, and the hat and booties I'd knitted him. I felt duty bound to keep them, since he would never grow into them. I'm not sure about the logic in that reasoning, but there it was. The blanket had long since lost his sweet, temporary smell, but at times I could almost imagine it.

I knew I would stay after I told Phoebe about Theo.

She didn't coax the story out of me; it was in me, waiting to be delivered just as he had been: painfully, and with little hope. I was barely at twenty-three weeks when the contractions came in earnest.

I simply started talking one night when Phoebe and I headed to our rooms for sleep, after the late-night comedy newscast we chose over the actual news. People had been doing this for years, substituting entertainment for fact. Nothing could be made of real knowledge anyway, since even our votes had stopped being more than metaphor, like saluting the flag, or burning it.

Phoebe trundled down the hall, singing, "Now it's time to say goodnight, goooooood-night, goooooood-night," which she did as habitually as she ate rye toast, but what I said stopped her before she disappeared behind her door.

"I had a child once. Not a stillborn, not a miscarriage—a live birth that didn't last much longer than thoughts I have these days."

Her heavy-lidded eyes stretched open. "Want to talk about it, Dess?"

"Why do you think I mentioned it?" I said this with a nasty edge, as though she were responsible for the whole ordeal. It was almost as if I wanted to punish her with my story because she'd been so kind to me. We humans, as a species, are prone to lash out at kindness and cower at cruelty. Not our finest tendency.

It all came burbling out of me, though: I hadn't really wanted a child at forty-one, although lots of other women of our era were having babies later in life with great joy and anticipation, and my husband, Jerry, was thrilled. He'd said, *I'm still shooting live ones*, and took me out dancing at the Hyatt Newporter, before it got turned into apartments. (All habitable space was now apartments—that, or Distress Centers.) But I didn't eat well, didn't take in enough fruits and vegetables and proteins, and succumbed to my cravings for ice cream, which did have calcium in it, after all, and shave ice, popsicles, anything cold because the hormonal surges caused me to sweat all the time. I was not a radiant pregnant woman. I didn't glow, except for the hot flashes. I especially didn't like the way my aging belly skin—damaged from years of being a sun goddess in southern California—started to stretch like the leather of an old satchel. (*Remember the lengths we went to fry ourselves, Phoebe?* I asked, and she nodded, pulling at the crepey skin on her forearm.) I slathered on the cocoa butter as an antidote to stretch marks, and when we'd go out for dinner and drinks with friends, they ordered tropical cocktails, even in February, because the smell was so suggestive, and I sipped on a sparkling water with lemon, feeling like a big bulging scratch 'n' sniff sticker. Jerry was the one who glowed, really. I sat around reading trashy tabloids. Couldn't possibly concentrate on anything else, with the flashes, and my feet up on the coffee table because my ankles were as big around as orchid pots. It was the only time he waited on me, popsicle after popsicle. Orange was my favorite. I tried not to think about the two years of stinky diapers I had ahead of me. Then I went into early labor, and they could tell this baby was coming at the hospital, coming fast. The pain was unbelievably awful, so intense I bellowed, and though he was barely a pound, he might as well have been full-term. The minute I caught sight of him, so tiny and perfect on the outside, I couldn't imagine not wanting him. I wanted him more than anything I'd ever wanted in my entire life, more than money or to be loved for my true self or world peace. I wanted that little purplish person. They rushed him out of the room, and Jerry followed. After what seemed like only a few minutes but was really more than an hour, I guess, Jerry came back. His mask was off. My regular doctor was gone, too, and there was a neonatal specialist in front of me, saying, *We're sorry, it's untenable*, and I said, *What? What's untenable? Be specific.* He said, *Your baby's survival. Intestinal malformation, lungs don't respond to treatment. We can keep him alive on machines he'll need for the rest of his life, or you can hold him until he passes.* I held him. I held Theo, wrapped in a blanket he didn't really need to keep him warm because he would never have a chance to get sick. His head was the size of a tennis ball. I held him until he stopped breathing, and then I kept holding him and wouldn't let anyone take him. I screamed and spit and threatened to kill anyone who touched him. I'm sure they sedated me because when I woke up, Theo was gone, and Jerry was looking at me with a stare as huge and blank as a blown wall monitor. A couple months later he left me after I made a remark about his "live ones" not being lively as he'd thought.

As I finished, Phoebe stood with her arms clutched to her torso, as if she were holding the child I'd just told her about, or maybe one she'd dreamed up herself. She wasn't crying. The premise of holding a dead baby goes beyond sadness, into a realm of emotion that's not suited to a single word, and that a collection of words would trivialize.

When we were girls, I razzed Phoebe about her sensitivity, as afraid of it as I was of my gift. I liked her for it now. Which is why I then told her that, several times during my unsuccessful pregnancy, I saw a vision of a small white shoebox, next to a pile of dirt.

"I'm not sure I understand," she said, and dropped her arms. "Are you saying you caused his death with a recurring hallucination?"

"No," I said. "I knew he was going to die. I have these visions a lot. Have had them my entire life."

Many questions were in her stare, and I said, "Yeah, as a child I had them. When Pierce tried to hang himself on Volare's leash, after your folks gave the dog away? I knew that would happen. And I don't know if I threw up because I knew it, and saw it for real, or because I was relieved he was still alive, despite the vision."

She tilted her head and looked at me for a long time. Finally she said, "Jesus God, Dessa. What a burden you've borne. All that, and two husbands." She put her arms around me, even though my body was rigid with the shock of showing myself to someone, and I was still a good half-foot taller than she was. Our spines had shrunk at the same rate, I suppose. Her head bumped against my chin and clacked my teeth together, and suddenly we both began laughing, then the laughter turned to confused tears.

I said, "I think I tried not to love him. You know, because I knew he was going to die, I tried not to." I sobbed in giant howls I'd been saving up for who knows how many years, calendars full of howls, unwritten journals of them.

Phoebe walked me over to the couch, sat me down and made some chamomile tea. She had tins of tea she stockpiled and used for specific events, like the hysterical, ranting revelations of old childless women.

I emptied myself out. I reminded her of the ambrosia incident, and told her of how I'd helped my first husband make money in telecommunications just as the cell phone came into being. The vision I had was one that became normal for a long while, of thousands of people driving in cars, or jogging on the beach, or walking through malls in the same pose of elbow bent with hand at ear. And how I'd helped Jerry by dreaming a block of houses—shacks, really, pastel shacks—in Laguna Beach, and describing them to him because the image kept interrupting my dreams like breaking news. We cruised around Laguna one weekend to see if we could find them, and, "Bingo! Look," I said. "For sale, too." He bought the entire block for 300 grand, and within four years the property was worth close to six million. By then, he'd snapped up a few other beach shacks.

I told her I was relieved each husband I divorced, because I'd stopped being a person for either man, but was more their personal Geiger counter. I spent the settlements fast in travel. "Running away," I said. "An art I've perfected, except I've never gone far enough away from myself." I'd counted on their pensions to get me through old age.

I could tell Phoebe was tired; her eyes sagged and she did her characteristic head dip once in a while, but she stayed awake listening until 3 a.m. when I finally slowed like a runaway truck hitting a gravel ramp.

She didn't seem the least bit shocked, by the time we went to bed. "Let's sleep till lunchtime," she said. "It takes a lot of energy to be old."

When my empty body stretched out on the mattress, I felt like it was levitating. I thought, as I dozed off to the hum of my own snores and the drone of a distant Emergicopter, that the only thing better than friendship is a second chance at one.

Willow Manor

Karen Paul Holmes

What's graceful about a nursing home?
Surely not the tang of applesauce on dry breath
or Lysol cloaking incontinence.

A wheelchaired woman perches in the hall,
chirps hello more than once.
Another sleeps in a child's bed
clinging to her doll.

And what of the sighing, sighing,
the fireworks behind closed eyelids,
the praying, praying for final reckonings?
The silence when breathing stops.

And when the soul escapes?
Grace.

Flight

Diane Porter Goff

In haunting rhythm   the owl
drops her hollow notes into the rise of darkness
outside your window
and I rush to sit beside your bed   praying
she has come to bear you away on her spotted back,

away from this place where your breath whimpers and cries
and you have lost the syllables of your own name,
where bedsores etch your flesh
down to the white shine of bone.

Morning light,   the owl flown
any hope of mercy pinned
in her cruel beak.
Your eyes beckon.   "Please," you whisper,
your voice soft as down.

Perhaps the pillow   underneath your head,
the one with the white casing
we bought together that spring day
for my trousseau,
you saying,   mother to daughter,
"I want you to have a white wedding night."
and laughing with joy   that we could
speak so plainly.

If I positioned it just right
centered above your face,
when I pressed down
its two sides   would rise like wings,
the lace on one edge
a scalloped fringe of feathers.

If I could fold up my heart
and tuck it away   for just those few moments,
perhaps that pillow bird
could be your ride   out of here.

Information on My Mother's Grave

Elaine Dugas Shea

I.

Grief is overwhelming;
it stretches beyond the
shadowed gray boxes
on the death certificate.

I wasn't looking for all
that I found. Those perfumed
envelopes people save in hope
chests, forever jaundiced papers,
the legal stuff heartbeats
eventually catch up to.

A baptismal certificate saved
since 1929, a proposal to carve
in granite, signed and dated.
Photos taken in low sunlight,
a Living Will paid in full.

I didn't know my brother
struggled for fifteen minutes,
gasping for air and an
autopsy was performed.

All that information, mine
now, the only survivor.
I'm the keeper of the
smelly envelopes. They make
me sick. I'll throw them away.

Instead, I choose a clear
plastic container, place
them inside, the things I
cannot change.

Do not die, I say to
my husband, a promise
he cannot keep.

Someone else will see
these, cry sometime later.
Too many flat spaces
as we begin and end life.

II.

Mix up cookie dough
plump for the oven,
chocolate soldiers ready,
send them off to war.

Come back changed,
how can they tell us
of events unspoken.
Conversations wait
until hair turns silver,

whispers soften, old
stories begin to flow.

His blue eyes sparkled
when he told the stories
remembering every detail,
each piece of lint
pressed in his mind.

I asked him
to salute one last time.
He did so proudly, smiling,
knowing he could.

His body began to wither,
dying, he worked every breath
moment by moment. Sadie, his nurse,
knew; *He's waiting for someone
else to come*, she said.

We looked at each other
not realizing he was waiting
for Al, his only son who walked
into the Spirit World three
years earlier. Soldiers together,
Dad needed help crossing over
to the Holy Road.

How do I lift my wings and fly? he
asked. *It's easy, Dad. I'll hold on
to you. When you're ready, we'll take off.
And then, you must let go my hand.*

Crossword

Elaine Handley

For Ginger Swanson

What transfiguration
manifested
as you sat on your couch
working a crossword?
Did you hear angels singing like Sinatra?
Did your life race
across the newspaper, MTV style?
Were you startled by white light
coming from the kitchen?

I am puzzled
by your sudden disappearance.
I thought you'd linger
for a goodbye, one more
cup of tea, a scan of our horoscope,
instructions
for a life down and across
without you.

But then, could there be
a better way
than your heart giving out
over finding
just the right
word?

A Certain Age

Jennifer Soule

When her friend Nora died
Mom finally learned her age
from the obituary page.
As young waitresses, they balanced
high those heavy trays on long nights
at the Minnekada Country Club.
Outside of work they shared
two-for-one Tuesday burgers
braved blizzards for *Cat on a Hot Tin Roof*
shopped Crazy Dayz bargains
drank a forest of coffee beans
but enjoyed a zinfandel as well.

Yet women of their generation
did not share the private details
worries and woes of spouse or bills.
Nora never mentioned cancer
until the month before her death:
I'm terminal. Enough. Not weaned
on talk show confessions, they smiled
through tears and laughed in the wind.
Secrets remained secrets.

Elegy for Yellow

Elizabeth Bernays

In April, the pale sulfur yellow of paloverde tree blooms drapes the lower slopes of the hills as far as I can see from the flat roof of my house in the Sonoran Desert, and it is so dense I am reminded of trees weighed down by heavy snowfall.

As the paloverdes begin, the Engelmann prickly pear flowers bejewel the gray-green expanses of cactus with their round spine-covered pads. Large, shiny, butter-yellow cups open as the sun rises high, attracting cactus bees to a dense pool of yellow pollen within. As evening falls, the petals close in, but open again next day an orange-yellow before their final demise. For miles, the spots of shiny yellow with the shrouds of sulfur above cover the desert with a glory that belies the harshness of the place. Deep storage roots of the paloverde and extensive opportunistic surface roots of prickly pears are strategies. Naturally, a good winter rainfall ensures an intensely yellow spring.

There are certain hillsides where brittlebush abounds, a small gray-leaved shrub that exudes a sticky resin from broken branches. In mid-April these shrubs shoot out an army of buds and one day, the hillsides are suddenly yellow with their big bright daisy flowers. Some have dark centers, but most are solid yellow. I don't have such a hillside in my four-acre patch of desert, but I planted a few and from my bedroom window in spring I can enjoy two brittlebushes, their dense daisy flowers a solid gold between two pale paloverde gowns.

But that is not all. In patches and along pathways and roadsides, long stems of desert sunflower pop up with a yellow flower so brilliant it makes one blink. Foot-high mounds of clear yellow paper-flower dot some areas, while tiny mounds of orange-yellow dyssodia take other spots, sometimes converging into extensive mats where no steps in between are possible. And there are lesser players. Dark yellow trixis daisies show up in sheltered corners or amongst prickly pears. Dull yellow catkins of flowers hang from the newly greened mesquite trees, creamy yellow rods of small flowers mass over catclaw acacia, and small orange-yellow balls make a scattering of decorations on white thorn acacia.

As the yellow springtime reaches a climax, paloverde blooms begin to fall. Yellow petals blow in the wind and under each tree a yellow carpet forms, slightly darker than the sulfur boughs above. The desert is now more yellow than ever, with little gray or green or brown to notice. Leafcutter ants collect the flowers, armies of them tromping from the carpets to their nest entrances, dropping yellow all along the way, until the desert floor is criss-crossed with yellow pathways. And one realizes how common are these underground dwellers, how abundant and how much a part of the desert. The final removal of so much material to their underground fungus gardens must be a major recycling event here.

By mid-May just a few dots of yellow remain on the trees, an occasional last prickly pear flower opens that will probably not be pollinated now that the cactus bees are done. The paper-flowers and desert sunflowers have faded to cream. Shriveled scraps of paper adorn prickly pear pads. The yellow show is over for now and gives way to searing heat and the high white flowers of the giant saguaros.

It was springtime in the desert when Reg died. As he weakened during April, the show was just beginning. I lay in bed beside him in the mornings, looking out onto the different yellows. We held hands but rarely spoke. Not that he was unable to, or that we had nothing to say, but rather that our hearts were full and our lives fulfilled together, and the unsaid words hovering around us were enough.

Sometimes he said, "Loves," and I replied, "Loves." Then he would squeeze my hand lightly and look the other way.

We drank early morning tea in bed in those weeks. Sitting up

one could see more of the yellow desert and watch Gila woodpeck-
ers at a nest in our closest saguaro. We could hear the baby birds
inside and noticed that, as days passed, the parents brought food more
frequently, between them returning to the hole high in the saguaro
twenty times an hour. We saw one of them chase off a kestrel. We
noticed how rare it was for the nest to be left with neither parent.

With my help, Reg had been struggling in to the research lab
for weeks, but now he rested: "Just don't want to do anything now,
Mom." And I thought about our thirty-seven years of partnership,
our long-lived love. We both knew we had been among the lucky
ones, but what was he thinking then? He never told.

It was when the United States invaded Iraq, and whenever I
heard a plane overhead from Davis-Monthan Air Force Base, I was
reminded of young people dying in a foreign place, innocent people
in Iraq dying violently, while Reg died slowly from a common disease. We had lived so many good years, and I felt the happiness of
what had been, even more as I felt his approaching death and saw
his weakness increase daily.

The hospice nurse came for the evaluation a month before he
died. She sat beside him as I stood at the foot of the bed and she
asked, "So you want to stay here?"

Reg turned to look through the sliding glass doors out to the
desert, a small pool, and the ramada we had built, and waved his
hand: "Look."

Then she turned to me with eyebrows raised, and I said, "Yes."

"Of course—we will arrange everything for you here."

And so she did. We had oxygen, wheelchair, commode, mattress
covers, shower stool, and, of course, drugs. Nurse Martha visited
every other day and provided phone numbers for emergencies.
There was a peaceful finality; friends left us alone. And all the time
we had the yellow desert to look at, the big paloverde tree across the
pool from the bedroom window with the first falling flowers floating
on the water under a clear blue sky.

Strange to think that more than a third of our life together was under the cloud of leukemia. It was diagnosed in July 1990. Two years later he had the first major chemotherapy, then splenectomy. Family came and went as years passed. It seemed that time was running out with determination: how to use our time and what was worth doing? I resigned from my busy job—we needed togetherness in that last yellow springtime, when the prickly pear flowers smiled in the mornings and the sulfur petals of paloverde flowers blew in the warm dry wind.

Gloom had come over us when we first knew about the leukemia.

"Oh, we can't leave our two cats," and we realized that our time left together was worth more than ever.

Reg decided to rewrite his big entomology textbook, somehow knowing the value of a major challenge. We lived each desert day with passion. We noted when the first white-winged dove arrived in spring, whether the orioles had bred successfully, or whether the cowbird had won. We watched the Harris's antelope squirrels and Gambel's quail always at the little pool and thrilled to the sight of a bobcat there one day, crouching by the hop bush alert to movement. One year we had a family of Harris hawks. The fledglings grew bigger than their parents before they succeeded in catching any prey, and squawking like spoiled children they chased after the hunting parents, until all four could share a cottontail rabbit on the ground. We measured rain and plotted out weather patterns. We monitored growth of our seventy-one saguaros, from those that were tiny seedlings to great monsters with arms. We pushed on with lab work and we rushed to operas, concerts, and plays. In New York and Santa Fe we knew it was the last time and loved them more than ever. Then monoclonal therapies, bone-thin legs, skin flaking, constant exhaustion.

All through the last winter I worked frantically on an experiment as he watched from his chair, struggling to assist, analyzing data at home. Blood calcium rose to danger levels, CT scans showed the tumors, coordination suffered. Insecurity, dependence. I got a cell phone at last. At chemotherapy sessions I took notes on all the conversations between the cancer nurse and the six or seven patients in the room. Finally treatment of last resort abandoned. We behaved as if it was not so bad, as if somehow this time would pass and a better time would come.

We sat in the Arizona room in the evenings enjoying cottontail rabbit foraging activities on the seed not yet eaten by quail and mourning doves on the patio, the last hummingbirds to feed at the chuperosa flowers, the first bats and night hawks to sweep across the dusk.

Each of us said, "Hasn't it all been wonderful, amazing, extraordinary?" And we held hands tightly. Then the last scan, the last visit to the doctor when massive tumors were shown, and Reg's pulse found to be 160. There in the doctor's office he said, "My darling Lizzie, I am glad it will be quick for you now."

As spring came he seemed to want to escape something.

"I am so anxious in my muscles, Lizzie."

"Lizzie, make my bed outdoors."

"Got to get out, got to get out," his slurred weak voice complained.

"I got lost in the night because the house is full of empty spaces."

He wanted to fix all the financial files but got so confused the papers became a jumbled heap. I had to leave him to it.

Everything tasted bad.

"No good," he said when I gave him his favorite pasta.

"Funny, you used to make such nice tea."

More Valium and morphine, and I had to keep watch—pills all over on the floor in the mornings.

It was early afternoon, and he had managed to get up, find socks (odd ones) and put on clothes from the heap of washing. He had the buttons of his shirt in the wrong buttonholes. I put on the video of the opera Falstaff. It seemed a good choice—not too taxing, funny but not too funny, and so tender a treatment of a silly old man. But his eyes closed soon and his face was gray. After the first act:

"Got to go to bed now."

"I feel terrible," came the muddy voice.

"Can't swallow."

The day came when he could no longer drink but the struggling continued. People came and went. Then he became unresponsive. I sat and held his hand as I gazed out at the yellow desert. The paloverde trees still in full bloom, late that year, after the cool spring, and the prickly pears covered in yellow cups. It was a perfect Tucson day with a bright blue sky. His eyes closed and he no longer responded to my putting his adored cat on him. I talked to him all our love words. I kissed his smooth face as his breaths became irregular, his hands cold.

He died in the early afternoon and I held his lifeless body for some time. I was glad to have time then to sit alone with him, to have him completely to myself, to look at the falling yellow flowers and know that he loved it here and that we had some of the best times in the leukemia-filled years. I thought of all the days of happiness we had in this desert place, the thirteen yellow springtimes, the increasing passion for the colors of life. I know he valued ever more the things he loved as death got closer—me, the cat, Schubert's octet, family, wild animals, and the desert scene. For all these things he cried with love, knowing that the great darkness would engulf him soon and forever.

I said to him a few days before he died, "Why did we think of the Hemlock Society?" And he answered unhesitatingly, "I suppose we thought it would be worse than it is." He had already thought about that.

At last I contacted the hospice nurse, who called the proper people and said the kindest words. I signed papers and she emptied morphine down the sink. In just an hour two women (mother and daughter, it turned out) came to take him for the medical school as part of the body donation program. "Say goodbye," said the mother as she readied the blanket. I kissed him for the last time. How quickly he had turned to ivory. His forehead was as smooth as glass on my lips.

I loved him, and most of what I did for all those years was to make him proud and happy. And I knew he had loved me too much. I wondered what motive there would ever be to carry on the research he loved, to analyze data, combat popular passing theories, to write the poems he loved to hear me read, to do anything, really. I wondered how I would be able to bear the sight of paloverde flowers.

Sometimes I wonder what it was that drew me to Reg in the first place and what it was that made everything work so well. Nothing about him fitted any vision of love or romantic idea of a mate. His appearance at thirty-five was plain. He had a round rather puffy face, prominent mole on one cheek, a large and somewhat flattened nose, slightly prognathous jaw with teeth that were clearly not his own. He stared out through horn-rimmed glasses and his expression at rest was one of dissatisfaction. He had an unathletic body as far as could be judged, and rolled-up sleeves revealed the silvery sign of psoriasis on his elbows.

We sometimes went to The Gloucester pub for lunch and one day we made a detour on the way back to work and sat for a while in Bloomsbury Square. We passed a desultory time in the lovely London scene, chilly, on a corner bench under a plane tree. I noticed how strangely muscular his arms looked because he wore his jacket over the rolled up sleeves of his shirt. I noticed his old cloth cap with a tear at the back. As we stood to leave he turned and kissed me on the mouth and I had never been so surprised. It was at that moment that my life changed forever, with a passion sudden and ferocious. The turmoil of that first and only love was shocking. And it grew for thirty-seven years.

Until that day in Bloomsbury Square I doubted the stories of excessive love; they had to be nonsense, the very idea of it a chimera. The experience I had always thought to be total exaggeration was exaggerated in myself to a degree more than worthy of Juliet.

We were also lucky to join hands in a career of entomology, to enjoy so much else together, share almost all our interests. Reg had trained me to be a scientist, guided my research, taught me how to experiment, made me love silly jokes, and we traveled the world for work and vacation. I think back through my life with him and remember watching grasshoppers together among yellow butter-cups in an English field, chasing locusts in the Australian outback, finding ecological answers to pest problems in Nigeria, in India, in the Philippines, emigrating to the United States and feeling so free in Berkeley, and ending up on the edge of Tucson, Arizona, where the desert became our happy home and the yellow flowers gave us such joy every spring.

It seems that yellow threaded through our lives, as if it bound us in some bright joyful place. Reg always maintained that dandelions were more important than all the rare orchids, and far from being a pest the little yellow suns in rich green sward were a source of great plea-sure for most people, ordinary people. He explained how yellow was a super-stimulus for plant-feeding insects, how yellow was the strongest floral color for pollinators, how yellow daffodils in an English spring made him so glad. He ran student experiments in the fields of Sussex, in which yellow-painted dishes full of soapy water became water traps for insects and a means of monitoring populations of certain bugs, a way of testing the attractiveness of added chemicals, a tool for testing the favored size of flowers for little insects.

"Yellow," he said, "is the brightest color, a symbol of color itself."

"Yes," I replied, "yellow is the symbol even of life: a yellow sun, a yellow moon, a strand of yellow poppies, a flight of pierid butterflies, a color to lighten loads."

We left it at that. Both of us were elated by the expanses of daffodils in Kensington Gardens that spring, but it was rare for Reg to say so much.

Of course, each color has its special appeal. The blue of jacarandas from my childhood still makes me think fondly of all my young days and the color of dark blue lobelia can send shivers down my spine. The orange of California poppies and the scarlet of flame trees pierce something in my brain, and the greens of grasses and trees give such peace to my heart. Yellow, though, makes me smile and gives joy, the joy of sunny days and golden sunsets. Yellow reminds me of buttercups in English fields where I felt so young and full of Wordsworth, of laburnum in the front garden of my childhood home where I lay and looked into the yellow heavens of my future, and of my very first memories being in the garden with Mama where she grew yellow roses that had a faint pink blush and were called, I think, "Peace."

We think of colors as fixed properties of things, and so they are as measured by instruments. And so they are as seen by eyes with color vision. And yet I have to think that people vary in how intensely they see or experience color, as Reg and I seemed to, except perhaps in the realm of yellows. There, I could tell, we both found a kind of glory that flooded our minds and hearts, pushing aside the countless details of our lives and bringing daylight to dark reflections.

In the spring of 1988 in California, we heard that the southern desert was springtime colorful and we drove south. The Tehachapi slopes were totally golden, Death Valley was a riot of yellows, and while all the other colors were there, it was the yellow that fixated itself on our memories, the yellow that shows best in all our photographs, the yellow that fills my heart now with the memories of that spring.

And so to Arizona and the years of desert yellows.

It is fitting that Reg died in spring, surrounded by all the shades of yellow that fill April and early May. And it makes me glad that he ended his life looking out onto the glory of it, that he loved it more each year, that he loved it more as he approached death. That somehow, he wanted to live to see another day of yellow, right until the last one. That he didn't want to cut the days short because he felt so bad. And all those years we talked of euthanasia, gave money to the Right to Die, and Death with Dignity, yet it was good to live the extra days, good to see that last golden sunset, good to see the paloverde one more time. One more time.

Now, with years passing and pain still potent, I look out at the desert and dream of that last spring, that time of yellow glory. And mixed with all the bittersweet of times gone, love past, is the still-strong, more-strong, always-strong ecstasy of all that I see from the window, all that I see in my desert walks, and always the springtime flowers—the yellows of the May-time Sonoran Desert.

Out of Pathos, Pothos

Mary Kolada Scott

The potted plant the office sent
after his second heart attack
grows rampant.

Vines take over the dining room.
Heart-shaped leaves spread
shadows across the nook.

Devil's ivy wraps around the hutch
like a shawl drawn over shoulders.

I can't bear to cut it back.

While I Was Dead

Phyllis J. Manning

On Friday in mid-April, my husband died with little pain and great dignity. The charge nurse at the hospital told me, "You need to call Social Security."

I nodded.

Then our longtime doctor hugged me. "You okay?"

Not really trusting my voice, I murmured, "This was . . . no surprise."

"But we're never really ready."

I nodded again.

She squeezed my hand with both of hers. "Soon as possible—early next week will do—phone Social Security."

"Social Security," I repeated as she disappeared down the hallway.

Then the funeral home counselor gave me a "To Do" list containing a bolded toll-free number with "SOCIAL SECURITY" in all caps.

I dialed the 800 number on Tuesday and went through a series of automated voices until a human tone reached my ear. "How may I help you?"

Identifying myself, I told her the situation.

"No notification yet," she said. "You need to mail in a death certificate immediately."

"The funeral home promised death certificates within ten working days."

An edge in her voice: "But you called here anyway?"

"I was told—by everyone—to call you as soon as possible."

"You say your husband died last Friday. This is Tuesday. That's 'as soon as possible'?"

I let my breath out slowly. "Yes."

She asked several routine questions about address and phone. Then: "Was this a first marriage?"

"Second, for both of us."

"Two prior divorces?" Disapproving. She asked for and I supplied the date of my divorce and the date of our subsequent marriage. Then: "And the date of your recently deceased husband's divorce?"

"I don't know."

"You don't know the date of your husband's divorce? Yet you married him?"

More deep breaths by me. "Yes. Almost forty years ago. I may have known once, but not now. Is—is it important?"

"Madam, I do not ask unimportant questions! Now, the date of his divorce—?"

"—Would have been well before we met. He and his former wife lived a thousand miles apart—and had for years."

"I cannot believe that you don't know the date of your husband's divorce."

My face heated. I felt embarrassed, guilty, stupid. But then I thought, How many second wives remember many years later a date unimportant to them in the first place? Tears were dropping onto my stack of papers, but I resented the tone of this disembodied voice coming across the line and decided to speak up.

"You know, ma'am, people who make this kind of call aren't in the best spirits, anyway. And when you scold and find fault—well—it's unpleasant."

Dripping sarcasm: "I am so sorry to wound your delicate sensibilities—"

My jaw clenched. "What is your name, please?"

Pause. "Carolyn."

"Well, Carolyn, I think I'll hang up now and call later to talk to someone else."

"But we're practically finished."

"We are finished, Carolyn."

"This is dumb, lady. Only about ten more questions—why?"

"Because I prefer a civil—uh—thank you." My shaking hand put down the receiver. Two hours later, I phoned again and started over. This time, my courteous agent was not unduly disturbed when I confessed to not knowing, more than four decades after the fact, the date of my husband's divorce. She tried, but located nothing online about the earlier Social Security phone conference.

My first clue that something was amiss came when I went for a scheduled doctor's appointment a few weeks later. "You're not listed on Medicare anymore," the secretary told me. She double-checked, then contacted my HMO.

"That person is deceased." I heard the words clearly across the line.

"But she's here, talking to me right now," the secretary protested.

Secure Horizons, however, was adamant.

Confused, I canceled my appointment "until we get things straightened out."

At home, I tried to inform Medicare, but could get no human voice and the nature of my query fitted none of their automated categories. When I myself phoned the HMO, the agent was confident that I had died in April.

"My husband did, but not me. I'm talking to you right now."

"We have no way of knowing who's talking to us. Medicare has the woman as deceased."

"Look, I'll come to your office and prove who I am, and you can make a copy of my husband's death certificate and get the record right."

"Not here. It's Medicare you have to convince."

"So where's Medicare actually located?"

"I have no idea."

A few days later arrived a letter from Social Security addressed "To the Survivors of . . . Phyllis J. Manning."

Since I could find in the phone book no local phone number, I had that mailing in hand when the Social Security office opened the next morning.

"Let me check." The pleasant worker punched some keys, frowned, punched some more, then swiveled to face me.

"You are recently deceased."

I nodded. "And yet, here I am—talking to you."

She grinned. "Can you prove it's you?"

Deliberately loaded with identification, I could and did.

"And your husband?"

I gave the name and presented the death certificate.

"A mix-up. According to the record, he's alive."

"Can you correct the record?"

"I can try." She didn't sound as hopeful as I might have wished.

There followed weeks of mail addressed to my "survivors"—and of my going daily to the Social Security office. It opens at nine, weekdays only. I was first to snap a number off the machine by the door.

"Yesterday," I told the attendant, "my family got papers to sign so they get the close-out on my life insurance. And you know that I presently have no health insurance, no Social Security check, no teaching pension."

"We've corrected the record at this office," the sympathetic woman told me, "but Medicare doesn't want to change—and it's that record people check."

Days passed. I watched Social Security employees open their service window, see omnipresent me waiting there, and walk away to be replaced by some agent who, presumably, had less tenure. I was pleasant. Patient. But also persistent—especially for a cadaver—and I was a perpetual reminder that all was not well with The System.

I heard one agent talk to State Teacher Retirement in Sacramento. "This office certifies absolutely that she is alive, apparently well, is in fact standing before me."

She hung up. "I think it worked, for now. Nothing's going to help if we can't get Medicare to respond."

"You're good," I told her. "You think you could convince my HMO?"

She just looked at me.

I thanked her and left, the morning routine complete. No money had come into my bank account for more than three months. My doctor's office was calling several times a week. "Phyl, we need to know you're okay. Just come in."

"Not until I have insurance. I'm fine physically, not depressed, just baffled. And I'm staying busy, believe me. Don't worry."

The physician herself called. "Come for a chat—old friends, no charge."

My pride is almost tangible. I don't rack up bills I may not be able to pay, and I don't take charity. Besides, what if something were wrong physically? "I'll call when I have insurance."

One thing was certain: I had to get some kind of job. Substitute teaching was the most logical and immediate possibility. So I called, took in papers and TB clearance to several districts, and was informed that because of recent national events (this was 2001), I now needed my fingerprints in the federal file.

No problem. I made an appointment at the county sheriff's office. Gone are the days when officers ink up your fingers and roll them across white paper. Now it's high tech—and the deputy charged with the task couldn't get prints from my fingers clear enough that the computer would accept them. She passed the task to others, who oiled and talcumed and soaped variously but to no avail.

One held my fingers up to the light and examined them one by one. "They're kind of smooth," she told me, "and a lot of the whorls are broken." She tried again. Nothing. "Look, the regular technician is off today. She can get prints off a billiard ball. Could you come back first thing tomorrow morning?"

I could and did. A confident deputy laughed about the inexpert efforts of her predecessors. "Everyone has fingerprints," she assured me. But after eight or ten tries, she too was mystified. "Did you ever sand off your prints for some reason?" she asked.

I laughed. "My fingers have been very busy for a long time," I told her. "Oh, and I also did stained glass for years. Lots of cuts, I suppose."

"You have no prints left."

"But I have to have something on file!"

She shook her head, shrugged.

I drove home close to despair. I thought I was still alive, even though the system didn't. But now—without fingerprints—should I just close my eyes and stop breathing and make all cyberspace giddy with joy? On impulse, I stopped in at the local school district office in Chico and explained my dilemma.

"Ridiculous!" the clerk told me. "Here, I'll phone the university." And she did. I was not hopeful three days later when I walked in for my appointment and saw the very same type of ornery machine which had eschewed my fingers in the nearby county. Especially when a snip of a student who looked twelve years old announced that she was the technician. Should I warn her that I'd had previous problems with this big black creature? That I was officially dead?

But I simply smiled and murmured, "Good luck."

She got acceptable prints on her first try. My fervent "Thank you!" made her raise her eyebrows. Now I could earn enough to tide me over until Medicare and the pension and health insurance got sorted out. Okay, Federal System—you're going to owe me so much money and maybe even an apology.

Soon, I had insurance through Blue Shield, a company which took its agent's word—as he stood facing me in our living room— that I did indeed exist. That important fact apparently seeped into

Medicare records, as well. Within a few weeks, my pension arrived at the bank—in fact several months' worth—along with Social Security.

The phone call from Secure Horizons came late one afternoon. "Mrs. Phyllis J. Manning?" A bouncing voice filled with enthusiasm.

"Yes."

"Mrs. Manning, I have terrific news for you."

"Oh?"

"Your health insurance is reinstated—retroactively!"

"Retroactively," I echoed.

"Isn't that wonderful?" All resonant with good cheer. "Your insurance is back, and it's retroactive!"

"But—why would I want it retroactive? I already canceled doctor appointments."

"But ma'am! Reinstated retroactively. As if it were never gone!"

I thought of the dozen or so hours I'd spent on the HMO line waiting, waiting, waiting for a human voice—only to be told that there was nothing to be done or—twice—that the workday was now concluded, and would I like to try tomorrow? And this woman had simply touch-toned my number and here we were talking.

"Can you give me one single advantage to me in what you're offering? I now have insurance with another company."

Silence.

Then it struck me: What a scam! "You've been taking automatic deductions from my inactive checking account? Even though I had no insurance—no need for it since you insisted that I was dead—you took the money, anyway?"

"An error. Two separate parts of our company. But now that you're reinstated retroactively—"

"—No reinstatement! Retroactively or otherwise! And please refund every penny you took from my account after mid-April."

"But our insurance—"

"—Was getting more expensive every quarter. May I expect a

refund check within this next week?"

"That's too soon—"

"—All right, I'll wait two weeks before I contact my attorney."

As if I had an attorney. . . . But the woman agreed and the refund actually did arrive in a mere twelve days.

That was it, then. I was officially back among the living with Medicare and Social Security and all of the agencies that follow their lead. I had health insurance now, and pension money coming in—and daily jobs besides, as many as I wanted. I had learned a valuable lesson, too: Don't ruffle the feathers of a federal bird with pecking capability. I'll always believe that the mix-up was caused deliberately by that coot who called herself "Carolyn."

All through this ordeal, putting one foot before the other, trying to do what had to be done and somehow get by, I had believed that the matter would be funny in retrospect, no longer a black hole— sure, blackly humorous, but amusing nevertheless. Medicare never did apologize. Still, after that last phone call from the HMO, I felt good. In fact, alive at last. Still, it has taken some time for the laughter to come.

Instructions upon the Occasion of My Death

Mary E. O'Dell

First, cry a lot.

But while you're crying, scoop out the litter box.
People will be coming in,
and you won't want the place smelling like cat pee.

Then, light candles.
Not the church kind but whatever's around the house—
those that smell like cookies baking, or apple pie.

That night, cook a big old pot roast
with carrots, potatoes, and onions
and maybe a turnip.

Do what you will with my body,
it's worn out anyway.
Likewise, my clothes and shoes and furniture.

But handle my books with reverence.
Screw up here,
and I'll find a way to haunt you.

When the day is over, put your feet up,
get a big bowl of ice cream and watch a few
M*A*S*H reruns. Hawkeye's going to miss me.

And finally, don't believe them
when they say life's too short.
It's just long enough.

PROSE POEM

News of My Death

Janet Sunderland

I woke suddenly, hearing chatter from a cop car radio, and discovered four policemen, dressed in blue and fully armed, surrounding my car, and one said, "What are you doing here?" and I said, "Taking a nap in the shade," and he said, "We got a report of a woman dead or passed out; you been drinking?" and I said, "No, I've been taking a nap," and he said, "Why here? Can I see your driver's license?" and I said, "Sure. My son lives here. Only he's not here," and as I gave the license to him, I reached for the registration to the car, since he'd want that next I figured, and my cell phone rang and it was my other son and he said, "Yo!" like he always says and then, "Happy birthday," and I said, "Thanks, but right now I have four cops surrounding me," and he said, "What happened?" and I said I'd taken an afternoon nap in front of his brother's apartment and somebody reported me dead and he asked if I wanted him to call me back and I said that would be good and he hung up, and then I handed the car registration to the cop, and he said, "This is a church's car," and I said, "Yes, I'm the pastor," and then I found my minister identification and handed that to him too and two of the cops got bored and said they'd go on somewhere else and the head cop said that was okay, so they did and then I was only surrounded by two cops, which isn't really surrounded but sort of anyway, and the lead cop leaned down and said this wasn't exactly a good neighborhood to fall asleep in with my car door open even if it was hot and why didn't I drive to the movie house and bookstore two blocks away so he wouldn't have to come back in case somebody really did rob or make me really dead and I said I would and then he went away, and my son, the one who lives in the apartment building from where I'd been reported dead, came striding across the grass saying he'd just got home and seen the cop cars but hadn't paid attention and then he'd gone inside and listened to his messages and had one from his brother saying, "Mom's outside your place surrounded by cops! Where are you?" and so he came downstairs and was I okay and I said yes and he said, "Happy birthday, Mom . . ." and then I laughed. Because what I really like about birthdays are surprises.

Writing a Paper on Silence

Janet McCann

taxonomy of silence
history of silence
silence in myth
       enforced silence (tongue cut out etc.)
       chosen silence (patient Griselda etc.)
       silence of the gods
silences of everyday life
pregnant silences
cold silences

footnotes fell to the bottom of the page, because the words died

the missed beat before "I love you, too" that says everything
the unanswered call down cellar steps
the humming void after he hangs up

her quiet in the face of his aggression
the nuns' peace in the long, tranquil hours,
their fingers speaking the beads

the spaces between words
the spaces where the Doctor removed the word God from all his speeches
the tree in the forest in total isolation falling

don't
shhh

When Last on the Mountain

Kaye Bache-Snyder

Late afternoon. Sun low. Shadows of alpine spruce edge across snow. My breath freezes in my nostrils. I dawdle, adjust my poles and goggles, then ski to the chairlift.

"Last ride," the operator says, as I load. "Have a good one, Ma'am."

I turn and watch him close the gate for today. Except for two men on a chair swinging above me, I ride up Big Burn Mountain alone. Cigarette smoke and French words drift back as we rise. Snowmass Peak glows on the western horizon. At the top, I unload, then pole across the ridge for my last downhill run.

From the shadows, I watch the men smoking. They wear black stretch pants with yellow stripes down muscular thighs and calves and look like racers. Will they take the expert runs through trees? I hope. I plan an easier, intermediate run down Mick's Gully, Coney Glade, than Velvet Falls. The men take their last puffs, tighten boots, stomp skis, explode downhill, and disappear in the trees.

I can hear the chairlift creaking, running empty until a few from the ski patrol ride up to scour the slopes for anyone lost or injured. I am alone here on the mountain. Snowmass Resort is a toy land below. Pushing off, I ski into my shadow. With speed, fear rises. I coach myself as I ride. "Pole, turn, edge, soft knees, eyes down-hill. Good. Good." I shed self-consciousness like dead skin, feel fire inside me. Body dances faster, faster. I stop to breathe and wipe frozen tears from my goggles. A raven lands on a bare aspen branch nearby and croaks.

I know.

Nevermore. One day, I will write my last downhill run, not on snow, but on paper. Not today. No. I dance, stop, dance, stop, dance, dance, dance down the mountain.

Practicing the Presence

Fredrick Zydek

I am sitting here, eyes closed, in silence
remembering that every one of my cells
is composed of the same atoms that make
up everything else in the universe. I am

one of the ways in which it has chosen
to be. What I am is a bit of it gathered
into one place. I am atoms and electrons
that have learned to ask questions, write

music, poetry, judicial prudence, the laws
of physics, and the recipe for apple pie.
I am present to all these atoms and they
are present to me. They are composed

of shades and strings of light. It is that
first light, that always light that burns in
them and in me. We are one in the light.
If the light were a vast ocean, I would be

one of its waves. Everything that is in
the sea is in the wave but the wave is not
the sea. It is in the presence of this truth
I practice. All that is is in me. I am its

visible manifestation, a way in which it
can contemplate itself, a place thinking
has found to dwell and a million ways
to keep itself occupied and happy.

The Editors

VICKY LETTMANN grew up in southeastern North Carolina near the Atlantic Ocean where she learned to love the smell of saltwater tides. She created Turtlehouse Ink and published *The Beach*, a collection of poems with artwork by her mother, Ruth, to capture some of those ocean smells and sounds of her childhood. For over thirty years, she taught writing and literature at a community college in Minneapolis, Minnesota, where she founded and edited the literary arts magazine *Under Construction*. She also served as an editor for *Speakeasy*, a literary magazine published by the Loft Literary Center. She writes poetry, stories, and short essays and teaches writing workshops in Minneapolis and in Sanibel, Florida, where she and her husband, John, spend the winters.

CAROL ROAN fell in love with the sound of words as a child and began singing them professionally at seventeen. Thirty years later she had begun to write her own words and was elected to Poets & Writers of New Jersey. Her two nonfiction books, *Clues to American Dance* and *Speak Easy: A Guide to Successful Performances, Presentations, Speeches and Lectures*, were written at the request of the publisher, Starrhill Press. Between those two phases of her life, she raised three children as a single mother by working as a corporate vice president and as a marketing consultant. She now teaches voice and stage presence in Winston-Salem, North Carolina, where she also edits and leads workshops in readings by writers.

Biographical Information

Diana Anhalt is a former teacher, newsletter editor and book reviewer for *The Texas Observer* and the author of *A Gathering of Fugitives: American Political Expatriates in Mexico 1948-1965* (Archer Books), recently translated into Spanish. Her short stories, poetry, and essays are published in both Mexico and the United States.

Kaye Bache-Snyder taught in universities in the U.S., Canada, and on board World Campus Afloat. A correspondent for the *Denver Post* and reporter and editor for the *Daily Times-Call* in Longmont, Colorado, she now devotes herself to writing, publishing, and teaching writing workshops at the Arvada Center for the Arts and Humanities. Finishing Line Press nominated her chapbook, *Pinnacles & Plains*, for the Pushcart Prize Anthology. She has a Ph.D. in English from the University of Wisconsin.

Bonnie Louise Barrett is a Los Angeles poet, novelist, short story writer, and playwright. An early novel, *The Badminton Court*, received a Eugene F. Saxton Memorial Award. Her poetry has appeared in *Southern California Review*, *Statement*, and *Chaparral*, among others. Her friend and high school classmate, Ray Bradbury, cites Ms. Barrett as an inspiration and dedicated his *Collected Poems* to her. She is working on her third novel, *Going to La Paz*, the story of a young girl's search for herself among the beach bums and beautiful people of Southern California in the wake of World War II. She lives in the Hollywood Hills with her husband, Laurence Wolfe.

Bruce Barton teaches writing and American literature at Mansfield University in Pennsylvania and lives in Wellsboro, Pennsylvania, with his wife, the poet Judith Sornberger. His poems and stories have appeared in a variety of literary journals over the past thirty years.

Elizabeth Bernays, who grew up in Australia, became professor of entomology at the University of California Berkeley and Regents' Professor at the University of Arizona. She also has an M.F.A. She has won several awards including the 2007 X.J. Kennedy prize for nonfiction. Website: elizabethbernays.com.

Zan Bockes earned an M.F.A. in Creative Writing from the University of Montana. Her fiction, nonfiction, and poetry have appeared in many magazines, including *Poetry Motel*, *Visions International*, *The Comstock Review*, *Cutbank*, and *Phantasmagoria*, and she has had three nominations for a Pushcart Prize.

William Borden's book-length poem *Eurydice's Song* was published by Bayeux Arts (Calgary) and St. Andrew's Press (Laurinburg, N. C.) His poems have appeared in over one hundred magazines and anthologies and in a chapbook, *Slow Step and Dance*. His novel *Dancing with Bears* was published by Livingston Press in 2008.

Betty Buchsbaum is professor emerita at Massachusetts College of Art and lives in Newton, Massachusetts, with her husband. Her book of poems, *The Love Word*, appeared in 2004 (Chicory Blue Press). Her work has appeared in two anthologies and various literary journals. She is the mother of three and grandmother of eight.

Dane Cervine's book *The Jeweled Net of Indra* was published by Plain View Press in 2007. His poems have won awards from Adrienne Rich and Tony Hoagland and have appeared in *The Sun*, the *Atlanta Review*, and *The Hudson Review*. He lives in Santa Cruz, California, along the Monterey Bay coast.

Barbara Diltz Chandler lives on ten acres of fir trees and wild meadow just outside a small Victorian-era seaport. Her poems, essays, photographs, and articles have appeared in literary magazines, newspapers and glossy monthlies. She is also the author of a nonfiction handbook on avalanche safety for backcountry travelers.

Ann Fox Chandonnet is a poet, food historian, and nonfiction writer. Raised in Massachusetts, she spent more than three decades in Alaska. She is now retired to North Carolina. Her poetry collections include *Auras: Tendrils* and *The Wife & Other Poems*.

Sharon L. Charde, a retired family therapist, has been published in over twenty journals and anthologies, and has two prizewinning chapbooks, *Bad Girl at the Altar Rail* (Flume Press) and *Four Trees Down from Ponte Sisto* (Dallas Community Poets Press). Her full-length collection, *Branch in His Hand*, was published in November 2008 by Backwaters Press. She has also edited and published the prizewinning *I Am Not a Juvenile Delinquent* (2004), an anthology of poems written by adjudicated adolescent girls with whom she has worked for ten years doing a weekly poetry workshop.

Beverly Cottman is a multidisciplinary performance artist who thrives on collaboration and finding ways to turn found objects into thought-provoking art. Life experiences and events inform and inspire her poetry.

Philip Dacey's most recent of ten books of poems is *Vertebrae Rosaries: 50 Sonnets* (Red Dragonfly Press, 2009). More of his work can be viewed at his website, www. philipdacey.com. A resident of Minnesota for thirty-five years, he now lives in New York City.

Karen de Balbian Verster, three-time cancer survivor, is the author of the novel *Boob: A Story of Sex, Cancer & Stupidity*. Many of her stories, essays, and poems have been published in literary reviews and anthologies. "The Bad Seed" won Honorable Mention in the 2007 UNO Writing Contest, and "Anne Frank Redux" will appear in the anthology *Writers and Their Notebooks*. To read excerpts and more about the author, visit: http://mysite.verizon.net/kdebv.

E. Michael Desilets was born in Framingham, Massachusetts, when FDR was president, and he now lives in Los Angeles. His work has appeared in numerous publications, including *Exit 13, Poesy,* and *The Rambler.* "In lieu of hymns," his e-chapbook, is available at the *Origami Condom* website (http://origamicondom.org/Chapbooks/Desilets.01.pdf).

Marsha Dubrow earned her M.F.A. in Fiction Writing and Literature from Bennington College, which published her book *Single Blessedness*. Her nonfiction and fiction are in anthologies including *Still Going Strong* (Haworth Press) and *Looking Back* (New Brighton Books). Her work has appeared recently in *National Geographic Traveler, Houston Chronicle,* and others.

Lois West Duffy was a newspaper reporter and columnist. Widowed at the age of forty-three, she stayed single long enough to work in the U.S. Senate, for a nonprofit organization serving inmates, and with a corporate foundation. She lives in Afton, Minnesota, with her husband, Joe Duffy, and is at work on her first novel. She has served on the board of the Loft Literary Center. She is the author of *Zillah's Gift*, a chapter book for young readers.

Donna Emerson is a college instructor, licensed clinical social worker, photographer, and writer of poetry and prose. Recent publications include *California Quarterly, The South Carolina Poetry Review, Phoebe,* and *So To Speak*. Her chapbook, *Body Rhymes,* was selected by Finishing Line Press for publication in May 2009. Donna lives with her husband and daughter in Sonoma County, California.

Carmen Anthony Fiore is presently a full-time writer living in the Toms River, New Jersey, area. He has also lived in Brevard County just north of Melbourne, Florida. He has published four adult novels, a juvenile novel, a historical nonfiction book about the young heroes of the Civil War, a co-written nonfiction book, short fiction, plus magazine and newspaper articles and essays.

Maureen Tolman Flannery's latest book is *Destiny Whispers to the Beloved*. Having grown up on a Wyoming sheep ranch, she and her actor husband Dan have raised their children in Chicago. Her other books are *Ancestors in the Landscape, A Fine Line, Secret of the Rising Up, Remembered into Life,* and *Knowing Stones.* Her work has appeared in fifty anthologies and over one hundred literary reviews, including *Atlanta Review, Birmingham Poetry Review, Out of Line, Santa Fe Literary Review,* and *Saranac Review.*

Gretchen Fletcher frequently travels to attend poetry readings, awards, and book signings, and leads writing workshops for Florida Center for the Book, an affiliate of the Library of Congress. Her chapbook, *That Severed Cord,* was published by Finishing Line Press. One of Gretchen's poems won the Poetry Society of America's Bright Lights, Big Verse competition; and she was projected on the Jumbotron as she read it in Times Square.

Elizabeth Gauffreau lives in Nottingham, New Hampshire. She administers individualized learning programs at Granite State College in Concord and teaches courses in self-directed learning. Her publications include the following: *The Long Story, Ad Hoc Monadnock, Rio Grande Review, Blueline,* and *Slow Trains.*

Sarah Getty's second book of poems, *Bring Me Her Heart* (Higganum Hill Books, 2006), received Pulitzer and National Book Award nominations. Her first, *The Land of Milk and Honey,* was part of the James Dickey Contemporary Poetry Series (University of South Carolina Press). Sarah has published fiction in *The Iowa Review* and has recently completed a novel, *Spend All You Have.*

Diane Porter Goff is a writer and photographer living in the mountains of Virginia. She has written a memoir, *Riding the Elephant,* about journeying with her mother through the landscape of Alzheimer's disease. Her work has appeared in places such as *Southern Distinctions* magazine, *The Sun,* and the *We'moon Calendar Book.*

Georgia A. Greeley is an artist and writer who lives and works in Saint Paul. Her passion for combining words and images frequently shows up as fine press broadsides or handmade artist's books. She enjoys teaching book arts and writing to adults, teens, and children.

Carla J. Hagen's work has appeared in *Gypsy Cab; Sing Heavenly Muse!; 100 Words; Voices for the Land; What Happened to Us? The Bush Years;* and online in *MindFire: War, Peace and Everything in Between.* She has just completed her first novel, *Hand Me Down My Walking Cane.* She lives in St. Paul, Minnesota, with her husband.

Elaine Handley is professor of writing and literature at Empire State College, State University of New York. She has published four chapbooks of poetry (two of which, in collaboration, won the Adirondack Center for Writing Best Poetry awards in 2006 and 2007). Her poetry and fiction have appeared in a variety of magazines and anthologies including *Stone Canoe, Journal of Family Life,* and *The Dos Passos Review.* She is a recipient of a NYS Council on the Arts grant and is presently finishing a novel, *Deep River,* about the Underground Railroad in upstate New York.

Tom Hansen taught English for thirty-five years before retiring to the Black Hills of South Dakota. His essays and poems have appeared in *The Bitter Oleander, The Literary Review, The Midwest Quarterly, Nimrod,* and *Poetry Northwest.* In 2006, BOA published his first book of poetry, *Falling to Earth.*

Mara Hart was born in New York City in 1933 and raised there. She has also lived in Cleveland; Minneapolis; Stockholm, Sweden; Claremont, California; and currently lives in Duluth, Minnesota. She writes memoir in prose and poetry, edits, and helps others write their life stories. She holds graduate degrees in Library Science, English, and Creative Writing (memoir). Her most recent book is Lovecraft's *New York Circle: The Kalem Club, 1924-1927.*

Karen Paul Holmes, a published poet and award-winning business writer, splits her time between Atlanta and the Southern Appalachians. She enjoys classical music, ikebana, contra-dancing, and her two Welsh terriers. She's married to Ken and has a twenty-two-year-old daughter, Katja (also a writer).

Ruth Harriet Jacobs, a gerontologist at Wellesley College (Wellesley Centers for Women), is the author of nine books, including *Be an Outrageous Older Woman* and *ABC's for Seniors.* She teaches in lifetime learning programs at Brandeis University and Regis College and speaks nationwide.

Louise Jaffe, professor emerita of English at Kingsborough Community College of the City University of New York, has published four poetry chapbooks and a collection of three novellas on the theme of female empowerment, as well as numerous other poems and stories in anthologies and literary journals.

J. Kates is a poet and literary translator who lives in Fitzwilliam, New Hampshire.

Cleo Fellers Kocol has been writing for thirty of her eighty-three years. She wrote three one-woman, many-character shows that she performed throughout the United States for five years. She has published short stories, poetry, essays, and novels. Her most recent novel is *Fitzhugh's Woman.* Her work appears in assorted anthologies, and she is the recipient of various writing awards.

Dahlma Llanos-Figueroa is a novelist, memoirist, and short story writer whose work is grounded in the Puerto Rican communities on the island and in New York City. Her novel *Daughters of the Stone* traces the lives of five generations of Afro-Puerto Rican women from the mid-19th century to the present. She is currently working on a collection of travel pieces called *Writing on the Road* and compiling her short stories and memoir pieces into a collection called *The Carisa Stories*. Her short pieces have been published in a number of literary journals, including the Fall 2007 issue of *Narrative* magazine at www.narrativemagazine.com.

John Lavelle is an assistant professor in the Humanities and Communication Department at Florida Institute of Technology. "Living in the Past" is from a short-story collection concerned with the working-class people of Buffalo, New York. The collection is still a work in progress, although he hopes to finish soon.

Larry Lefkowitz's stories, poems, and humor have been published in the U.S., Israel, and Britain. He has completed a novel, *The Peddler*, about a 19th century Jewish peddler looking for the Lost Tribes of Israel among the American Indians.

Sharon Anderson Lewis is an assistant professor of African American Women Writers at Montclair State University in Upper Montclair, New Jersey.

Christina Lovin is the author of *What We Burned for Warmth* and *Little Fires*. She is an award-winning poet and two-time Pushcart nominee, and her work has been widely published and anthologized. Her work has been generously supported by the Elizabeth George Foundation, the Kentucky Foundation for Women, and the Kentucky Arts Council.

Charles Henry Lynch, from Baltimore, Maryland, has lived in Brooklyn, New York, with his wife Gayle since 1969. He teaches English at New Jersey City University, is a Baha'i, and was a Cave Canem Fellow. "Wrong Color, Right Size" is based upon his cousin "Aunt" Barbara Hawkins's account of how absurd segregation could be.

Arlene L. Mandell, a retired English professor whose work has appeared in more than 300 publications and fourteen anthologies, lives in Santa Rosa, California.

Phyllis J. Manning is originally from Nebraska. She is a widely traveled longtime educator who started teaching at age sixteen in a one-room rural schoolhouse but did much of her adult service (classroom, counseling, administration) at international schools overseas. Widowed, Phyl has a married daughter and family in Chico and a married son and family in San Diego.

Deborah Marshall's words are informed by her life experiences. Her professional work has been as a teacher, photojournalist, visual artist, and art therapist keeping company with grieving children and adolescents at a local hospice. She remains grateful for her family, friends, and dog.

Janet McCann is a Texas poet, born in 1942. Journals publishing her poems include *Kansas Quarterly, Parnassus, Nimrod, Sou'wester, New York Quarterly, Tendril, Poetry Australia*, and others. She has won three chapbook contests, sponsored by Pudding Publications, Chimera Connections, and Franciscan University Press. A 1989 NEA Creative Writing Fellowship winner, she has taught at Texas A & M University since 1969. She has also co-edited anthologies, including *Odd Angles of Heaven* (1994) and *Place of Passage* (Story Line, 2000). Her most recent poetry collection is *Emily's Dress* (Pecan Grove Press, 2004).

Ed Meek has published articles, fiction, and poetry in magazines and newspapers including *The North American Review, The Paris Review, Yankee, North Dakota Quarterly*, and *The Boston Globe*. His latest book of poems, *What We Love*, was published by Blue Light Press and is available at Amazon. He teaches composition and creative writing at Austin Preparatory School.

Ilze Klavina Mueller, a native of Latvia, lives in Minneapolis. *Gate*, a collection of her poems, was published by Laurel Poetry Collective in 2003. Her work has also appeared in *Looking for Home* (Milkweed), *Calyx, Water~Stone*, and *Hedgebrook Journal*, while some of her literary translations were included in *Latvian Literature* and *World Literature Today*.

David Mura has written three books of poetry, *After We Lost Our Way, The Colors of Desire*, and, most recently, *Angels for the Burning* (BOA Editions). His memoirs are *Turning Japanese* and *Where the Body Meets Memory*. His book of criticism is *Song for Uncle Tom, Tonto & Mr. Moto: Poetry & Identity*. His most recent work is the novel *Famous Suicides of the Japanese Empire* (Coffee House Press).

Sheryl L. Nelms is from Marysville, Kansas. She graduated from South Dakota State University. She published over 4,500 articles, stories, and poems, including thirteen individual collections of her work. She served as the essay editor of *The Pen Woman Magazine*, the National League of American Pen Women publication, for the past ten years.

Karen Nelson's first book of poems, *The Woman You Think I Am*, was published in 2006 (Northwoods Press); and her second, *Wise Woman and Her Co-Pilot*, was published in March 2009 (Borrego Press). Her poems reflect her life in California, New Hampshire, and most recently in Tullahoma, Tennessee. She has been published in *The Larcom Review*, *Earth's Daughters*, and *Poetry Motel*.

Mary E. O'Dell has been writing and publishing poetry for thirty-five years and has three poetry collections, *Poems for the Man Who Weighs Light* and *Living in the Body*, both by Mellen Poetry Press, and *The Dangerous Man* by Finishing Line Press. She is founder and president of Green River Writers, Inc., a twenty-five-year-old nonprofit organization.

Ann Olson and her husband Steve, together for forty years, grew up on the plains and coteaus of South Dakota. She teaches writing and literature at Heritage University within the Yakama Reservation in Toppenish, Washington. She holds an M.A. in literature from the University of Illinois, Urbana, and an M.F.A. in Creative Writing from Eastern Washington University.

Susan Peters grew up in the Midwest and graduated from the University of Kansas. After fifteen years living in Europe and Asia, she returned to the U.S. for her "Vegas Wedding." A member of the Kansas City Writers Group, she has published poetry and nonfiction, won awards at local and regional competitions, and teaches academic writing at a local community college.

Carlos Reyes is a noted poet and translator. His most recent book of poems is *At the Edge of the Western Wave* (2004). Most recent book of translations: *La señal del cuervo / The Sign of the Crow* by Ignacio Ruiz Pérez. He lives in Portland, Oregon, with his wife Karen Checkoway, who is a noted book designer and editor.

Susan Pepper Robbins lives with her husband in rural Virginia across the road from the farm where she grew up. Her first novel was published when she was fifty (*One Way Home*, Random House, 1993), and she is working on a collection of stories about older women. She wrote a dissertation on Jane Austen's novels, and she teaches at Hampden-Sydney College.

Tracy Robert, a native of Southern California, has taught writing for over two decades. She won the Pirate's Alley Faulkner Prize for Fiction, was a finalist for the Flannery O'Connor Award for Short Fiction, and has been published in various anthologies and periodicals. The selections included here are excerpts from her novel, *The Curse of Ambrosia*.

Brent Robison lives in the Catskill Mountains of New York. His stories have appeared in various literary journals and have won awards from *Literal Latté*, *Chronogram*, and the New Jersey Council on the Arts, as well as a Pushcart Prize nomination. He is the editor and publisher of the Hudson Valley literary annual, *Prima Materia*.

Frances Saunders's work had been published in *Acorn, Passager, Tea: An International Anthology*, and *Reflections*. An essay, "Not Our Kind," will be published in an anthology about inclusion/exclusion from Wising Up Press. Frances, who was born in 1915, lives in Cambridge, Massachusetts.

Mary Kolada Scott, a writer and artist from Ventura, California, has written and published poetry since she was a teenager. Her work has appeared in numerous periodicals, journals, and galleries. Both her husband and the pothos plant continue to thrive. Visit her website at www.marykoladascott.com.

Dan Seiters was the publicity manager for Southern Illinois University Press for more than two decades, during which time he wrote the jacket copy for about 1,500 books plus a mountain of news releases. His publications include a novel entitled *The Dastardly Dashing of Wee Expectations* and *Image Patterns in the Novels of F. Scott Fitzgerald*.

Judith Serin's collection of poetry, *Hiding in the World*, was published by Diane di Prima's Eidolon Editions. Her work has appeared in *Bachy, The Ohio Journal, Writer's Forum, Nebraska Review, Woman's World, Colorado State Review, Barnabe Mountain Review*, and recently in *Proposing on the Brooklyn Bridge* (Grayson Books), *The Paterson Literary Review, First Intensity, Paragraph*, and *the blink*. She lives in San Francisco with her husband, Herbert Yee. "Sharing a Room with Your Sister" is part of her "Family Stories" series.

Thomas Shane, writer, editor, and leading-edge boomer living in Alexandria, Virginia, has had his share of experience. He has been a lawyer, park ranger, lobbyist, trail-crew cook, government official, farm hand, actor, and Franciscan monk, not necessarily in that order. Judy Barrett, his graphic-designing wife, with the help of their two grown kids, keeps him honest.

Elaine Dugas Shea, born in New England, has lived in Montana for thirty-seven years. She has enjoyed a career in social justice, especially working in civil rights and serving American Indian tribes. Her writing was featured in *Montana Voices Anthology, Intermountain Woman, Third Wednesday*, and the *Missoulian*.

Michael Shorb is a poet, technical writer, editor, and children's book author who lives in San Francisco. He writes frequently about environmental issues and historical topics. His work has appeared in over 100 publications, including *Michigan Quarterly, Kansas Quarterly, The Nation, Commonweal, Rattle, The Sun, Salzburg Poetry Review, European Judaism, Queen's Quarterly,* and *The Shakespeare Newsletter.* He has also appeared in a number of anthologies, including *Discover America* (San Jose, California, 1976), *A Bell Ringing in the Empty Sky* (San Diego, California, 1985), *The Dolphin's Arc: Poems on Endangered Creatures of the Sea* (College Park, Maryland, 1989), *To Be a Man: In Search of the Deep Masculine* (Los Angeles, California, 1991), and *Names in a Jar* (Portland, Oregon, 2007).

Thomas R. Smith lives in River Falls, Wisconsin, and teaches at the Loft Literary Center in Minneapolis. His first book, *Keeping the Star* (New Rivers Press), was published in 1988 when he was forty. His recent volumes include *Waking Before Dawn* (Red Dragonfly Press) and *Kinnickinnic* (Parallel Press).

Glen Sorestad is a well-known Canadian poet who has more than fifteen volumes of his poems published. His poems have appeared in poetry magazines, journals, and online sites in many countries and have also been translated into a half-dozen languages. He lives in Saskatoon, Saskatchewan, and was that province's first poet laureate (2000-2004).

Judith Sornberger has four collections of poems. *Open Heart*, her full-length collection, is from Calyx Books. *Bones of Light*, a chapbook from the Parallel Press, is her most recent. Her poems appear frequently in journals such as *Poems & Plays, Calyx, Prairie Schooner,* and *Pilgrimage*. She is a professor of English and women's studies at Mansfield University of Pennsylvania.

Jennifer Soule has published in various journals including *South Dakota Review, North Dakota Quarterly, Coal City Review, Modern Haiku, The Sow's Ear,* and the anthology *Crazy Woman Creek*. She obtained her writer's license with an M.F.A. in Writing from the University of Nebraska in 2008 at the age of sixty-one. She has been a nurse's aide, community organizer, social worker, and professor.

James E. Stanton, who was born in 1945 and grew up in the Midwest, served in the U.S. Army from 1967 to 1971 in Thailand as a Lao/Thai translator-interpreter. He married a Thai girl from Isan (the Northeast), and he is still married to her. He spends winters in Thailand writing short stories and the rest of the year at his lake cabin in Minnesota doing everything but writing short stories.

Ann Struthers is currently the writer-in-residence at Coe College in Cedar Rapids, Iowa. She has published poetry widely in journals and fourteen anthologies and she has two collections and two chapbooks. The latest chapbook, *What You Try to Tame*, is based on her life in Sri Lanka as a Fulbright Fellow. She has five poems in the Summer 2008 issue of *The Southern Humanities Review*, and Ted Kooser recently featured one of her poems in his weekly column.

Janet Sunderland is an essayist and poet whose work has appeared in a variety of small presses and anthologies. She is also a priest and co-pastors with her husband Cliff in Kansas City, Missouri. She recently completed a spiritual memoir, *Standing at the Crossroad*, and is now working on an essay collection, *Kansas Chronicles*.

Joyce Sutphen's first book of poetry, *Straight Out of View*, won the Barnard New Women Poets Prize (Beacon Press, 1995). Her second book of poems, *Coming Back to the Body* (Holy Cow! Press, 2000), was a finalist for a Minnesota Book Award; and her third book, *Naming the Stars* (Holy Cow! Press, 2004), won the Minnesota Book Award in Poetry. Her poems have recently appeared in *The Gettysburg Review*, *The Kean Review*, *Magma*, and other journals. She teaches literature and creative writing at Gustavus Adolphus College in St. Peter, Minnesota.

Barbara Wade teaches literature and creative writing at Berea College. Her poetry has appeared in *Appalachian Heritage Magazine*, *Appalachian Journal*, *Florida Review Chapbook*, *Perigee*, *River Walk Journal*, and *Women's Studies Quarterly*. *Inside Passage*, a poetry chapbook, is forthcoming from Finishing Line Press.

Dody Williams received a Master's degree in Liberal Studies in May 2009 from the University of North Carolina, Greensboro. Her stories have appeared in *The Rambler Magazine*, *Carolina Woman Magazine*, *Read This Magazine*, and *Memoirs Ink*. She is dedicating "Her Benevolent Concern" to Meghan, who prompted its writing.

A. D. Winans's poetry, prose, articles, and book reviews have appeared in numerous literary magazines and anthologies, including *Poetry Now*, *Tule Review*, *City Lights Journal*, *Poetry Australia*, *the New York Quarterly*, and the *Outlaw Bible of American Poetry*. His poetry has been translated into eight languages. In 2004, a song poem of his was performed at Tully Hall, New York City. In 2006, he was awarded a PEN Josephine Miles award for literary excellence. In 2007, Presa Press published a book of his selected poems, *The Other Side of Broadway: Selected Poems 1965-2005*.

Diana Woodcock's chapbook, *Mandala*, is forthcoming from Foothills Publishing. Her poems have appeared recently in *Best New Poets 2008*, *Crab Orchard Review*, *Nimrod*, *Atlanta Review*, and *Portland Review*. Recipient of first and second prizes in 2008 from Artists Embassy International and the 2007 Creekwalker Prize for Poetry, she teaches at Virginia Commonwealth University in Qatar/School of the Arts.

E. Lynne Wright is a Florida resident whose short stories, essays, and nonfiction articles have appeared in the *Cleveland Plain Dealer*, *The Hartford Courant*, *Women's World*, *Mature Lifestyles*, the *Chicken Soup* books, and numerous anthologies and literary magazines. She has published three nonfiction books for the Globe Pequot Press: *More Than Petticoats: Remarkable Florida Women*, *It Happened in Florida*, and *Disasters and Heroic Rescues of Florida*. She has recently completed a collection of linked short stories and a novel and is at work on another Florida book.

Cherise Wyneken is a freelance writer whose stories, poems, and articles have appeared in a variety of publications. She has published two books of poetry, *Touchstones* and *Seeded Puffs*; a memoir, *Round Trip*; a novel, *Freddie*; and a poetry chapbook, *Old Haunts*.

Fredrick Zydek is the author of eight collections of poetry. Formerly a professor of creative writing and theology at the University of Nebraska and later at the College of Saint Mary, he is now a gentleman farmer when he isn't writing. He is the editor for Lone Willow Press.

Acknowledgements

Putting together this book has brought an appreciation for all the folks who are still out there slugging away at the writing business. Many of us started out in our twenties, caught the writing bug, and after years of hard work (with little bits of recognition sprinkled in to keep us going) still love the feel of words making their way onto the page in the shape of stories, poems, and essays.

This book is dedicated to all those who (even into their nineties) keep on making artistic sense as best they can from the everyday experiences of life. To the writers from all over the world who sent us work, thank you. Without you, this book would not have been possible.

Many people helped us. We offer a special thanks to friends and gifted writers Marge Barrett, Mary Junge, and Paulette Bates Alden, who offered support and advice along the way. We'd also like to thank the writers in Vicky and Marge's private class who helped read and evaluate some of the many pieces sent to us: Wendy Henry, Jerry McAllister, Bill Nemmers, Sharon Spartz, Janet Tripp, Jacquie Trudeau, Jan Denham, Lee Orcutt, Nancy Christensen, Mary Sue Comfort, Bonnie West and especially Pamela Bonk, who put in hours creating and maintaining our database.

Thanks also to Nora Erickson for her help with the database, to Jan Hempel for her support in launching the project, and to Carolyn Holbrook and Ed Southern for pointing us to many excellent writers who may have missed our initial call for submissions.

A special thank you to Vicky's mother, Ruth Hodges, a visual artist in her nineties, who uses paints to find focus, meaning, and structure in a sometimes blurry world and who continues to inspire us to have faith in the power of words to do the same.

We would especially like to thank Carol's adman son Tim Roan, who expanded our vision of the market for this book, and Carol's daughter-in-law, Vicki, whose ideas about cover design made the book come alive for us.

A huge thank you to Ilze Mueller, poet and copy editor extraordinaire. We so appreciate your keen eye!

And finally to Jim Perlman of Holy Cow! Press, who encouraged us and agreed to publish our anthology, thank you for having faith in our project.